Korean Grammar for *Beginners*

Learn How to Read, Write, and Speak Korean through Concise
Lessons with Fun Facts about Korea
to Keep You Engaged

WorldWide Nomad

TABLE OF CONTENTS

Korean Grammar for Beginners

Learn Conversational Korean For Adult Beginners

Korean Short Stories For Language Learners

FREE GIFTS

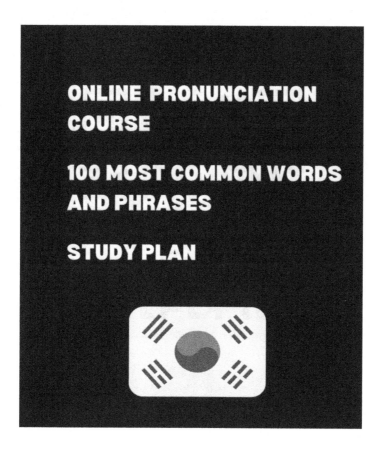

Inside this gift you'll find:

Online Pronunciation Course: Easily perfect pronunciation through an online video course for audio learners

100 Most Common Words and Phrases: Increase your vocabulary through some of the most common words and phrases in use

Study Plan: A custom study plan for maximum retention and learning

TO CLAIM BONUSES:

Scan the QR Code below

OR

Visit the link below:

https://worldwidenomadbooks.com/korean-grammar-free-gift

Introduction

Have you ever found yourself in a bustling Korean restaurant, surrounded by the symphony of sizzling meats and lively chatter, only to be utterly bewildered when handed a menu written in intricate Hangul characters? Imagine being able to navigate such a scenario with ease, ordering your meal in fluent Korean, much to the delight of the restaurant staff. For many, this seems like a distant dream, especially when the Korean language is often perceived as one of the most challenging languages to master, with its unique script and complex grammar structures. In fact, it's estimated that for an English speaker, learning Korean could take approximately 2,200 class hours, highlighting the complexity and depth of the language.

However, *Korean Grammar for Beginners* is here to transform this seemingly insurmountable challenge into an achievable and enjoyable journey. This workbook is not just another language guide; it is a companion designed to make learning Korean a breeze for those who prefer short, concise, and interactive lessons. Whether you are a student, a working professional, a traveler, or simply someone with a keen interest in the Korean language and culture, this book is crafted just for you.

We understand that diving into a new language, especially one as intricate as Korean, can be overwhelming. The fear of mispronunciation, the complexity of the grammar structures, and the alien nature of the script can make the journey seem daunting. Additionally, the overwhelming sea of resources available can leave learners confused and lost, not knowing where to start. And let's not forget the struggle to maintain focus during extended lessons, a common pain point for many, particularly in today's world of constant distractions.

Moreover, learning a language isn't just about memorizing vocabulary and rules; it's about understanding the cultural context and nuances that come with it. A lack of cultural insights can make the learning experience feel incomplete and less fulfilling. Traditional textbooks often fail to address this, focusing solely on the language aspects without providing the cultural flavor that makes learning truly immersive.

This book aims to address all these concerns by offering concise and engaging lessons interspersed with fun facts about Korean culture. The lessons are designed to be clear and straightforward, making them accessible to everyone, even those completely new to language learning. The workbook format ensures that you are actively involved in the learning process, allowing you to practice as you learn, and making the journey interactive and enjoyable.

The benefits of traversing through this book are manifold and extend far beyond mere language acquisition. Here are some of the profound impacts this workbook aims to have on your learning journey:

1. **Enhanced Comprehension:** The clear, concise, and structured lessons will ensure a smooth learning

curve, allowing you to grasp complex grammatical concepts with ease and build a strong foundation in Korean.

2. **Interactive Learning Experience:** The workbook format, coupled with engaging exercises and quizzes, will facilitate active learning, enabling you to practice and reinforce your knowledge as you progress through the chapters.

3. **Cultural Enrichment:** The cultural insights and fun facts interspersed throughout the book will provide you with a deeper appreciation of Korean traditions, values, and way of life, making your learning journey more meaningful and enjoyable.

4. **Increased Focus and Retention:** The bite-sized lessons tailored for short attention spans will keep you focused and motivated, ensuring consistent progress without feeling overwhelmed or bored.

5. **Enhanced Communication Skills:** Armed with essential vocabulary and phrases, you will be able to communicate effectively in various everyday situations, whether it's ordering food, asking for directions, or making new friends.

6. **Personal Fulfillment and Empowerment:** Mastering a new language can be incredibly rewarding. It opens up new horizons, allows you to connect with people from different cultures, and boosts your confidence and sense of achievement.

7. **Adaptability in Real-Life Situations:** The practical knowledge and skills acquired from this book will empower you to navigate real-world scenarios with ease, whether you are traveling in Korea or interacting with Korean speakers elsewhere.

Chapter One
The Building Blocks of Korean Grammar

Korean, with its rich history and cultural significance, offers an intriguing linguistic landscape for beginners. The language might seem complex at first glance, but with the right approach, it becomes more accessible and enjoyable to learn.

At the heart of the Korean language lies its unique script known as Hangeul. Created in the 15th century, Hangeul stands out due to its logical and systematic design. Each character represents a sound, making it phonetic in nature. This script serves as the foundation upon which the entire language is built. Once you get a grasp on Hangeul, reading Korean becomes much simpler. But understanding the alphabet is just the starting point. To truly communicate in Korean, you need to be familiar with its sentence structures. Korean follows a subject-object-verb order, which might be different from what English speakers are used to. For instance, while in English we say, "I eat apples," in Korean, the structure would be more like "I apples eat." Recognizing this pattern early on can greatly aid in constructing and understanding sentences.

Another pivotal aspect of Korean grammar is the use of particles. These are small words or syllables that give context to a sentence. They can denote various relationships, like possession, direction, or purpose. Grasping the role of particles can be a bit challenging, but they play a crucial role in giving depth and clarity to your sentences.

1.1 Korean Alphabets (Hangeul)

Hangeul (한글), the Korean script, stands as a testament to the ingenuity of linguistic design. Unlike many other writing systems, Hangeul was crafted with the explicit intent of ensuring literacy for everyone. Its creation in the 15th century was motivated by a desire to have a script that was intuitive and easy to learn, diverging from the complex Chinese characters previously in use.

Origin and Design

King Sejong the Great, along with a group of scholars, introduced Hangeul to the Korean people in 1443. The design was rooted in simplicity. Each symbol corresponds to a sound, making Hangeul a phonetic script.

Furthermore, the shapes of the letters are not arbitrary; they were designed to mimic the shape the mouth makes when producing that particular sound.

1.2 Consonants (자음 - Ja-eum)

Hangeul's consonants, or "Ja-eum," form the backbone of the script. They are the building blocks of Hangeul characters and are designed to represent the sounds of spoken Korean as accurately as possible. Unlike the complex Chinese characters that were the only used language in the country before, Hangeul consonants are remarkably simple and easy to learn.

The Korean language consists of 19 consonants that were made representing the shape of the parts of the mouth that form their respective sounds. In a syllable, consonants always come first, followed by a vowel.

Consonants	Sound Value
ㄱ	G as in gift / K as in Kite
ㄴ	N as in name
ㄷ	D as in Door / T as in tango
ㄹ	R as in River / L as in lake
ㅁ	M as in moon
ㅂ	B as in boy / p as in pen
ㅅ	S as in shoes / T as in Ted

ㅇ	(silent) / ng as in lo<u>ng</u>
ㅈ	J as in jar / T as in tango
ㅊ	Ch as in church / T as in tango
ㅋ	K as in kite
ㅌ	T as in tango
ㅍ	P as in pen
ㅎ	H as in house / T as in tango

Notice that there are consonants with 2 (two) sound values. You will learn in "The Rule of Final Consonant (Batchim) which sound value to pronounce depending on the consonant's location in the syllable.

1.2.1 Double Consonants

In the Korean alphabet, these twin consonants are called Double Consonants and are considered as one. These are pronounced strongly from the throat by tensing the vocal cords.

Consonants	Sound Value
ㄲ	kk
ㄸ	tt

ㅃ	pp
ㅆ	ss
ㅉ	jj

Yes, we know exactly what you are thinking! Many consonants when placed as the final consonant changes from their original sound value to "T". You might be quite confused, but it only takes a few minutes to memorize these consonants, and soon you'll get the hang of it.

*ㄷ, ㅌ, ㅅ, ㅆ, ㅈ, ㅊ, ㅎ when placed as final consonant, they are all pronounced as [t].

For **Double Final Consonants**, only one sound value is pronounced. There is no general rule of the choice of sound value to use and it only depends on the specific word and its meaning.

Example:

값 (only ㅂ is pronounced and ㅅ is ignored)

1.3 Vowels (모음 - Mo-eum)

Just as consonants are crucial to forming the skeleton of Korean words, vowels are the heart and soul, providing meaning, emotion, and rhythm to the language. Understanding these fundamental elements will lay the groundwork for our exploration of character combinations, and deepen our understanding of the concept of the Korean language.

Let's start by learning the basic vowels and their unique sound values.

Basic Vowels

Vowel	Sound Value
ㅏ	a as in father

ㅑ	ya as in yacht
ㅓ	eo as in call
ㅕ	yeo as in young
ㅗ	o as in horse
ㅛ	yo as in yoga
ㅜ	u as in pool
ㅠ	yu as in you
ㅡ	eu (as in smiling with teeth showing and clenched)
ㅣ	i as in fill

*Tip: 2 (two) vertical or horizontal lines in vowels means the sound value starts with "y"

Example: ㅛ(yo), ㅕ (yeo), ㅑ (ya), ㅠ(yu)

Four Complex Vowels

Vowels	Sound Values
ㅔ	e
ㅖ	ye
ㅐ	ae
ㅒ	yae

Vowels ㅔ and ㅐ sounds very similar when pronounced, same case for ㅒ and ㅖ. And that is why so many Koreans cannot distinguish their difference in pronunciation because it is hard to tell them apart.

Combined Vowels

The following vowels are combinations of the basic vowels.

ㅘ	ㅗ + ㅏ = wa
ㅙ	ㅗ + ㅐ = whe
ㅝ	ㅗ + ㅓ = wo
ㅞ	ㅗ + ㅔ = weh
ㅚ	ㅗ + ㅣ = weh
ㅟ	ㅜ + ㅣ = wi

ㅓ	— + ㅣ = ui

The combined vowels "ㅙ", "ㅞ" and "ㅚ" do not have much difference in pronunciation and only through writing/spelling can be distinguished.

1.4 Syllables

As we immerse ourselves in the fascinating world of learning, have you ever wondered how Korean words are pieced together to form meaningful units of communication?

In Hangeul, the notion of syllabification is different as it represents a visually distinguishable unit.

Let's uncover the rules and principles that govern the arrangement of consonants and vowels within a syllable.

As mentioned earlier, consonants and vowels are combined to make a syllable block, which fundamentally consist of one (1) consonant and one (1) vowel. A consonant alone cannot make a syllable. Likewise, vowels cannot make a syllable alone too.

Here are the possible components of a Korean syllable:

1.   Consonant + Vowel

2.   Consonant + Vowel + Consonant

3.   Consonant + Vowel + Consonant/Vowel

Order placement of the consonants and vowels in a syllable:

1. Consonant + Vertical Vowel:

나 (ㄴ + ㅏ)

2. Consonant + Horizontal Vowel:

노 (ㄴ + ㅗ)

3. Beginning Consonant + Vertical Vowel + Final Consonant:

밥 (ㅂ + ㅏ + ㅂ)

4. Beginning Consonant + Horizontal Vowel + Final Consonant:

문 (ㅁ + ㅜ + ㄴ)

5. Consonant + Vertical Vowel + Final Consonant:

한 (ㅎ+ㅏ+ㄴ)

6. Consonant + Vertical Vowel + Double Final Consonant:

값 (ㄱ+ㅏ+ㅄ)

The construction chart below will help you practice what we've learned so far in terms of consonants and vowel combinations.

	ㅏ (a)	ㅔ (e)	ㅣ (i)	ㅗ (o)	ㅜ (u)
ㄱ(g)	가(ga)	게(ge)	기(gi)	고(go)	구(gu)
ㄴ(n)	나(na)	네(ne)	니(ni)	노(no)	누(nu)
ㄷ(d)	다(da)	데(de)	디(di)	도(do)	두(du)
ㄹ(r)	라(ra)	레(re)	리(ri)	로(ro)	루(ru)

ㅁ(m)	마(ma)	메(me)	미(mi)	모(mo)	무(mu)
ㅂ(b)	바(ba)	베(be)	비(bi)	보(bo)	부(bu)
ㅅ(s)	사(sa)	세(se)	시(si)	소(so)	수(su)
ㅇ(_)	아(a)	에(e)	이(i)	오(o)	우(u)
ㅈ(j)	자(ja)	제(je)	지(ji)	조(jo)	주(ju)
ㅊ(ch)	차(cha)	체(che)	치(chi)	초(cho)	추(chu)

ㅋ(k)	카(ka)	케(ke)	키(ki)	코(ko)	쿠(ku)
ㅌ(t)	타(ta)	테(te)	티(ti)	토(to)	투(tu)
ㅍ(p)	파(pa)	페(pe)	피(pi)	포(po)	푸(pu)
ㅎ(h)	하(ha)	헤(he)	히(hi)	호(ho)	후(hu)

To help you with correct pronunciation and character writing order, practice reading and writing the following real Korean vocabularies:

1. 사자 (sa-ja) = lion

2. 아기 (a-gi) = baby

3. 다리 (da-ri) = legs

4. 가수 (ga-su) = singer

5. 노래 (no-re) = song

6. 새우 (se-u) = shrimp

7. 모자 (mo-ja) = hat

8.   오이 (o-yi) = cucumber

9.   비누 (bi-nu) = soap

10.   치마 (chi-ma) = skirt

1.5 Re-syllabication

When a syllable ends in a consonant and is followed by a vowel (example: an empty consonant ㅇ), the final consonant sound value is transferred to the place of the next beginning consonant.

밥 을 → 밥 을 : [바블]

먹 어 요 → 먹 어 요 : [머거요]

If there are two consonants in the batchim, the very last consonant sound is shifted to the next syllable and the closer consonant becomes the batchim sound of the first syllable.

음액[으맥]	한국어[한구거]	할아버지[하라버지]
집에[지베]	꽃이[꼬치]	이름이[이르미]
걸어요[거러요]	앉아요[안자요]	읽어요[일거요]

Practice the following words by yourself. Listen and check if your pronunciation matches with the instruction mentioned above about batchim.

1.   물이

2.   문을

3.   앞에

4.   닫아요

5.   싫어요

6.	있어요

7.	깎아요

8.	읽어요

9.	앉아요

Practice and read the following sentences applying the batchim rule.

1.	창문을 닫으세요.

2.	사진을 찍었어요.

3.	책에 이름을 쓰세요.

4.	물을 마시고 싶어요.

5.	아침에 병원에 갔어요.

Additional points to remember when writing Korean:

Understanding the common writing conventions and formatting in Korean is essential for effective communication in the language. To ensure clarity, it's crucial to keep these key points in mind.

Left-to-Right, top-to-bottom: Korean follows a left-to-right, top-to-bottom writing direction, which is similar to English. This means that when you write in Korean, you start on the left side of the page and move horizontally from left to right. Subsequently, you proceed to the next line below, and so on. Each syllable is stacked vertically within a line, and pages are read from top to bottom, just as you would in English or other Western languages.

Spaces: Like in English, spaces are used in Korean to separate words. This practice contributes to improved readability and comprehension.

Capitalization: Korean Language has no capitalization concept.

Punctuation: Korean employs punctuation marks similar to those found in English, such as periods (.), question marks (?), and exclamation marks (!). These marks serve the same purposes as in English: to indicate the end of a sentence, to form questions, or to convey emphasis or excitement. Proper usage of punctuation is crucial for maintaining clear and coherent writing in Korean.

Honorifics: Honorifics play a significant role in Korean language and culture. When writing, it's essential to pay attention to honorifics as they reflect the level of politeness and respect conveyed in the language. The choice of honorifics should be based on the context and the relationship between the writer/speaker and the recipient. Using the appropriate honorifics demonstrates respect and familiarity, enhancing the effectiveness of your written and spoken communication.

Cultural Significance

Hangeul is more than just a writing system; it's deeply embedded in Korean culture and identity. Every October 9th, South Korea celebrates Hangeul Day, commemorating the script's creation and its significance in promoting literacy and cultural expression.

For those new to Korean, Hangeul might seem daunting initially. However, its logical design means that with consistent practice, it can be mastered in a relatively short period. One effective approach is to start by familiarizing oneself with each consonant and vowel, practicing their sounds, and then moving on to combining them into syllables. Writing out characters repeatedly can also aid in retention.

So, with all the basic alphabets and rules you learned, let's try and see if you remembered what we discussed so far with these exercises:

Exercises

1.1 Korean Alphabets

1.   How many consonants are there in Korean?

a. 10   b. 14   c. 19   d. 16

2.   What is the English equivalent of *m* in Korean?

a. ㄴ   b. ㅈ   c. ㅁ   d. ㅍ

3.   All of these consonants sounds like a *t*
if placed as the final consonant, **except:**

a. ㅇ   b. ㅎ   c. ㅊ   d. ㅌ

4.   All of these consonants sounds like a ㅅ
if placed as the final consonant, **except:**

a. ㄷ   b. ㅆ   c. ㄱ   d. ㅈ

5.   What consonant does not have a sound value when placed as the beginning consonant?

a. ㄹ   b. ㅂ   c. ㅅ   d. ㅇ

1.2 Pronunciation and Writing Exercises:

A. Read the following syllables/words and try to write their equivalent romanization or sound value in English:

1.   곰, 공

2.   달, 답

3.   목, 몸

4.   방, 발

5.   삼, 산

6.   눈, 산, 편지

7.   밤, 마음, 몸무게

8.   공, 양, 강아지

9.   집, 잎, 수업

10.   옷, 낮, 꽃

1.3. Write the correct Korean word based on the English romanization/sound values provided:

1.   Han-guk

2.   Sa-ram

3.   Bap

4.   Han-gang

5.   De-han Min-guk

6.   U-ri Nara

7.   Se-u

8.   Chi-ma

9.   A-beo-ji

10.   Ban-chin-gu

Fun Fact Breather Section

Beware The Fan

Superstition alert! Many Koreans believe leaving the fan on while you sleep will bring the grim reaper for a visit

Heads Up, Gentlemen!

Valentine's Day in Korea is mostly for the guys. That's right, men are the ones getting chocolates and gifts. Ladies, don't worry—White Day is coming for you!

It's Just A Number?

Tetraphobia is a thing in Korea! The number four is avoided like the plague, and you'll often see elevators skipping the number altogether.

Chapter Two
Korean Sentence Structure

Korean, like all languages, has its unique rhythm, pattern, and structure. Understanding the basic sentence structures in Korean opens doors to meaningful conversations and deeper insights into the language's essence.

2.1 Word Order

At the core of Korean sentence structures lies the Subject-Object-Verb (SOV) order. The verb is placed at the end of a sentence, which is clearly distinct from English, where the verb immediately follows the subject. In Korean, the verb typically comes at the end of the sentence.

So technically speaking, you will only know what your Korean friend is talking about at the end of the sentence, so you better listen carefully.

English Structure: SUBJECT (S) + VERB (V) + OBJECT (O)

Korean Structure: SUBJECT (S) + OBJECT (O) + VERB (V).

(SOV Structure is used in Korean, Japanese and partly German)

To understand the English and Korean difference in terms of sentence structures, take a look at these samples:

English	Korean
I have a pen.	I pen have.
She gave me a cake.	She cake gave me.
I don't know her.	I her don't know.

If you are quite confused now, don't worry. The best tip we can give you is "**always finish your sentence with a verb or an adjective**".

Here are some sentence structure examples of Korean to help you get familiar with this grammar rule:

Example 1:

English: I ate an orange.

저는 오렌지를 먹었어요.

(Jeo-neun o-ren-ji-rul mo-go-sso-yo)

I + orange + ate

Example 2:

English: My big brother plays football.

오빠가 축구를 해요.

(op-pa-ga chuk-gu-rul he-yo)

Big brother + football + to do

Example 3:

English: I meet my friend.

저는 친구를 만나요.

(Jeo-neun chin-gu-rul man-na-yo)

I + friend + to meet

This pattern remains consistent across various sentence types, whether they're statements, questions, or commands.

The next step that you need to learn is **conjugating verbs** because it is not quite enough that you know Korean common verbs and where they should be placed in a sentence. You should also know how to cut and groom these tricky verbs so that when you use them in a sentence, you would not sound like a talking dictionary or an emotionless robot.

Conjugating is very, very important but we will dive into this more complex topic later. For now, here is a quick introduction to the other fundamental parts of speech in the Korean language.

Before we delve into the world of parts of speech, you should be familiar with the most common Korean sentence ending as a beginner first, for easier understanding. Let's take a quick look at *To be* verb as our example below:

이에요/ 예요

This verb ending means "**am, is** or **are**" depending on the context of the sentence. This ending is used when speaking in a casual form, not too formal. **이에요 (i-yeyo) is used when the noun's last syllable ends with a consonant and 예요 (yeyo), if it ends with a vowel.**

이에요:

저는 송혜진이에요   (I am Song Hyejin)

(jeo-neun song-hye-jin-iyeyo)

저는 **김윤경이에요**   (**I am** Kim Yoongyung)

(jeo-neun kim-yoon-gyung-iyeyo)

예요:

저는 이민호예요.   (**I am** Lee Minho)

(jeo-neun ee-min-ho-yeyo)

저는 박민수**예요**.   (**I am** Park Minsoo)

(jeo-neun pak-min-soo-yeyo)

This rule also applies to the subject or nouns of the sentence. So, the meaning is not fixed, it depends on the verb's usage.

화장품**이에요**.

(hwa-jang-pumi-iyeyo)

It **is** cosmetics.

기숙사**예요**.

(gi-suk-sa-yeyo)

It **is** the dorm/Here **is** the dorm.

The ever-popular **입니다** (im-nida) ending, however, is very easy to use because you don't have to check the ending of the previous syllable. It works the same for vowels and consonants.

저는 수치입니다.

(jeo-neun su-ji-imnida)

I am Suzy.

저는 한국 사람**입니다**.

(jeo-neun han-guk sa-ramim-nida)

I am Korean.

If this verb is used to ask a question, as in "**Are** you a Korean?",

입니다 transforms into **입니까** (im-nik-ka)

한국 사람**입니까**?

(han-guk sa-ramim-nik-ka?)

Are (you) Korean?

The verb 이에요/ 예요 stays the same for statements and questions. We will have a separate chapter discussing how to ask questions, so don't panic yet.

In any language, the very first fundamental part of speech that we learn is the **noun**. We start building our vocabulary and knowledge of the language with nouns.

Even if you know a bunch of verbs, prepositions, adjectives and grammar rules in general, you would not be able to create a sentence if you do not know any vocabulary, so only after building up our vocabulary, we can then easily make simple sentences.

And in reality, regardless if you are a beginner, intermediate or advanced or even a near-native speaker, you will be learning a new word every day for the rest of our lives.

2.2 Korean Nouns (명사 - Myeong-sa)

Similar to English and other languages, a Korean noun refers to a person, object or thing, which may be tangible or intangible. They can be replaced by pronouns.

There are three (3) types of nouns in Korean Language:

1. Sino-Korean Nouns:

About 60% of the nouns fall under this category. This is because of the long history of Chinese language being used in the country before, thus words originating from Chinese characters.

생활 (seng-hwal) from Chinese word 生活 (shēnghuó) which means *life or living*

정신 (jeong-shin) from Chinese word 精神 (jīngshén) which means *mind or soul*

항상 (hang-sang) from Chinese word 恒常 (héngcháng) which means *always or all the time*

혹시 (hok-shi) from Chinese word 或是 (huòshì) which means *by chance or incidentally*

2. Native Korean Nouns

Approximately 35% of the entirety of nouns are purely native Korean. These are usually words originating from traditional culture and fundamental elements of Korean lifestyle.

Examples:

하늘 (Ha-neul which means *sky*)

고양이 (Go-yang-i which means *cat*)

바다 (Ba-da which means *ocean*)

나래 (Na-re which means *wing*)

3. Korean Borrowed Words

The remaining 5% of the nouns are the words that are borrowed or adapted from other languages which commonly are Japanese, English, partly German and French. These nouns are also called "exotic words" or "konglish" which is a combination of Korean-English.

Examples:

앨리게이터	(el-li-ge-i-teo from *Alligator*)
택시	(tek-shi from *Taxi*)
피자	(pi-ja from *Pizza*)
비타민	(bee-ta-min from *Vitamin*)
초콜릿	(cho-kol-lit from *Chocolate*)

These words are very easy to spot because the pronunciation is very recognizable and the meaning of the words are the same. For people whose native language is English, these nouns are very easy to understand even without studying Korean.

Here are some of the most common Korean nouns, their romanization and meaning to help you begin your journey with Korean vocabulary:

Korean Nouns	Meaning	Korean Nouns	Meaning
아이 (a-yi)	Child	세상 (se-sang)	World
남자 (nam-ja)	Man	집 (jib)	House
여자 (yeo-ja)	Woman	신문 (shin-mun)	Newspaper
가족 (ga-jok)	Family	가방 (ga-bang)	Bag
나라 (na-ra)	Country	사랑 (sa-rang)	Love
언니 (eon-ni)	older sister	동생 (dong-seng)	younger sibling
누나 (nu-na)	older sister	형 (hyeong)	older brother

Classroom Nouns:

Korean	Sound Value	English
선생님	seon-seng-nim	teacher
학생	hak-seng	student
반 친구	ban chin-gu	classmate
칠판	chil-pan	blackboard/whiteboard
의자	ui-ja	chair
연필	yeon-pil	pencil
지우개	ji-oo-geh	eraser
필통	pil-tong	pencil case
시계	shi-gye	clock

달력	dal-yeok	calendar
창문	chang-mun	window
문	mun	door
공책	gong-chek	notebook
책상	chek-sang	book

Occupation Nouns:

Korean	Sound Value	English
운전기사	un-jeon-gisa	driver
점원	jeom-won	clerk
회사원	hwe-sa-won	office staff
주부	ju-bu	housewife
경찰관/경찰	gyeong-chal-gwan/ gyeong-chal	police officer
의사	ui-sa	doctor
기술자	gi-sul-jja	technician
소방관	so-bang-gwan	firefighter
간호사	gan-ho-sa	nurse
목수	mok-su	carpenter
공무원	gong-mu-won	public official

요리사	yo-ri-sa	cook/chef
어부	eo-bu	fisherman
검사	geom-sa	prosecutor
농부	nong-bu	farmer
변호사	byeon-ho-sa	lawyer

Country Nouns:

Korean	Sound Value	English
한국	han-guk	Korea
필리핀	pil-lip-pin	Philippines
호주	ho-ju	Australia
네팔	ne-pal	Nepal
일본	il-bon	Japan
몽골	mong-gol	Mongolia
미얀마	mi-yan-ma	Myanmar
베트남	be-teu-nam	Vietnam
미국	mi-guk	US
중국	jung-guk	China
캄보디아	kam-bo-di-a	Cambodia
방글라데시	bang-geul-la-de-shi	Bangladesh

파키스탄	pa-ki-seu-tan	Pakistan
태국	te-guk	Thailand
인도네시아	in-do-ne-shi-a	Indonesia

Community Nouns:

Korean	Sound Value	English
여기	yeo-gi	here
회사	hwe-sa	office
거기	geo-gi	there
저기	jeo-gi	over there
화장실	hwa-jang-shil	bathroom
식당/레스토랑	shik-dang/re-seu-to-rang	restaurant
우체국	u-che-guk	post office
집	jip	house
시장	shi-jang	market
기숙사	gi-suk-sa	dorm/dormitory
마트	ma-teu	mart
세탁소	se-tak-so	laundry shop
쇼핑 몰	sho-ping-mol	shopping mall
편의점	pyeon-i-jeom	convenience store

미용실	mi-yong-shil	beauty salon
슈퍼마켓	shu-peo-ma-ket	supermarket
공원	gong-won	park
백화점	bek-hwa-jeom	department store
커피숍	ko-pi-shop	coffee shop
노래방	no-re bang	karaoke
서점	seo-jeom	bookstore
PC 방	pi-shi-bang	internet cafe
도서관	do-seo-gwan	library
영화관	yong-hwa-gwan	movie theater

Nouns for everyday stuff:

Korean	Sound Value	English
열쇠	yeol-swe	key(s)
가족사진	ga-jok-sa-jin	family picture
가방	ga-bang	bag
지갑	ji-gap	wallet
여권	yeo-gwon	passport
우산	u-san	umbrella
화장품	hwa-jang-pum	cosmetics/make-up

베개	be-ge	pillow
헤어드라이어	he-eo-deu-ra-yo	hairdryer
이불	i-bul	blanket

Don't worry, as we go on with all the other grammar rules, you will pick up vocabularies one by one and in no time, you'll be able to switch and choose words from your vocabulary stash.

2.3 Korean Particles

Korean Particles may be a small fragment of the Korean grammar but this is essentially where beginners get their first head-scratch-of-confusion.

This part of Korean grammar is so important to learn and master because these particles work as labels attached to nouns to help you understand what the noun is all about.

To put simply, these Korean particles can tell you if the noun is the subject, the object, or if the noun is related to the other noun in the sentence.

Here are the most common and useful Korean particles:

Type of Particles	Korean Particles
1. Topic	은 (eun)
	는 (neun)
2. Subject	이 (ee)
	가 (ga)
3. Object	을 (eul)
	를 (rul)

4.	Combining	와 (wa)
		과 (gwa)
		랑 (rang)
		이랑 (ee-rang)
		하고 (ha-go)
5.	Plural	들 (deul)
6.	Possessive	의 (ui)
7.	Location/Time	에 (eh)
		에서 (es-seo)
		으로 (eu-ro)
		로 (ro)
		부터 (bu-teo)
		까지 (kkaji)
8.	Only	만 (man)
9.	Too	도 (do)
10.	Offering/Receiving	께 (kke)
		에게 (e-ge)
		한테 (han-te)
		께서 (kke-seo)
		에게서 (e-ges-seo)
		한테서 (han-tes-seo)

1. Korean Topic Particles: 은 and 는

A topic particle tells everyone what's being talked about. Any noun followed by 은 (eun) or 는 (neun) is emphasized as the topic of the sentence.

은 and 는 are the same.

However, 은 is used if the noun's last syllable is ending in a consonant. 책 (chek), which means "book," and 집 (jib), which means "house," both end in consonants, so we use 은 for them:

집은 크다.

(Ji-beun keu-da.)

The house is big.

On the other hand, for easier pronunciation, 는 is used for nouns with syllable that ends in a vowel. 저 (jeo), honorific form "I/Me" ends with the vowel ㅓ (eo) so we use 는 with it.

저는 한국인이에요.

(Jeo-neun han-gu-gini-yeyo.)

I'm Korean.

2. Korean Subject Particles: 이 and 가

Another essential Korean Particle that helps us identify the subject of the sentence are the particles 이 and 가.

When the subject is often related to the verb or adjective, these markers help answer the following questions:

Who is the doer of the action?

Who/what is being described?

The subject particle is either 이 (ee) or 가 (ga). They're basically the same thing. Similar to the topic particles, we use 이 if the noun's last syllable is ending in a consonant and 가 if it's a vowel.

날씨가
가방이
e
날씨가 좋다.
(Nal-shi-**ga** jo-tta.)
The weather is nice.

가방이 예쁘다.
(Ga-bang**i** ye-ppeu-da.)
The bag is pretty.

3. Korean Object Particles: 을 and 를

To find the object in Korean sentences easier, just follow the S-O-V (Subject-Object-Verb) pattern, and it will lead you to find the object before the verb.

Both 을 (eul) or 를 (rul) are the same.

Similar to Topic and Subject particles, we use 을 if the noun's last syllable is ending in a consonant and 를 if it's a vowel.

저는 김치를 먹었다.
(Jeo-neun kim-chi-rul meo-got-dda.)
I ate kimchi.

그녀는 물을 마신다.
(Geun-yeo-neun mu-rul ma-shin-da.)
She drinks water.

저는 개를 봤어요.
(Jeo-neun ge-rul bwa-sseo-yo.)
I saw a dog.

4. Korean Linking Particles: 와, 과, 랑, 이랑 and 하고

The following particles are the English equivalent of "and" or "with"

They're used to indicate the grouping or pairing of nouns. For example:

you **and** me

cheese **and** pizza

Due to its formality, 와 and 과 is often used for speeches, presentations and written forms while 랑, 이랑 and 하고 are used in daily conversation since they convey a little more casual tone.

과 is used if the noun's last syllable is ending in a consonant and 와 for vowels.

사과와 오렌지
(Sa-gwa-wa o-ren-ji)
Apples **and** oranges

소금과 후추
(So-geum-gwa hu-chu)

Salt **and** pepper

이랑 is used if the noun's last syllable is ending in a consonant and **랑** for vowels.

오늘 윤경**이랑** 놀거야.
(O-neul Yoon-gyung-i-rang nol-geo-ya.)
I'm going to play **with** Yoon Gyung today.

난 친구**랑** 영화보는 걸 좋아해.
(Nan chin-gu-rang yeong-hwa-bo-neun-geol jo-wa-he.)
I like to watch movies **with** friends.

하고 can be used for both vowels and consonants.

개, 고양이**하고** 새
(Ge, go-yang-i-ha-go se)
Dogs, cats **and** birds

5. Korean Plural Particle: 들

Making plural form of nouns is quite easy, you just have to add "들" after the noun. But there are always exceptions. Just like in the English language, there are certain nouns that do not need the plural marker because they are already known to be plural without it.

Making nouns plural is not as common in Korean as it is in English because there is really not much difference between singular and plural, and Korean speakers have no problem with this because the context of the sentences is often already enough to be understood by the listener or reader.

So, a sentence like 저는 사과를 샀다 (Jeo-neun sagwa-rul sat-da) can either mean "I bought an apple" or "I bought apples."

들 is really only used for people or living things—it's rarely used for objects. You use it when you want to make clarity and emphasize that there is only **one thing**. Here are some examples:

친구 →친구들 (Friend/Friends)
남자 → 남자들 (Man/Men)
사람 → 사람들 (Person/People)
학생 → 학생들 (Student/Students)
꽃 → 꽃들 (Flower/Flowers)

학생들은 집에 갔다.
(Hak-seng-deu-run ji-be gat-da.)
The students went home.

6. Korean Possessive Particle: 의

This last Korean particle is the equivalent of the English apostrophe and s ('s) which expresses ownership or possession.

의 (ui) is placed between nouns and determines the relationship between them.

The order of the nouns is very, very important. The first noun is the owner, and the second noun—the one following 의—is the thing owned.

Here is an example:

언니의 차 (Eon-ni-ui cha). 언니 means "older sister" and 차 means "car." So, it means "elder sister's car."

Here are some more examples:

오늘의 게임
(Oneu-ri ge-im)
Today's game

민재의 머리카락
(Min Jae-ui meo-ri-ka-rak)
Min Jae's hair

우리 아버지의 친구가 왔다.
(U-ri a-beo-ji-ui chin-gu-ga wat-da.)
My father's friend came.

In speaking, 의 is often pronounced as 에 (e).

Adding 의 to get the possessive forms of the pronouns results in a new combined sound for short and easier pronunciation:

나의 (na-ui) becomes 내 (ne) which means "**my**"

저의 (jeo-ui) becomes 제 (je) which means "**my**"

너의 (neo-ui) becomes 네 (ne) which means "**your**"

Here are some more examples:

오늘은 **내** 생일이야.

(O-neu-reun ne seng-i-ri-ya.)

Today is **my** birthday.

네 생일은 언제야?

(Ne seng-i-reun on-je-ya?)

When is **your** birthday?

7. Korean Location Particles

There are 5 Korean location particles and all of which helps in determining the location in sentences. They emphasize where the subject or object is going, or what direction or movement the action has or is taking place.

Some of the Korean location particles may also be used as time markers.

7.1 -에 (eh | Time/Location)

When the verb of the sentence is 있다 (it-da), 에 (eh) is used to indicate location or time.

저는 학교**에** 있어요

(jeo-neun hak-gyo-ye is-seo-yo)

I am **at** school.

7.2 -에서 (eseo | Location)

에서 (eseo) also indicates location but its use is quite different from 에 (eh). You use 에서 when you are emphasizing the location you are doing or where you did something in, when describing how something is like somewhere, or when expressing the where something or someone is from. However, when the verb of the sentence is 있다 (it-da), in in this case 에 (eh) is used.

Example:

카페**에서** 숙제를 했어요

(kha-peh-eseo suk-je-reul hes-seo-yo)

I did my homework **in the** cafe.

저는 한국**에서** 왔어요

(jeo-neun han-gu-ge-seo was-soyo)

I am **from** Korea.

7.3 -로/으로 (ro/eu-ro | Direction and multiple other meanings)

로/으로 (ro/eu-ro) is a multi-use particle. For beginners, you can use it to express the location where something is happening similar to 에 (eh).

For example:

우유를 슈퍼**로** 사러 가려고 해요
(u-yu-rul shu-peo-ro sa-ro ga-ryeo-go he-yo)
I intend to go **to** the supermarket to buy milk.

You can also use it to express the *tool, method, language,* and so on.

For example:

기차로 대구**에** 갈 거예요
(gi-cha-ro de-gu-ye gal-ko-ye-yo)
I will go to Italy **by** train.

수채화**로** 그림을 그렸어요
(su-che-hwa-ro geu-ri-meul geu-ryos-soyo)
I painted **using** watercolors.

그 사람한테 한국말**로** 대답을 줬어요
(geu sa-ram-han-te han-guk-mal-lo de-da-beul jwos-soyo)
I answered that person **in** Korean.

맨날 아침식사**로** 죽을 먹어요
(men-nal a-chim-shik-sa-ro ju-geul mo-go-yo)
I eat porridge for breakfast **every** morning.

그쪽으**로**
(geu-jjo-keu-ro)
that way

남쪽으**로**
(nam-jjo-keu-ro)
toward south

7. 4 -부터 (bu-teo | From/Start)

부터 (bu-teo) is used to indicate when something starts.

Example:

저는 지난달**부터** 한국어를 배웠어요
(jeo-neun ji-nan-dal-bu-teo han-gu-geo-reul bae-wos-soyo)

I started to learn Korean last month.

부터 (bu-teo/**start**) is usually reserved for Korean sentences where you would it includes 까지 (kka-ji/**end**) in its structure and the two particles indicates the starting and the ending point.

For example:

집**부터** 학교**까지** 걸어 다녀요
(jib-bu-teo hak-gyo-kka-ji go-ro dan-yo-yo)
I walk from home to school.

기말고사는 내일**부터** 다음주말**까지** 있을거에요
(gi-mal-go-sa-neun ne-il-bu-teo da-eum-ju-mal-kka-ji i-sseul-ko-yeyo)
Our final exams will start tomorrow and last until the end of next week.

For both time and place, 까지 basically means *end* or specifically *until*. You can also use it together with 에서, but combining it with this particle is isn't always necessary because 까지's meaning will still remain clear in even when used alone.

Example:

집**에서** 여기**까지** 걸어서 왔어요
(ji-be-so yo-gi-kka-ji gor-ro-so was-seo-yo)
I walked from home up to here.

8. Korean Particle "Only"

This particle is attached to the noun to express the word *only*.

어제 우유**만** 마셨어요
(o-je u-yu-man ma-shos-so-yo)
I only drank beer yesterday.

하루종일 공부**만** 했어요
(ha-ru-jong-il gong-bu-man hes-so-yo)
I did nothing but study all-day.

9. Korean Particle "Also"

도 (**do**) is used to indicate addition or similarity in the form of *too* and *also*. When using the additive particle 도 you can skip the subject/object or other particles.

Examples:

나도 빅뱅을 좋아해요

(na-do big-beng-eul jo-wa-heyo)

I like Big Bang, **too.**

나도 필리핀사람이에요

(na-do pil-lip-pin-sa-ra-mi-ye-yo)

I am **also** from the Philippines.

10.   Offering/Receiving Particles

께, 에게, 한테 (kke/e-ge/han-te) are particles added to express offering or giving someone something.

Examples:

언니**한테** 돈을 빌려줬어

(eon-ni han-te do-neul bil-yos-seo)

I lent money to my elder sister.

께, 에게, 한테 all mean the same, the only difference between each one is basically their level of politeness.

께 (**kke**) is of honorific level, 에게 (**e-ge**) is formal polite form, and 한테 (**han-te**) is informal and casual.

Don't worry, we will have a separate topic about Korean honorifics, so you don't have to panic yet.

께서, 에게서, 한테서 (kke-seo/e-ges-seo/han-te-seo) are particles used to receive something from someone)

These particles have the same level of politeness as their counterparts above.

Phew! That was quite the topic, don't you think? As you discover Korean grammar, learning the particles will essentially improve your knowledge of Korean sentences which will make you more confident to talk to your native Korean friends!

So, now you know a couple of the most common Korean particles and you're a step closer to mastering these important Korean markers!

Let's try to test your understanding and memory power through the following exercises!

Exercises

2.1 Sentence Structure Exercises

Choose the correct answer.

1. What is the typical sentence structure order in Korean?

a. SVO   b. SOV   c. VSO   d. OSV

2. What do you need to add to a word if you want to make it plural?

a. 의   b. 를   c. 들   d. 만

3. What is the particle that expresses *too or also*?

a. 은   b. 는   c. 도   d. 두

4. What is the particle that expresses possession?

a. 을   b. 의   c. 하고   d. 에

4. What is the subject particle pair?

a. 은 / 는   b. 와/과   c. 에/에서   d. 이/가

2.2. Fill in the blanks with the correct particle:

1. 오늘 친구__을 만나요.

2. 오늘 남자친구__ 영화를 보러 가요.

3. 하루안에 그 책을 처음부터 끝__ 읽었어요.

4. 저는 인도네시아__ 왔어요.

5. 주말에 친구와 영화__ 볼 거예요.

6. 바나나__ 먹어요.

7. 화장실__ 어디예요?

8. 이름__ 뭐예요?

9. 샤워__ 잠을 잘 거예요.

10. 어제 맥주___ 마셨어요.

2.3. Write 1 example each where the 10 particles are applied, totalling to 10 sentences. The words or sentences provided in Part B should be excluded. Please include what type of particle it is.

Examples:

1. Subject Particle 가 = 엄마가

2. Topic Particle 은 = 그 사람은

Fun Fact Breather Section

Housewarming Gifts, Korean Style

Moving to a new place in Korea? Save your money on toilet paper and laundry detergent. Your housewarming guests have got you covered!

Tentacles, Anyone?

Live octopus is not just a Korean delicary; it's an experience! Feel the thrill of tasting a delicacy that fights back.

Swiping the Plastic

South Korea is a haven for credit card lovers. It's one of the world's most wired countries with an affinity for plastic money.

Chapter Three
The Art of Korean Pronouns

Korean Pronouns (대명사 - De-myeong-sa)

The Korean language offers a fascinating perspective on pronouns. This distinction is deeply rooted in the culture, reflecting the importance of respect and hierarchy in social interactions. By understanding the pronouns in Korean, learners can communicate more effectively and navigate various social settings with ease.

Unlike many other languages, Korean pronouns (can change based on the level of formality in a conversation, **so we will also tackle a little bit about honorifics.**

In this chapter, you will learn about:

Subject pronouns which are used to indicate who is performing an action. In English, we use terms like "I", "**you**", and "**they**". In Korean, these pronouns have different forms based on the relationship between the speaker and the listener. It's crucial to select the appropriate form to ensure the conversation remains respectful and appropriate for the context.

Object pronouns which are used to refer to the receiver of the action. In the Korean language, the way these pronouns are used is slightly different from English.

Lastly, **possessive pronouns** which indicate ownership or association. They help in understanding who or what something belongs to. In Korean, these pronouns also come with their nuances, which can be mastered with practice.

The world of Korean pronouns is intricate, but with a systematic approach, it becomes manageable. This chapter will guide you through each type of pronoun, offering clear explanations and examples. By the end, you'll have a firm grasp of the role and usage of pronouns in the Korean language, setting a strong foundation for more advanced grammar concepts.

3.1 Subject Pronouns

Korean subject pronouns hold a unique position in the language's grammar. Unlike the English language, Korean has different levels of politeness or honorifics.

Again, compared to English where there is often only one pronoun – such as "you" when addressing somebody, there are different ways of doing so in Korean. Due to the importance of respect, age, and hierarchy in Korean culture, you'll have to learn these levels in pronouns as well.

So, the next time you try to talk to your friend or boss in Korean, you'll have to be careful which pronoun to use.

Here is a quite detailed overview of all the pronouns that we will be discussing:

1. First-person singular

2. First-person plural

3. Second-person singular

4. Second-person plural

5. Third-person singular and plural

6. Usage and absence of pronouns

7. Practice

Yup! Those titles might be a bit scary for beginners, but when you read each section you're going to understand them immediately!

3.2 Addressing Yourself: First-Person Singular

Let's start by discovering how you would address or talk about yourself.

There are 2 ways of referring to yourself.

*   저 (jeo) which is the <u>formal</u> *I*

*   나 (na) which is the <u>informal</u> *I*

Unlike in English where pronouns can change depending on their position in the sentence, in Korean, the pronoun remains the same regardless of its position.

Comparison:

English:

I gave him the bag.

He gave the bag to **me**.

Korean:

저는 메리에게 가방을 주었다

(**I** gave the bag to Mary.)

메리는 **저**에게 가방을 주었다

(Mary gave the bag to **me**.)

The Korean particles that you just learned in the previous chapter will be your helpful partner to denote the position of the pronouns.

Here is a table to help you understand the usage of these personal pronouns:

Formal "I"	Informal "I"
저는 (I)	나는 (I)
저를 (me)	나를 (me)
저의 (my)	나의 (my)
제가 (I)	내가 (I)

3.3 Addressing a group including Yourself: First-Person Plural

Similar to the singular, Korean has two different ways of addressing yourself as part of a group.

저희 (jeo-hee) which is the **formal *we***

우리 (u-ri) which is the **informal *we***

These pronouns work exactly like the singular ones. What a relief! As we continue with the topic, you'll see the same rules over and over again. Phew!

Formal "we"	Informal "we"
저희는 (we)	우리는 (we)
저희가 (we)	우리가 (we)
저희를 (us)	우리를 (us)

저희의 (our)	우리의 (our)

Good to know:

In Korean, if 우리 is used without the possessive particle 의 it conveys usage as a singular possessive pronoun. You might have heard this often in Korean dramas and tv shows.

우리 엄마는 김치를 엄청 좋아해요

(U-ri eom-ma-neun kim-chi-rul eom-cheong jo-wa-he-yo)

(**My** mother really likes Kimchi.)

나는 **우리** 선생님을 좋아해요

(Na-neun u-ri seon-seng-ni-meul jo-wa-he-yo)

(I like **my** teacher.)

This is why you always have to watch out or listen intently because the meaning of the sentence will depend on this context. So the next time you'll be talking to a friend, and they are only referencing themselves, you'll most likely hear **우리** being used as a singular possessive.

3.4. Addressing Others: Second-Person Singular

Again, we have two ways of saying "you".

- 당신 (dang-shin) which is the **formal** of *you*

- 너 (noh) which is the **informal** of *you*

You just have to apply the same particle rules that you have learned for pronouns *I* and *we*.

Formal "you"	Informal "you"
당신은 (you) as subject	너는 (you) as subject
당신이 (you) as topic	네가 (you) as topic
당신을 (you) as object	너를 (you) as object

당신의 (your)	너의 (your)

3.5. Addressing Groups: Second-Person Plural

Addressing groups are quite easy. You just have to add the plural particle 들 after the pronouns you learned above.

Formal "you" as group	Informal "you" as group
당신들은 (you) as subject	너희는 (you) as subject
당신들이 (you) as topic	너희가 (you) as topic
당신들을 (you) as object	너희를 (you) as object
당신들의 (your)	너희의 (your)

Now, you might have already recognized the patterns for the pronouns we discussed so far. You can tap yourself in the back because you are definitely doing a good job!

3.6. Talking about Others: Third-Person Singular and Plural

Talking about other people in Korean is very simple. We use 그 (geu) for men and 그녀 (geu-nyo) for women.

- 그 (geu) for He

- 그녀 (geu-nyo) for She

He	She
그는 (he as subject)	그녀는 (she as subject)
그가 (he as topic)	그녀가 (she as topic)
그를 (him as object)	그녀를 (her as object)
그의 (his as possessive)	그녀의 (her as possessive)

To make these pronouns plural, you just have to add plural 들 particle.

Honestly, you won't see or hear these pronouns in use very often. They're only commonly used in written Korean.

Now that you have already learned the different pronouns and their levels of formality, you might be surprised if we tell you that Koreans do not use them that much. Yes! You've heard it right. They usually omit the subject of a sentence specially in informal speech or conversation, but this is not acceptable in written or formal speech of course!

You must have heard an actress or an actor saying "배고파요!" while touching their stomach. This word literally means just "**hungry**". However, the real meaning of the sentence would be "**I'm hungry!**"

Fun Facts about Korean Pronouns:

Just thinking about making a mistake with pronouns in Korean makes you panic? Oh, don't.

Beginners are always forgiven for these mistakes, but be sure not to make the same mistake again, especially for pronouns!

Here are some worth-knowing facts about pronouns:

Even polite form of "you" which is 당신 can sound rude at times. You'll most likely hear people use this when they are making a point, if someone is upset or couples in the middle of an argument.

So the best way with Korean is to avoid addressing people directly with pronouns, especially in spoken language. Instead, you can use a term of endearment (if accepted by the counterpart), call them by their job title or just by their names.

Question:

How do I address people that I don't know?

Answer:

Here are the ways to address them:

1. **Add 님 after their names.** This particle is mostly used for teachers or other professionals but if you need to talk to a stranger they would understand if you use this to address them because it conveys respect.

2. **아저씨**. For men (whom you think are married or older), you can use this to address them such as taxi drivers or restaurant staff.

3. **사장님**. This literally means "owner" but you can use it to call men and women in a very polite manner. Use this instead of 아줌마 when addressing women (whom you think are married or older) since they

usually **do not** like to be called 아줌마 because of the connotation of being old associated with it.

4. Add 씨 after their names. This particle literally means "miss" or "mister", and can be used in either casual or formal settings. This is a little less polite than 님, so 님 would still be a better choice specially for business conversations.

Hopefully, by this time, you already have a good understanding of Korean pronouns. There aren't as many rules to remember as it is in English, so you can simply practice and start using pronouns today!

Exercises

3.1 Subject Pronouns Exercises

1. Which pronoun is used as an informal way to refer to "I" or "me"?

a. 나   b. 저   c. 그   d. 우리

2. In a formal setting, which pronoun would you use to address someone older than you?

a. 너   b. 저는   c. 당신   d. 우리

3. How do you say "we" or "us" in Korean?

a. 그들   b. 저희   c. 우리   d. 그분들

4. True or False: In Korean, the pronoun is always present in a sentence.

3.2 Writing Practice

Write the Korean equivalent of the provided English sentences.

1. I am Suzy.

2. She is Mina

3. They are the Korean Team.

4. He is hungry.

5. I am a student.

3.3 Composition Practice

Write at least 3 sentences introducing yourself which includes your name and your nationality and occupation. Write the sentences in both Casual polite and honorific form. There should be 6 sentences in total.

Fun Fact Breather Section

Internet Paradise

Internet in Korea is no joke! Try not to get too envious when you experience internet speeds that feel like a dream.

Delivery Champions

In Korea, your delivery doesn't just arrive; it sprints to your doorstep! Speed and quality are the name of the game and Korea takes this very seriously

Floor Warmth

Feeling chilly? In Korea, the heating method of homes focuses on the floor! Keep yourself warm in the cold months by turning on the heater and sticking to the ground

Chapter Four
Verbs and Conjugation

Korean Verbs (동사 - Dong-sa)

In Korean language, verbs stand as powerful pillars. They drive the action, convey emotions, and shape the direction of conversations. These Verbs start with their root form which needs to be conjugated in order to be used in a conversation.

Conjugation is the art of modifying these verbs to express different tenses, moods, and levels of formality. Together, verbs and their conjugation form an essential duo, enabling rich and varied expressions in Korean.

Verbs in Korean are broadly categorized into **regular** and **irregular** types.

Regular verbs follow standard conjugation patterns, offering predictability and ease to learners.

Irregular verbs, while fewer in number, introduce unique conjugation patterns. These verbs often involve changes in their stems or endings when modified, adding layers of complexity. Yet, they're essential for a holistic understanding of Korean, as they frequently appear in everyday conversations.

Conjugation rules, the backbone of this chapter, provide a systematic approach to transform verbs. The rules to consider are:

1. the verb's ending,
2. the intended tense and;
3. the desired level of politeness.

Mastering these rules allows learners to form sentences with precision, ensuring their Korean is both grammatically correct and contextually appropriate.

This chapter aims to demystify the world of Korean verbs and their conjugation. Let's get started.

4.1 The Root Verb

The **root verb** or sometimes called *infinitive* or *dictionary form* is a verb when it is <u>NOT YET conjugated</u>. You'll find the verbs in a dictionary in this form, which cannot be used in a conversation because it sounds unnatural and robotic, that is why we need to conjugate it to sound more smooth and natural.

These unconjugated verbs end in **다**.

Here are some of the most common verbs that we use in our daily lives:

Verbs for Senses	Movement Verbs	Action Verbs
보다 (bo-da) To see/watch	점심을 먹다 (jeom-shi-meul meok-da) To eat lunch	들어오다 (deu-ro-o-da) To enter
말하다 (mal-ha-da) To talk/speak	오다 (o-da) To come	나가다 (na-ga-da) To exit
묻다 (mud-da) To ask	가다 (ga-da) To go	기다리다 (gi-da-ri-da) To wait
대답하다 (de-dap ha-da) To answer	걷다 (geot-da) To walk	그만하다 (geu-man ha-da) To stop
생각하다 (seng-gak ha-da) To think	앉다 (an-ja) To sit	서두르다 (seo-du-reu-da) To hurry
자다 (ja-da) To sleep	일어나다 (i-ro-na-da) To wake up	움직이다 (um-jik-i-da) To move
요리하다 (yo-ri-ha-da) To cook	춤추다 (chum-chu-da) To dance	돌아오다 (do-ra-o-da) To return
꿈꾸다 (kkum-kku-da) To dream	만나다 (man-na-da) To meet	여행하다 (yeo-heng ha-da) To travel
만들다 (man-deul-da) To make/create	운동하다 (un-dong ha-da) To exercise	하다 (ha-da) To do

듣다 (deut-da) To listen/hear	운전하다 (un-jeon ha-da) To drive	배우다 (be-u-da) To learn
놀다 (nol-da) To play	타다 (ta-da) To ride	공부하다 (gong-bu ha-da) To study
필요하다 (pil-yo ha-da) To need	열다 (yeol-da) To open	쓰다 (sseu-da) To write
이다 (i-da) To be	닫다 (dat-da) To close	읽다 (ik-da) To read
되다 (dwe-da) To become	도착하다 (do-chak ha-da) To arrive	일하다 (il-ha-da) To work
할수있다 (hal-su-itda) To be able to do	출발하다 (chul-bal ha-da) To depart	

Below, let's take a quick look at the three basic levels of formality or honorifics. It is important to get familiar with the verb endings because it will tell you what level of politeness to convey the relationship of the speaker and counterpart.

(There's actually more, including a special one for speaking with royalty! We won't be covering those as they aren't commonly used.)

Let's take a look at how the verb 가 which means "to go" looks in the 3 different levels of formality:

Informal	Casual Polite	Honorific
Verb + 아 or 어	Verb + 아요 or 어요	Verb + 습니다 or Verb + ㅂ니다
가	가요	갑니다

Here is the detailed explanation of the table above.

4.2 CONJUGATING BASED ON POLITENESS LEVEL

1. **Conjugating verbs in Informal Form**

Informal is used with those younger than you and with family and friends.

All you need to do is drop the 다 add 어/아/여 to the stem of the verb:

Example:

먹다 (To eat)

먹 + 어

먹어

When adding something to a word stem, if the <u>last vowel</u> in the stem is ㅏ or ㅗ, you must add **아**. For all the other vowels (except the 2 mentioned vowels) you must add **어**. If the syllable of the stem is **하**, you add **하여** which can be shortened to just **해**.

가다 =	**가**	(가 + 아)
오다 =	**와**	(오 + 아)
배우다 =	**배워**	(배우 + 어)
끼다 =	**껴**	(끼 + 어)
나서다 =	**나서**	(나서 + 어)
켜다 =	**켜**	(켜 + 어)
하다 =	**해**	(하 + 여)

These verbs, although short, are already stand alone words and can be considered as a whole sentence by itself. You will most likely hear them within friends, families or couples because these relationships do not require the honorific level of speech.

In Korean, you only really have to conjugate the verb **considering tense**, which makes it a much easier process than in English. Let's start conjugating regular verbs in Casual Polite Form.

2. **Conjugating Regular Verbs in Casual Polite Form**

Casual Polite is a safe level for a new learner of Korean. You are not going to offend anyone but you're also not being overly polite.

In English Language, you have to match the verb and the subject in the sentences such as person or number.

However, in Korean, you don't have to worry about this.

English:

The cat eats.

The cats eat.

Korean:

고양이는 먹어요 (The cat **eats**)

고양이들은 먹어요 (The cats **eat**.)

Notice how in Korean, the verb stayed exactly the same.

To conjugate a Korean verb, the first step is to get rid of the 다 ending. Let's look at how to do that.

The final vowel gets to decide whether 아 or 어 is used.

Level Guide:

Use 아요	Use 어요	Combine
if the last vowel in the verb is ㅏ or ㅗ. Ex: 가다 (to go) → 가요	if the last vowel in the verb is all the other vowels. Ex: 먹다 (to eat) → 먹어요	If the verb stem ends in a vowel, the 아 or 어 that you add to the verb stem will combine with the previous syllable. Ex: 가다 (to go) = 가요 주다 (to give)= 주워요 오다 (to come)= 와요 서다 (to stand)= 서요 배우다 (to learn) = 배워요

하다 (To Do)

하다 is one of the most common verbs in Korean. but it is a bit different to conjugate than the other verbs. Instead of becoming *하요* as you'd expect from the rules above, it becomes **해/해요**, except at the highest formality level.

Informal: 해

Casual Polite: 해요

Honorific: 합니다

Here's how you will see it:

운전 (noun, drive) + 하다

운전하다 (to drive) – 운전해요

Here is a final look at this verb in different politeness levels:

운전하다 (to drive)

Informal: 운전해

Casual Polite: 운전해요

Honorific: 운전합니다

There are a lot of **하다** verbs so whenever you learn new noun or vocabularies, you'll be able to use this verb form.

3. Conjugating regular Verbs using Honorific Level

This level is used in public service announcements, on the news, to superiors in a workplace, to teachers and parents, and to those older than you.

This is done similarly to the conjugation you learned for Informal form and casual polite which means, we have to look at the word stem as well.

To conjugate using the honorific ending, you add ㅂ니다/습니다 to the end of the word stem.

After dropping 다, if the word stem ends in a vowel, you add -ㅂ니다.

Examples:

보다

보 + ㅂ니다 = 봅니다

운동하다

운동하 + ㅂ니다 = 운동합니다

After dropping 다, if the word stem ends in a consonant, you add -습니다 to the word stem.

먹다

먹 + 습니다 = 먹습니다

Let's practice all the levels!

1. **있다** (to have)

Informal: 있어

Casual Polite: 있어요

Honorific: 있습니다

2. **가다** (to go)

Informal: 가

Casual Polite: 가요

Honorific: 갑니다

4.3 Conjugating Irregular Verbs

In the world of Korean verbs, irregular verbs stand out as intriguing anomalies. Unlike their regular counterparts, these verbs don't always play by the conventional rules, often introducing unique conjugation patterns.

Types of Irregular Verbs

Irregular verbs in Korean can be categorized based on the final syllable of the verb stem or specific changes they undergo.

Here are a few common categories include:

1. ㅂ Irregulars:

When present tense verbs with stems ending in 'ㅂ', this consonant is dropped and 워요 (wo-yo) is added

Example:

Root Form: 돕다 (dop-ta) - to help

Conjugated form: 도와요 (do-wa-yo) - helps

2. ㄷ Irregulars:

When present tense verbs with stems ending in 'ㄷ', the character often disappears during conjugation and is replaced by 'ㄹ'

Example:

Root Form: 걷다 (geot-da) - to walk

Conjugated form: 걸어요 (geo-ro-yo) - walks

3. 으 Irregulars:

Verbs that have '으' stems during conjugation.

Example:

Root Form: 끄다 (kkeu-da) - to turn off

Conjugated form: 꺼요 (kkeu-eo-yo) - turns off

Examples of commonly used Irregular Verbs:

Root Form: 앉다 (antta) - to sit

Conjugated form: 앉아요 (an-ja-yo) - sits

Root Form: 놓다 (not-da) - to put

Conjugated form: 놔요 (nwa-yo) - puts

Root Form: 오다 (o-da) - to come

Conjugated form: 와요 (wa-yo) - comes

The Challenge of Irregular Verbs

While the majority of verbs follow the rules outlined above, some irregular verbs deviate. These verbs, though fewer, have unique conjugation patterns and there is no easy way around memorizing stuff like this. The only tip we can give you is that – as you become more and more familiar with the language, it does become second nature. You might not believe that now, but it will be.

Exercises

4.1. Verb Exercises

Match the English words to the corresponding verbs:

1.   To Exercise 2. To Cook 3. To eat lunch   4. To sleep

a. 자다   b. 운동하다   c. 요리하다   d. 점심을 먹다

4.2. Conjugation Exercises

Conjugate the provided verbs in 해요/아요/어요 form and provide their English meaning:

1.   텔레비전을 보다

2.   일하다

3.   커피를 마시다

4.   운동하다

5.   장을 보다

4.3. Politeness Level

Conjugate the provided verbs in 합니다/ㅂ니다/습니다 form and provide their English meaning:

1. 쉬다

2. 도착하다

3. 돌아오다

4. 집에 오다

5. 회사에 가다

Fun Fact Breather Section

Drinking Freedom

Fancy a drink on a bus or on a leisurely stroll in the middle of the road? Korea says, "Why not!"

Toilet Etiquette

Whatever you do, don't throw that toilet paper into the toilet. Korea 's sewage is not built like that. Make sure to throw you toilet paper in trash cans

Two Worlds in One

In Korea, you don't have to choose between urban and natural beauty—you can have both, often within the same cityscape.

Chapter Five
Understanding Tenses

Tenses (시제 - Shi-je)

Tenses in the Korean language provide a fascinating window into the progression of events, actions, or states. Just as in many languages, Korean tenses are divided into three primary categories: **present, past, and future.** However, the way these tenses are constructed and used in Korean offers a distinctive experience for learners.

While the concept of tenses may appear straightforward, Korean tenses intricately weave the action's timing with the speaker's perspective. This combination helps convey not just when something occurs, but also the speaker's relationship to that event.

The **present tense**, as the name suggests, deals with actions that are happening right now or general truths. It's the foundational tense and getting a good grasp on it can significantly aid in understanding the language's structure.

The **past tense**, on the other hand, recounts events that have already taken place. In Korean, the past tense is not just a statement of a bygone action; it's also about reflecting on the event's relevance or implications in the present.

Lastly, the **future tense** deals with actions that are yet to happen. It carries with it a sense of anticipation or prediction. In Korean, the future tense can also express a speaker's determination or intent regarding an action.

This chapter will guide you through each tense, offering insights, structures, and nuances to enrich your grasp of the Korean language.

5.1 Present Tense

The present tense in Korean is an essential stepping stone in the learning process. It describes actions that are currently happening or stating general truths.

We have discovered how to conjugate verbs in present tense to 3 different levels in the previous Chapter: **Informal, Casual Polite and Honorific.**

Take advantage of this practice as we go through them once again.

1. Conjugating verbs in Present Tense

The present tense has different conjugation patterns based on the verb stem's final syllable. Here's a simple breakdown:

A. For verb stems ending in a vowel:

Drop the 다 then add 아요 (a-yo)

Example:

보다 (bo-da) - to see

보 + 아요 = 봐요 (bwa-yo) - see/s

B. For verb stems ending in a consonant:

Drop the 다 then add 어요 (eo-yo)

Example:

읽다 (ik-da) - to read

읽 + 어요 = 읽어요 (il-geo-yo) - read/s

These patterns form the casual polite present tense, suitable for many everyday situations. We won't be discussing the 2 other levels, but you can always go back to the previous page to review how to conjugate using the Informal and Honorific forms.

Let's look at some of these present tense verbs in a conversation:

수지: 지안 씨, 지금 뭐 **해요**?

(Jian what are you doing now?)

지안: 텔레비전을 **봐요**. 수지 씨는 뭐 **해요**?

(I'm watching TV. What about you?)

수지: 저는 지금 요리해요.

(I'm cooking.)

Surely, you are quite ready to delve into the world of Past tense. Let's go!

5.2 Past Tense

To conjugate verbs into past tense, same with the ever-famous Korean grammar rule we discussed in the previous chapters, you have to look at the last vowel in the verb stem, just like in conjugating present tense.

If the verb ends in ㅗ or ㅏ , you add **았다** to the verb stem.

If the last vowel **isn't** one of those two, you add **었다**.

Just like present tense verbs, some verbs that end in a vowel will *combine*.

Example:

가다 + 았어요 becomes 갔어요, not 가았어요.

The main reason for this combination is for easier pronunciation. Since we already have an ㅏ sound value, might as well, remove the other ㅏ to remove redundancy in sound values.

Level Guide:

Informal	Casual Polite	Honorific
Verb + 았어 or 었어	Verb + 았어요 or 었어요	Verb + 았습니다 or 었습니다

Quick Examples of verbs in past tense:

가다 (to go)

Informal: 갔어

Casual Polite: 갔어요

Honorific: 갔습니다

있다 (to have)

Informal: 있었어

Casual Polite: 있었어요

Honorific: 있었습니다

Again, the case is different for 하다 verbs.

After the stem (which might be a noun, an adjective, adverb or a verb stem), just add 했어 for Informal, 했어요 for casual polite and 했습니다 for honorific.

Informal: 했어

Casual Polite: 했어요

Honorific: 했습니다

Let's look at some of these past tense verbs in a conversation:

수지: 지안 씨는 언제 미국에 **왔어요**?
(When did you come to the U.S, Jian?)

지안: 올해 2 월 10 일에 한국에 **왔어요**. 수지 씨는 언제 미국에 왔어요?
(I came here on February 10th. What about you?)

수지: 저는 작년 7 월에 **왔어요**.
(I came here last July.)

Easy, isn't it? Now, it's time to learn how to make sentences in the future tense!

5.3 Future Tense

If you remember the grammar rules in conjugating present and past tense, future tense wouldn't be a hard thing for you because the same rule applies when making a sentence for future plans and things that will happen in the future.

There are quite a few ways to make sentences in the future tense but we will discuss the most common way.

A. Again, same with conjugating present tense and past tense verbs, we have to drop the 다 ending form of the verb and *add* ㄹ *if the verb ends in a vowel or* 을 *if it ends in a consonant.* You don't need to add anything to verbs that are already ending in ㄹ.

Level Guide:

Informal	Casual Polite	Honorific
Verb + ㄹ or 을거야	Verb + ㄹ or 을거예요	Verb + ㄹ or 을겁니다

Here are some examples:

가다 (to go)

Informal: 갈 **거야**

Casual Polite: 갈 **거예요**

Honorific: 갈 **겁니다**

있다 (to have)

Informal: 있**을거야**

Casual Polite: 있**을거예요**

Honorific: 있**을겁니다**

In future tense, this format is applied to **하다** verbs too unlike for present and past tense.

하다 (to do)

Informal: 할**거야**

Casual Polite: 할**거예요**

Honorific: 할**겁니다**

Let's look at some of these future tense verbs in a conversation:

수지: 지안 씨는 뭐 할 **거예요**??
(What are you going to do, Jian?)

지안: 운동할 **거예요**.

 (I am going to exercise.)

수지: 언제 갈 **거예요**?

 (When will you go?)

지안: 내일 갈 **거예요**.

 (I will go tomorrow.)

수지: 누구랑 영화를 볼 **거예요**?

 (Who will you watch the movie with?)

지안: 수민이랑 영화를 볼 **거예요**.

 (I will watch the movie with Sumin.)

수지: 뭐 먹을 **거예요**?

 (What will you eat?)

지안: 고기 먹을 **거예요**.

 ((I / We) will eat meat.)

B. There is another way of making future tense. After dropping the 다 of the root verb, just add 겠다 to the stem of the word.

Examples:

I will eat.
나는 먹겠다
I will learn.
나는 배우겠다

The three conjugations based on the level of politeness should be simple for you now:

Informal	Casual Polite	Honorific
Verb + 겠어	Verb + 겠어요	Verb + 겠습니다

Examples:

I will eat

나는 먹겠어 = (먹 + 겠어) Informal

저는 먹겠어요 = (먹 + 겠어요) Casual Polite

저는 먹겠습니다 = (먹 + 겠습니다) Honorific

I will learn

나는 배우겠어 = (배우 + 겠어) Informal

저는 배우겠어요 = (배우 + 겠어요) Casual Polite

저는 배우겠습니다 = (배우 + 겠습니다) Honorific

Notice that the pronouns should match the level of politeness.

Learning different tenses of the verb and to add levels of formality is a bit of a challenge. But always remember, you can never go wrong with the casual polite form, so you might want to focus on that area first.

5.1 Choose the correct present tense conjugated verb.

1. Sleeping

a. 자요   b. 일어나요   c. 쉬어요   d. 회사에 가요

2. **Going to the office**

a. 장을 봐요   b. 저녁을 먹어요   c. 와요   d. 회사에 가요

3. Watching TV

a. 전화해요   b. 아침을 먹어요   c. 와요   d. 텔레비전을 봐요

4. Singing

a. 쇼핑해요   b. 공부해요   c. 노래해요   d. 게임해요

5. Meeting (a) friend

a. 영화를 봐요   b. 책을 읽어요   c. 와요   d. 친구를 만나요

5.2 Past Tense Practice

Write 5 SOV sentences about the activities you did last week, using conjugated past tense verbs. 5 sentences per level of politeness. 15 sentences in total. Write their equivalent English meaning too.

5.3 Future Tense Practice

Write 5 SOV sentences about the schedule/activities you planned for the coming week, using conjugated future tense verbs. 5 sentences per level of politeness. 15 sentences in total. Write their equivalent English meaning too.

Fun Fact Breather Section

DMZ, The Animal Kingdom

The DMZ may be a no-man's land, but it's a paradise for wildlife. Yes, you read that right. Wildlife is flourishing in this tense environment

Island Galore

South Korea isn't as small as you think!; it has over 4,000 islands!

Mountain High

If you love mountains, you're in the right place. Korea has them all over the place and they are quite accessible

Chapter Six
Questions and Answers

As one navigates the Korean language, the ability to ask and answer questions is a vital skill. By understanding a few key patterns and words, one can easily transform statements into questions or express negative sentiments. While the basic sentence structures provide the foundation, this chapter delves into the nuances of turning those structures into inquiries or negative declarations.

Questions and answers in Korean can often have the *same structure*, the only difference is a slight modification or a change in intonation. The addition of specific particles or question words can transform a simple statement into a question.

Negations, on the other hand, involve modifying the verb or adjective to convey the opposite meaning. Korean offers systematic ways to negate statements, making it relatively straightforward once you recognize the patterns.

Just as in many languages, Korean possesses a set of question words designed to extract specific details, whether they're about people, places, reasons, or times.

In this chapter, we will take a closer look on making questions, negative sentences, and utilizing various question words.

Asking Questions

In the realm of human interactions, questions act as bridges, connecting gaps in understanding and sparking meaningful exchanges. In the Korean language, crafting questions is an art, one rooted in structure and expression.

Basic Structure

Forming questions in Korean often involves little more than a change in intonation.

Unlike the complicated question structure in English, Korean is quite simple. The initial question words "do/did/will" are not required to be present in order for the listener to understand that you are indeed asking a question. These words are unnecessary.

All you need to do is simply raise your tone at the end and make it sound like a question.

Let's uncover the ways of making questions without the use of "question" words first.

For example, you already know how to say "**My mother ate**".

엄마는 먹었어요

But, how would you ask "**did mom eat?**"

You only have to raise your intonation at the end and make it sound like a question.

엄마는 먹었어요?

Remember that Koreans almost avoid saying "you", so this pronoun can be just omitted.

6.1 Informal Question Form

If you are asking a question to someone younger than you or to your friends and siblings, this would be the common format to use. Remember how you conjugated verbs under informal form? That's what you will do and add the intonation at the end to make it sound like a question.

Examples:

밥을 먹었어? = Did (you) eat?

집에 갔어? = Did (you) go home?

소식을 들었어? = Did (you) hear the news?

You can also add 니 at the end of the stem, which is an informal way to ask a question, and you can do this in all tenses.

For example:

Present	Past	Future	Future
하니	했니	하겠니	할 거니
먹니	먹었니	먹겠니	할 것이니
가니	갔니	가겠니	먹을 거니
이니	이었니	가겠니	먹을 것이니

Questions ending with 니 have a slight feminine vibe and are usually used by older people to younger ones.

Examples:

시험을 잘 봤**니**? = Did you write the exam well (did you do well on the exam)?

부산에 가겠**니**? = Are you going to go to Busan?

몇 번이**니**? = What number are you?

이미 졸업했**니**? = Did you already graduate?

뭐 만드**니**? = What are you making?

마음에 드**니**? = Do you like it?

어디 사**니**? = Where do you live?

6.2 Casual Polite Form

You can use this form in casual or business settings.

Examples:

남동생은 울었어요? = Did your brother cry?

한국은 좋은 나라야? = Is Korea a good country?

엄마도 올 거야? = Will mom come too?

6.3 Honorific Question Form

In the case of the formal honorific form, we have to make a slight tweak in the ending part of the verb.

습니다 is never used as a question. When asking a question in this form, instead of using 습니다 you must use ㅂ/습니까.

6.3.1 -ㅂ니까

Gets added directly to stems ending in a vowel, and 습니까 gets added after a stem ending in a consonant. This applies to all the tenses:

Examples:

방학 동안 집에 안 갔**습니까**? = You didn't go home during vacation?

그 사람을 만나고 싶**습니까**? = Do you want to meet that person?

내일 학교에 갈 겁**니까**? = Are you going to school tomorrow?

내일 학교에 갈 것입**니까**? = Are you going to school tomorrow?

6.3.2 ㄴ/은가, ㄴ/은가요

Just like 니 you can also use ㄴ/은가(요) to make questions. Adding 요 to the end makes it more formal but less formal than ㅂ/습니까 form.

ㄴ/은가, ㄴ/은가요 is normally added to the stem of adjectives. Using this form gives a little bit of a softer vibe than using the forms described previously. The exact difference cannot be translated perfectly, but the nuance is like asking "would it be fine if I eat now?" rather than "can I eat now?".

The same method is used just like when you are conjugating verbs:

예쁘다 + ㄴ/은 = 예쁜

작다 + ㄴ/은 = 작은

And then attach 가(요) after that combination:

Informal	Casual Polite
예쁜가	예쁜가요
작은가	작은가요)

It is only used in present tense and therefore not suitable for past and future tenses. For example:

여자는 예쁜**가**? = Is that girl pretty?

이것은 너무 작은**가요**? = Is this too small?

그 사람이 우리 엄마**인가**? = Is that person our mom? (Is that our mom?)

그 사람이 선생님**인가**? = Is that person a teacher?

아닌가(요)? Is very commonly used at the end of a full sentence to say "no?" when you are asking yourself a question. It contains a nuance of doubt. For example:

그 여자는 한국에서 가장 유명한 연예인야. **아닌가?**
(That girl is the most famous celebrity in Korea... no?/isn't she?)

6.3.3 나/나요

Using **나/나요** at the end of a sentence to ask a question is the same with ㄴ/은가, ㄴ/은가요.

It can be used to make a question sound slightly softer. However, **나/나요** is more frequently used with verbs and with 있다 and 없다 root verbs.

For example:

Notice that the ㄹ irregular needs to be applied in appropriate situations again:

음식이 있**나**? = Is there food?

과일도 여기서 파**나요**? = Do you sell fruits here too?

지하철을 타고 있**나요**? = Are you on (riding) the subway now?

The main difference between ㄴ/은가, ㄴ/은가요 is that 나/나요 form can be used in the past tense as well.

For example:

그 소식을 들었**나요**? = Did you hear that/the news?

만화책을 샀**나요**? = Did you buy the comic book?

어제 병원에 입원했**나요**? = Did you go to the hospital yesterday?

교통카드가 있었**나요**? = Did you have your bus (transportation) card?

6.4 Question Words

Just as English has "who," "what," "where," "when," "why," and "how," Korean also boasts the same set of question words to elicit specific information. These words can be placed in sentences to replace the information you're seeking.

1. **누구 (Who)**: Refers to people.

누구를 만났어? (Who did you meet?)

누구와 함께 갔어요? (With whom did you go?)

2. **무엇 or 뭐 (What)**: Refers to things or activities.

뭐하고 있어? (What are you doing?)

무엇을 보고 싶어요? (What do you want to see?)

Other sets of what:

뭐라고- used to confirm something heard

어떤- **which**

그 파티에 *어떤*옷을 입을거야?

Which clothes will you wear to that party?

무슨- used to ask to clarify something

무슨 일 있어요?

(What's going on?)

뭐예요 used to convey questions like "what is this?"

이게 *뭐예요*?

(What is this?)

3. **어디 (Where)**: Indicates location.

어디에 가? (Where are you going?)

어디서 왔어요? (Where did you come from?)

4. **언제 (When)**: Refers to time.

언제 올 거야? (When will you come?)

언제 만나요? (When will we meet?)

5. **왜 (Why)**: Seeks a reason.

왜 그렇게 생각해? (Why do you think that way?)

왜 늦었어요? (Why were you late?)

6. **어떻게 (How)**: Inquires about the manner or method.

어떻게 해결했어? (How did you solve it?)

어떻게 그렇게 했어요? (How did you do that?)

Unlike English, where question words often begin the sentence, in Korean, they're usually positioned where the answer would be in a statement.

Comparison:

English: Where are you going?

Korean Structure: You are going where?

In more formal settings or written contexts, the full forms of words, like "무엇," are preferred. In casual conversations however or chats among friends shorter versions are most common such as "뭐."

Exercises

6.1 Forming Questions Exercises

Choose the best question word to complete the dialogues.

1. **Speaker 1**: 저기가 _____?

Speaker 2. 기숙사예요. (It is a dorm.)

a. 누구입나까   b. 어디예요   c. 뭐예요   d. 왜요

2.   **Speaker 1**: 이거 _____예요?

Speaker 2: 가방이에요. (It is a bag.)

a. 뭐   b. 어디   c. 누구   d. 왜

3.   **Speaker 1**: 이 사람은 _____입니까?

Speaker 2: 그녀는 여동생입니다. (She is my sister.)

a. 뭐 b. 어디   c. 왜   d. 누구

6.2 Composition Practice

Write the following sentences in Korean using the informal level/form.

1. Where do you live?
2. When did you arrive in Vietnam?
3. What are you eating?

6.3 Composition Practice

Write the following sentences in Korean using the honorific level/form.

1. What is your favorite food?
2. Are you going to eat now?
3. Where are you going?

Fun Fact Breather Section

River Trio

South Korea is crisscrossed by three major rivers, each with its own unique charm. The famous Han river is not the only one nor is it even the biggest!

Hot August

Thinking of visiting Korea in August? Prepare for a heatwave, as it's the hottest month of the year.

Shop 'til You Drop

The world's largest department store calls South Korea home. Get ready for a shopping marathon!

Chapter Seven
Adjectives and Adverbs

Diving into the colorful world of the Korean language, adjectives and adverbs shine brightly, adding depth, detail, and vibrancy to conversations.

Adjectives (형용사-Hyeong-yeong-sa), the descriptors of nouns, give life to objects, people, and places, allowing for more precise and vivid descriptions.

Adverbs (부사- Bu-sa), on the other hand, act as the modifiers of verbs, adding nuance to actions and painting a clearer picture of how something is done.

In this chapter we will unravel these two linguistic tools, exploring their various forms and uses.

7.1 Descriptive Adjectives

In the vast landscape of the Korean language, descriptive adjectives stand out as vibrant splashes of color, giving depth and character to nouns and subjects of the sentences.

Descriptive adjectives, as the name suggests, are words that describe or modify nouns and pronouns.

To get started, here are some commonly used descriptive adjectives in Korean:

Adjectives For People	Qualities	Colors and Taste	Shapes and Sizes
조용한/quiet	좋은/good	검정/black	큰/big
시끄러운 /loud	나쁜 /bad	하얀/white	작은/small
아름다운/beautiful	깨끗한/clean	쓴/bitter	두꺼운 /thick
못생긴/ugly	더러운 /dirty	짠 /salty	긴/long

행복한/happy	부드러운/soft	신/sour	짧은/short
슬픈/sad	딱딱한/hard	매운/spicy	좁은/narrow
건강한/healthy	비싼/expensive	달콤한/sweet	넓은/wide
똑똑한/smart	싼 /cheap	새로운/new	얇은/thin
멍청한 /stupid	빠른/fast	늙은/old	둥근/round

Like English, Korean adjectives can be placed before or after the noun. But the adjectives look a little different, depending on their placement.

Positioning in Sentences

Unlike English, where adjectives typically precede the nouns they modify, in Korean, descriptive adjectives can act like verbs. They often appear at the end of a sentence or clause and are conjugated depending on the tense and formality level.

In the following examples the adjective is placed in the middle of the sentence.

그 사과는 **빨간색**이에요.

(Geu sa-gwa-neun **ppal-gan-sek**-iye-yo.)

The apple is **red**.

이 청바지는 **긴** 것 같아요.

(I cheong-baji-neun **gin** got gat-ta-yo.)

These jeans seem **long**.

Adjectives can also be placed before the noun. For instance, the word '큰' (keun) means 'big' and can be used to describe a noun like '집' (jip), which means 'house'. If we put them together, '큰 집' translates to 'big house'.

작은 얼굴 (small face)

큰 얼굴 (big face)

Conjugating Adjectives

Adjectives in Korean need to be conjugated, much like verbs. The way to conjugate them is based on the ending syllable. For example, if an *adjective stem ends in a vowel, '아요' (a-yo) is added for the present tense. If it ends in a consonant, '어요' (eo-yo) is added.*

Let's use the adjective '예쁘다' (yeppeuda), meaning 'to be pretty' as an example:

예쁘 + 어요 = 예뻐요

(yeppeo-yo)

This rule applies to **있다** verbs and adjectives.

멋있다 (To be cool/amazing)

Informal: 멋있어

Casual Polite: 멋있어요

Honorific: 멋있습니다

7.2 Types of Adverbs

Korean adverbs 부사 (bu-sa) are used to describe a verb or an adjective. They work the same as in other languages.

Let's look at the Korean grammar rules with which adverbs are formed.

1. **Adverbs of Manner**

    1.1 **(Using -히)**

The conjugation 히 (hi) is used when you form adjectives into adverbs. This is usually added to adjectives that end with -하다 (hada). To do that, you replace -하다 (hada) with 히 (hi).

Examples:

막연하다	=	막연**히**(magyonhi)
(mag-yeon-hada)		(mag-yon-hi)
to be vague		**vaguely**

성급하다	=	성급**히**
(seong-geup-ha-da)		(seong-geup-hi)
to be hasty		**hastily**

Here are the most common adverbs under this rule:

Adverb	Sound Value	Meaning
대단히	de-dan-hi	greatly
분명히	bun-myeong-hi	clearly
솔직히	sol-jik-hi	honestly/ frankly
열심히	yeol-shim-hi	diligently
빨리	ppal-li	fast
완전히	wan-jeon-hi	completely
우연히	u-yeon-hi	by chance
자세히	ja-se-hi	in detail
천천히	cheon-cheon-hi	slowly
특별히	teuk-byeol-hi	especially
확실히	hwak-shi-ri	certainly
간단히	gan-dan-hi	simply
편히	pyeon-hi	comfortably
신중히	shin-jung-hi	carefully

Let's take a look at some example sentences:

빨리 움직여요
Move **fast**

신중히 골라요
Pick one **carefully**

편히 있어요
Make yourself **comfortable**

1.2) Using 게 (ge)

This type of adverb expresses purpose, conveys "in order to" or state/degree meaning. With 게 (ge) conjugations, you can make an adverb in Korean from adjective. In this case, you keep the entire word stem and simply replace 다 (ge) with 게 (ge).

For example:

크다	=	크게
(keu-da)		(keu-ge)
big		immensely

건조하다	=	건조하게
(geon-jo-hada)		(geon-jo-hage)
dry		dryly

나쁘다	=	나쁘게
(na-peu-da)		(na-peu-ge)
bad		badly

As you can see in the examples above, 다 is dropped and 게 is added.

REMEMBER that for 하다 verbs, 히 rule is used.

Here is a list of the most commonly used adverbs of this form.

Adverb	Sound Value	Meaning
이쁘게	ip-peu-ge	prettily
위험하게	wi-heom-ha-ge	dangerously
맛있게	ma-shit-ge	deliciously
무례하게	mur-ye-ha-ge	rudely
바쁘게	bap-peu-ge	busily
재미있게	je-mi-it-ge	entertainingly
자연스럽게	ja-yeon-seu-reop-ge	naturally
아름답게	a-reum-dap-ge	beautifully
어렵게	eo-ryeop-ge	with difficulty

Let's take a look at some example sentences:

빠르게 움직여요
Move **fast**

신중하게 골라요
Pick one **carefully**

편하게 있어요
Make yourself **comfortable**

집을 예쁘게 꿈이었어요.
The house is **beautifully** decorated.

질서를 어지럽히지 **않게** 줄을 서세요.

(In order) **to not cause** disorder, please line up.

1.3. Using 으로

으로 (eu-ro) means "in some way" or "partly" Actually, it's a postposition, not an adverb, but it becomes an adverb when you translate Korean into English. This type of adverb is used to indicate method or means, a reason or cause which conveys "due to/because of" meaning.

Examples:

일반적	=	일반적**으로**
(il-ban-jeok)		il-ban-jeo-geu-ro
general		generally

자동적	=	자동**으로**
(ja-dong-jeok)		(ja-dong-eu-ro)
automatic		automatically

Let's take a look at some example sentences:

과학적으로 해결해보세요

Solve it **scientifically**

무의식적으로 버튼을 눌렀어요

I pressed the button **unconsciously**

본능적으로 움직였어요

I moved my body **instinctively**

영어로 쓰세요.

Please write **in English**.

그는 독감**으로** 죽었다.

He died **from the** flu.

후문**으로** 가세요.

Please go **to the** back door.

1. Adverbs of Frequency and Time

항상, 늘, 언제나	always
계속	continuously
자주, 흔히	frequently
보통, 대개	usually
가끔, 때로는	sometimes
종종, 때때로	occasionally
좀처럼	seldom
드물게	rarely
결코, 절대	never
곧	soon
아직	yet
최근에	lately
마침내, 드디어	finally
전에	before, previously

어제	yesterday
오늘	today
내일	tomorrow
지금	now
그때	then (back then)
나중에/후에	later
오늘밤	tonight
바로 지금 / 지금 바로	right now
지난 밤	last night
다음 주	next week

나는 고기를 **좀처럼** 먹지 않아.

(na-neun gogi-reul **jom-chorom** mok-ji ana.)

I **seldom** eat meat.

These adverbs do not follow any rule. You can use them in a sentence just as you would in English.

2. **Adverbs of Degree**

아주, 매우	very
완전히	perfectly
단순히	simply
엄청	enormously
불과	only

절대로	absolutely/completely
정말(로) / 진짜(로) / 참(으로)	really
특히	particularly
상당히	fairly

Good to know:

You must have heard these adverbs in Korean dramas and tv shows a hundred times, so you might already have an idea on how to use them in a sentence. For native Koreans, 아주 has a bit of more positive vibe compared to 너무. The latter tends to be used in negative and a bit exaggerated sentences. It may even be used to sound sarcastic. So, when complimenting people it would be safe to use 아주 instead.

Let's take a look at some example sentences:

담배를 절대로 피우지 않겠습니다

I will never smoke

김치를 매우 좋아해요

I like Kimchi very much

김치를 진짜 좋아해요

I like Kimchi very much.

Adverbs vs. Adjectives: A Clear Distinction

It's worth noting the distinction between adverbs and adjectives. While adjectives describe nouns, adverbs describe how an action is performed. For clarity, consider this:

김치는 **매워요**.

(Kim-chi-neun me-wo-yo)

The kimchi is spicy

김치를 **매워게** 먹어요.

(Kim-chi-reul me-wo-ge mo-go-yo)

I eat the kimchi spicily.

In the first sentence, "매워요" (spicy) is an adjective describing kimchi. In the second, "매워게" (spicily) is an adverb describing how one eats the kimchi.

Concluding Thoughts

Adverbs play an essential role in providing depth and clarity to Korean sentences. They offer insights into the manner, frequency, and context of actions. Recognizing their formation, placement, and usage is crucial for anyone aspiring to master the nuances of the Korean language. By understanding and incorporating adverbs, one can convey thoughts with added precision, making conversations richer and more engaging.

Let's see if you remember all the rules and types of adverbs through the following exercises.

Exercises

7.1 Descriptive Adjectives Exercises

A.   Match the adjectives to the corresponding English adjectives.

1.   Cool   2. Tall   Short   Pretty

a.   예쁘다   b. 멋있다   c. 키가 크다   d. 키가 작다

7.2. Conjugate each given adjective into informal, casual polite and honorific levels and write their sound value and English equivalent.

Example: 예쁘다 = 예뻐요 (ye-peo-yo) which means pretty

1. 재미있다
2. 통통하다
3. 행복하다
4. 아름답다
5. 드물다

7.3. Conjugate each given adjective and write their sound value and English equivalent.

Example: 가깝다 = 가까이 (kak-ka-i) which means *near*

1. 완벽하다
2. 깨끗하다
3. 촉촉하다
4. 특별하다
5. 가만하다

7.4. Write 3 SOV sentences using an adjective or adverb about yourself, introducing your personality, liking, looks or appearance.

Example.

1. I am pretty.
2. I love sandwiches.

Fun Fact Breather Section

Holidays Unwrapped

New Year's is for family gatherings, but Christmas? Oh, that's date night in Korea! Good luck to those without significant others!

Feast Mode

Korean traditional meals aren't just meals; they're feasts complete with an array of side dishes, soups, and stews.

Shoe Taboo

Thinking of gifting shoes in Korea? Think again! It's considered a bad omen as it is believed that the ones who receive the gift will run away

Chapter Eight
Prepositions and Particles

Korean Prepositions (조사- *jo-sa*) guide the listener or reader through the spatial, temporal, and logical relationships between words. They help illustrate where something is, when an event occurs, or how two concepts relate. In contrast, particles play a pivotal role in indicating grammatical relationships. They help determine the subject, object, or topic of a sentence and add nuance to statements.

8.1 Common Prepositions

In Korean, prepositions play a central role in this task, helping depict the connections between objects, places, and time. By giving context and orientation, prepositions act as signposts, guiding listeners and readers through the narrative landscape.

Locomotive Verbs that are commonly used together with prepositions:

Korean	English
내려가다	to go down
내려오다	to come down
올라가다	to go up
올라오다	to come up
나가다	to go out
나오다	to come out

들어가다	to go in/enter
들어오다	to come in

옥상에 **올라가면** 카페가 있어요.

There is a cafe if you go up to the rooftop.

잠깐 **나가** 주세요.

Please go outside for a moment:

내일 고향에 **돌아가요**.

I will return to my hometown tomorrow.

3월에 동생이 미국에서 **돌아와요**.

My brother comes back from America in March.

These locomotive verbs will be a big help in making the whole sentence clearer.

Understanding Prepositions in Korean

In the Korean language, prepositions, often known as *postpositions*, typically come after the noun they modify. This positioning is a distinctive feature, setting Korean apart from many Western languages where prepositions precede the noun.

Below is a list of the most common Korean prepositions.

Korean	English	Korean	English
안	in/inside	속	inside/among
밖	outside	가운데	in the middle
앞	in front of	사이	between
옆	next to	근처	near
위	over/on/above	건너편	across from

뒤	behind	왼쪽	left
아래	under/underneath	오른쪽	right
밑	under/underneath	바로	directly

Below is image description of some prepositions to help you better understand the usage:

8.2 Types of Prepositions

Place Prepositions

Prepositions of place, also called as Spatial prepositions describe the *location or direction of an object in relation to another.*

1. **위에 (on, above)**: Indicates something is on top of or above something else.

Example:

테이블 위에 책이 있다.

There is a book on the table.

2. **아래 (under, below)**: Used to describe something beneath or under another object.

Example:

침대 아래 고양이가 있다.

There's a cat under the bed.

3. **앞에 (in front of)**: Denotes an object or place located in front of another.

Example:

집 앞에 정원이 있다.

There is a garden in front of the house.

4. **뒤에 (behind)**: Refers to an object or place situated at the back or behind another.

Example:

건물 뒤에 주차장이 있다.

There's a parking lot behind the building.

Time Prepositions

Prepositions of time, also called Temporal prepositions provide information about *when an event occurs in relation to another time frame.*

1. **전에 (before)**: Indicates an event occurring prior to another event or time.

Example:

학교 가기 전에 아침을 먹었다.

I ate breakfast before going to school.

2. **후에 (after)**: Describes an event happening after a particular time or event.

Example:

운동 후에 샤워했다.

I took a shower after exercising.

Connecting Prepositions

These prepositions establish a logical connection between ideas or events.

1. **와/과 (with)**: Denotes accompaniment or inclusion. 와 is used when the preceding noun ends with a vowel, while 과 is used when it ends with a consonant.

Example:

나는 친구와 영화를 봤다.

I watched a movie with a friend.

2. **없이 (without)**: Indicates the absence of something.

Example:

우산 없이 비를 맞았다.

I got wet in the rain without an umbrella.

Let's look at some of these preposition in a conversation:

수루: 이 **근처에** 약국이 있어요?

    Is there a pharmacy around here?

지안: 네, 있어요.

    Yes, there is.

수루: 약국이 어디에 있어요?

    Where is it?

지안: 저 사거리에서 **오른쪽으로** 가세요.

    Turn right at that intersection.

    그러면 병원 **옆에** 약국이 있어요.

    Then there is a pharmacy next to the hospital.

Practical Applications

While these prepositions provide a foundational understanding, Korean boasts a rich array of prepositions that cater to various contexts and nuances. As beginners become more adept, they'll encounter these variations and learn to apply them effectively.

In essence, prepositions in Korean serve as anchors, grounding sentences in context and clarity. They transform simple statements into descriptive narratives, enabling speakers to convey their thoughts with precision and depth.

In Korean, particles are attached directly to nouns and verbs to provide vital grammatical context. Think of them as markers, indicating various roles that words play within a sentence. Whether it's denoting the subject, object, or even the location, particles are there, ensuring the sentence's structure and intent are clear.

8.3 Combining Prepositions and Particles

The magic of the Korean language lies in its ability to craft meaning through a combination of words and grammar. Within this intricate tapestry, the blending of prepositions and particles stands out as a crucial element offering depth, context, and clarity to expressions.

Location and Direction:

에 vs. 에서 with 이/가 The preposition 에 indicates a static location, whereas 에서 specifies the starting point or origin of an action. When combined with the subject particles 이/가, they provide a complete spatial context.

Example:

공원에 사람이 있다.

There is a person in the park.

학교에서 학생이 나온다.

A student comes out of the school.

Action and Object: 로/으로 with 을/를

로 and 으로 denote direction or means. Paired with the object particles 을/를, they describe the action upon an object moving in a direction or by a means.

Example:

서울로 기차를 타다.

Take a train to Seoul.

Possession and Subject: 의 with 이/가

When denoting possession, the preposition 의 can be paired with the subject particles 이/가 to emphasize the possessor.

Example:

나의 친구가 학교에 간다.

My friend goes to school.

Complex Relations: From Purpose to Time

The combination of prepositions and particles isn't limited to simple spatial or possession relationships. They can illustrate complex ideas, from purpose to time intervals.

Example:

공부하기 위해 도서관에 간다.

(purpose)   (action)

Go to the library to study.

주말동안 여행을 가다.

(plan)   (time)

Go on a trip for the weekend.

Nuances in Combinations

In many cases, the combination of prepositions and particles brings subtle nuances to expressions. For instance, using 에서 instead of 에 might shift the emphasis from the action's location to its origin. Such nuances enrich the language, allowing speakers to convey their thoughts with precision.

For beginners, it's advisable to start with basic combinations, gradually exploring more complex structures as their proficiency grows. Over time, the intuitive understanding of when and how to use specific prepositions and particles together will develop.

Exercises

8.1 Common Prepositions Exercises

Complete the sentences with the correct preposition.

1. 차가 회사 _____에 있어요. (front)

2. 차가 회사 _____에 있어요. (behind)

3. 약국이 백화점 _____에 있어요. (inside)

4. 약국이 식당 _____에 있어요. (beside)

8.2 Help Suji find the pharmacy by choosing the correct instructions in the choices provided.

a. 은행 옆에	d. 약국 옆에	g. 병원 건너편에
b. 병원 옆에	e. 우체국 맞은편에	h. 은행이 있어요
c. 학교 뒤에	f. 마트가 있어요.	i. 학교가 있어요

8.3 Write 5 sentences using the prepositions you learned in describing your location/house/office/school to your friend.

Fun Fact Breather Section

Jeju Certificate

Reach the peak of Hallasan on Jeju Island, and you'll earn more than just bragging rights—you'll get a certificate!

Lucky Rice Cakes

Got an exam? Time to munch on some rice cakes. They're considered a good luck charm in Korea.

Group Blind Dating

Yes, group blind dating is a real thing in Korea. Spice up your social life in a group setting!

Chapter Nine
Numbers, Dates, and Time

Korean, like many languages, has its unique system when it comes to numbers, dates, and time. Understanding these is fundamental to daily life, be it shopping, making appointments, or celebrating special occasions. Grasping the basics will also provide a richer understanding of Korean culture and traditions, as numbers often play significant roles in festivals, customs, and even superstitions.

Korean has two main number systems: the **native Korean system** and the **Sino-Korean system**.

The native Korean system is primarily used for counting objects up to 99 and age, while the Sino-Korean system is used for dates, money, phone numbers, and numbers above 100. It's crucial to familiarize oneself with both systems, as they are used interchangeably in different contexts.

Dates in Korean are typically expressed in the Year-Month-Day format. The months and days are numbered from one to twelve, using the Sino-Korean number system. It's essential to note that Koreans often use the lunar calendar for traditional events, so some dates might differ from the Gregorian calendar familiar to most Westerners.

Telling **time** in Korean involves a mix of both number systems. Hours are told using the native Korean numbers, while minutes are expressed using the Sino-Korean system.

The world of numbers, dates, and time in Korean is a fascinating blend of the old and the new, the traditional and the modern. By mastering this chapter, you will be equipped to navigate daily life in Korea, from catching a bus on time to enjoying traditional festivals with a deeper appreciation.

9.1 Counting in Korean

The beauty of the Korean language lies in its intricacies, especially when it comes to numbers. There's an intriguing blend of the native Korean system and the Sino-Korean system. Both systems are integrated into daily life and have their own distinct applications.

9.1.2 Native Korean Numbers: An Insight

The native Korean system has its roots deep in Korea's history. It's primarily used for everyday tasks like counting objects, expressing age, or discussing quantities up to 99. It's a more intimate system, closely tied to Korea's cultural fabric.

To begin, let's learn the numbers 1 to 10 in native Korean:

Number	Native Korean	English
1	하나 (han-na)	one
2	둘 (dul)	two
3	셋 (set)	three
4	넷 (net)	four
5	다섯 (da-seot)	five
6	여섯 (yeo-seot)	six
7	일곱 (il-gop)	seven
8	여덟 (yeo-deol)	eight
9	아홉 (a-hop)	nine
10	열 (yeol)	ten

As we move beyond ten, the system becomes a matter of combining the basic numbers. For instance:

열하나 (yeol han-na) – eleven (10 + 1)

열둘 (yeol dul) – twelve (10 + 2)

Continue this pattern up to nineteen, and then the twenties introduce a new structure:

스물 (seu-mul) – twenty

스물하나 (seu-mul han-na) – twenty-one (20 + 1)

스물둘 (seu-mul dul) – twenty-two (20 + 2)

This combination pattern persists up to twenty-nine. As we approach thirty, the word for thirty in native Korean is '서른' (seoreun), and the counting continues similarly. This pattern holds true for the forties, with the term '마흔' (maheun) representing forty.

9.1.3 Sino-Korean Numbers: A Glimpse

The Sino-Korean system, derived from Chinese numerals, finds its place in modern contexts like dates, money, measurements, and larger quantities.

Starting with numbers 1 to 10 in Sino-Korean:

Number	Sino-Korean	Translation
1	일 (il)	one
2	이 (i)	two
3	삼 (sam)	three
4	사 (sa)	four
5	오 (o)	five
6	육 (yuk)	six
7	칠 (chil)	seven
8	팔 (pal)	eight
9	구 (gu)	nine
10	십 (ship)	ten

Constructing numbers beyond ten in the Sino-Korean system is systematic. For instance:

십일 (ship il) – eleven (10 + 1)

십이 (ship i) – twelve (10 + 2)

The pattern continues similarly up to nineteen. For the twenties:

이십 (i-ship) – twenty

이십일 (i-ship il) – twenty-one (20 + 1)

Continuing this structure will help you understand numbers up to fifty and beyond.

The Interplay Between Systems

While it may seem complex to have two systems, it's this duality that adds depth to the Korean language. The native system, with its cultural ties, adds a touch of authenticity to conversations. On the other hand, the Sino-Korean system, with its broader applications, provides a bridge to modern contexts.

Tips for Mastery

Consistent practice is the key. Engage in activities like counting objects using both systems or noting down numbers seen during the day and translating them into Korean. Additionally, listening to native Korean speakers will further solidify understanding.

9.2 Expressing Dates

Dates play a pivotal role in any language and culture. They mark special occasions, historical events, and the passage of time. In the Korean language, the art of expressing dates intertwines both the native and Sino-Korean number systems, showcasing the language's versatility and richness.

Year, Month, Day: The Korean Format

Korean dates typically adhere to the Year-Month-Day format. This sequence, though different from many Western conventions, offers a logical progression from the broadest time measurement to the most specific.

Years in Korean

Years are expressed using the Sino-Korean number system. For instance, the year 2023 would be broken down as '이천이십삼년' (i-cheon i-ship sam-nyeon), which translates directly to "two thousand twenty-three year."

It's interesting to note the use of the term '년' (nyeon) after the number. This is the Korean word for "year" and is always used to indicate that the numbers preceding it represent a year.

Months in Korean

Months, simple and systematic, are numbered from one to twelve. There's no variation or unique names for each month; they are expressed using the Sino-Korean system followed by the term '월' (wol), which means "month." For example:

일월 (il-wol) – January

이월 (i-wol) – February

삼월 (sam-wol) – March ... and so forth, up to December, which is '십이월' (ship i-wol).

Days in Korean

Days of the month range from the first to the thirty-first, and just like months, they utilize the Sino-Korean numbering system. After stating the number, the term '일' (il), meaning "day," follows. A few examples include:

일일 (il-il) – the first day

이일 (i-il) – the second day

삼일 (sam-il) – the third day

Let's take a look at this example conversation:

A: 너 몇년생이야?

Noh myeon-nyeon-seng-iya?
Which year were you born in?

B: 나? 2010 년.

Na? i-cheon-shim-nyeon.
Me? In 2010.

A: BTS 의 슈가는 몇년도생이었더라?

BTS-ui shu-ga-neun myeon-nyeon-do-seng-i-yeot-dora?
What year was Suga from BTS born in?

B: 1993 년!

Cheon-gu-bek-gu-ship-sam-nyeon!
In 1993!

---

9. 3 Days of the Week

English	Korean	Sound Value
Monday	월요일	wor-yo-il
Tuesday	화요일	hwa-yo-il
Wednesday	수요일	su-yo-il
Thursday	목요일	mo-gyo-il
Friday	금요일	geum-yo-il

Saturday	토요일	to-yo-il
Sunday	일요일	ir-yo-il

Notice how all the days ends with 요일 (yo-il). This is because Korean has the same structure as English, only the first syllables are different.

Traditional vs. Modern Calendars

While the Gregorian calendar is the standard for most modern purposes in Korea, the traditional lunar calendar still holds cultural significance. Many traditional festivals and holidays, such as the Lunar New Year (설날, Seol-lal) and the Mid-Autumn Festival (추석, Chu-seok), are based on this lunar calendar. It's a testament to how Korea seamlessly blends tradition and modernity.

Practical Usage

When stating a full date, Koreans typically follow the sequence of year, month, and then day. For instance, September 23, 2023, would be articulated as "**이천이십삼년 구월 이십삼일**" (i-cheon i-ship sam-nyeon gu-wol i-ship sam-il).

However, in casual conversations or written formats, sometimes only the day and month are mentioned, especially if the year is understood from the context.

9.4 Telling Time

Time, the omnipresent aspect of our lives, threads moments and memories together. In the Korean language, the manner of expressing time brings forward both the native and Sino-Korean numerical systems, painting a harmonious blend of tradition and modernity.

"Hours" in Korean is 시간 (shi-gan). If you want to express how many hours you spent writing an essay, you use native Korean system for the numeral and add 시간, with no space.

Let's take a look at the following conversation:

A: 비행기가 2 시간이나 지연됐어.
Bi-heng-giga du-shi-ga-nina ji-yeon-dwes-so.
The plane got delayed for two hours.

B: 아 정말? 그럼 2 시간 뒤에 픽업하러 갈께.

A jeong-mal? Geu-rom du-shi-gan dwi-e pi-geop-haro gal-kke.

Oh really? I will come and pick you up after two hours then.

A: 하루 한시간은 꼭 요가를 하려고 해.

Haru han-shiga-neun kkok yoga-reul ha-ryeo-go he.

I am trying to do yoga at least one hour per day.

B: 그건 좋은 생각인것 같아. 나는 일주일에 3 시간은 꼭 조깅을 하고 있어.

Geu-geon jo-eun seng-ga-gin-geot gat-ta. Na-neun il-ju-i-re se-shiga-neun kkok jo-ging-eul hago is-seo.

That's a great idea. I jog three hours per week.

Hourly Distinctions

When conveying hours, the native Korean number system is used. One starts the day with '하나' (hana) for one o'clock and moves forward to '열두' (yeol-du) for twelve o'clock. This pattern applies for both the 12-hour and 24-hour clock systems.

Yet, there's an essential distinction to keep in mind. The term '시' (shi) follows the number to indicate that it's an hour. For instance, '세 시' (se shi) means three o'clock.

Minute Details

Minutes, on the other hand, utilize the Sino-Korean system. Starting from '일' (il) for one minute, the progression continues up to '육십' (yuksip) for sixty minutes. To signify minutes, '분' (bun) is used after stating the number. For example, '십오 분' (ship o bun) represents fifteen minutes.

The AM and PM Conundrum

Korean language makes a clear distinction between AM and PM. For the hours before noon, '오전' (o-jeon) is used, translating to "morning." For the hours post-noon, '오후' (o-hu) means "afternoon." Thus, 3:00 PM would be expressed as '오후 세 시' (ohu se shi).

Seconds in a Moment

For more precise timekeeping, seconds are sometimes mentioned, especially in contexts like sports or scientific experiments. Here, the Sino-Korean system is employed, followed by the term '초' (cho) to indicate seconds. For example, '이십 초' (i-ship cho) denotes twenty seconds.

Asking and Stating Time

When inquiring about the current time, Koreans often use the phrase '지금 몇 시예요?' (jigeum myeot shi eyo?), which translates to "What time is it now?" In response, one might answer '지금 세 시오 분이에요' (jigeum se shi o bun-ieyo), meaning "It's three o'five now."

Half Past and Quarters

For common time expressions like "half-past" or "quarter-to," Korean has specific phrases. '반' (ban) refers to the half-hour mark. So, 2:30 would be '두 시 반' (du shi ban). For quarters, Koreans typically state the exact minutes, like '십오 분' (ship o bun) for a quarter past.

에 is attached after the time marker whether it ends in a final consonant or a vowel.

Examples:

가: 몇 시에 점심을 먹어요?
What time do you have lunch?

나: 12 시에 먹어요.
I have lunch at 12.

가: 언제 운동해요?
When do you work out?

나: 저녁에 운동해요.
I work out in the evening.

Tip:

언제 is used when you ask about the time, day, and date.

English uses prepositions which come before nouns like in 'at 3 o'clock' while particles in Korean come after nouns as in '3 시에'. Therefore, they are called *postpositions* or markers rather than prepositions.

Cultural Observations

In Korea, punctuality is highly regarded. Whether it's a business meeting, a casual hangout, or a train schedule, being on time reflects respect and professionalism. This cultural emphasis on punctuality makes understanding and expressing time in Korean even more critical.

Moreover, many Korean events, especially traditional ones, start at specific auspicious times, further underscoring the importance of time in the culture.

Time, a universal concept, gets a unique flavor in every language. In Korean, the dance between the native and Sino-Korean systems when expressing time offers learners a glimpse into the language's rhythmic beauty. As the clock ticks and moments pass, one's understanding of Korean time deepens, opening doors to richer interactions and cultural experiences.

Exercises

9.1 Counting in Korean Exercises

Provide the time and each English sound value based on the pictures provided.

1. 7:00 AM

2. 11:00AM

3. 1:00 PM

4. 10:00 PM

9.2 Write the following dates in Korean

1. July 15, 1967

2. March 27, 1992

3. February 12, 2015

4. November 19, 1950

5. May 27, 1972

9.3 Composition Practice

Write 10 sentences describing your daily routine. Every sentence should include time, (day of the week is optional) and the corresponding action verb.

Example:

7 시에 일어나요.

9 시에 회사에 가요.

Fun Fact Breather Section

Taxi Code

White or grey taxis are basic, but a black cab means you're riding in style with an expert driver.

Red Names

Seeing a name written in red ink? It's a no-no in Korea, signifying death or impending doom.

The Big Six-O

Turning 60 in Korea isn't just a milestone; it's a grand celebration called 'hwangap.'

Chapter Ten
Family and Honorifics

At its core, Koreans value family a lot and love to talk about their family. In this chapter we will discuss important tips about describing your family as well as the titles of each family member to expand your vocabulary. We will also dive into the world of honorifics as these elements, essential in everyday communication, mirror the Korean society's emphasis on respect, hierarchy, and relationships.

Formality levels in Korean play a crucial role in determining the tone and politeness of a conversation. They adapt based on the relationship between speakers, ensuring that interactions remain appropriate and respectful. From casual chats among friends to formal discussions with superiors, these levels guide the flow of conversation.

Honorifics are specific words and verb endings that convey respect. They are employed when addressing or talking about someone of a higher status or older age. The presence or absence of honorifics can significantly alter the meaning and tone of a sentence.

Choosing the correct level of formality and the appropriate honorifics is akin to selecting the right attire for an occasion. It requires awareness, understanding, and sensitivity. This chapter delves deep into the nuances of honorifics and formality, illuminating their significance and usage in the Korean language. Through insights and examples, it aims to equip learners with the knowledge to communicate with grace and respect, reflecting the true essence of Korean interactions.

Here are the nouns that you'll be needing in order to talk about your family:

할아버지 (Grandfather) 할머니 (Grandmother)

아버지 (Father)   어머니 (Mother)

If you are a **man**	형 older brother	누나 older sister	나 me	부인 wife	남동생 younger brother	여동생 younger sister
If you are a	오빠	언니	나	남편	남동생	여동생

woman	older brother	older sister	me		younger brother	younger sister

아들 (son)	딸 (daughter)

Notice that there are different versions of how you call your siblings if you are a man or a woman. If you are a woman (여자), you can just use the pink to introduce your family members. If you are a man (남자), the yellow row is for you. It would still be recommended to memorize both versions for general understanding of the language.

Talking about your family members in Korean often starts with details on how many members there are. Here are some common ways on how to ask and answer these questions.

10.1- "How many are there in your family?"

This is a common question about family. There are many ways to ask this question:

Formal:

가족이 모두 몇 명이에요?

Ga-jo-gi mo-du myeot myeo-ngi-ye-yo?
How many family members are there in total?

가족이 몇 분이세요?

Ga-jo-gi myeot bun-i-se-yo?
How many family members do you have?

가족이 몇 명입니까?

Ga-jo-gi myeot myeo-ngim-nikka?
How many family members do you have?

Informal:

가족이 모두 몇 명이야?

Ga-jo-gi mo-du myeot myeo-ngi-ya?

가족이 몇 명이야?

Ga-jo-gi myeot myeo-ngi-ya?

How many members are there in your family?

All of these family phrases in Korean mean the same thing. The only difference is that some are used in formal settings, and others in informal settings.

10.2- "There are [number] in my family."

Let's say that you have four people in your family. To say "*There are four people in my family,*" in Korean, you should say: 우리 가족은 네 명이에요 (U-ri ga-jo-geun ne myeong i-ye-yo).

Alternatively, you can say, 가족은 모두 [number] 명 입니다. (ga-jo-geun mo-du [number] myeong im-nida), which means "There are [number] family members in total."

Formal:

A: 가족이 몇 명입니까?

Ga-jo-gi myeot myeo-ngim-nikka?
How many family members do you have?

B: 우리 가족은 세 명이에요.

U-ri ga-jo-geun se myeo-ngi-yeyo.
There are three members in my family.

Informal:

A: 가족이 모두 몇 명이야?

Ga-jo-gi mo-du myeot myeo-ngi-ya?
How many are there in your family?

B: 우리 집? 아빠, 엄마, 언니 있으니까, 총 네 명있어.

Uri jib? Ap-pa, eom-ma, eon-ni is-seu-nik-kan, chong ne myeo-ngis-seo.
My house? There's dad, mom, and a younger sister, so a total of four.

10.3 Talking About Your Siblings

1- "I have siblings." and "I am an only child."

To ask someone whether he or she has siblings, ask them with the phrase 형제 자매가 있어요? (hyeong-je ja-me-ga is-seo-yo?), direct translation being "Do you have brothers and sisters?"

However, these days, we slightly shorten the sentence and we say **형제 있어요?** (Hyeong-je is-seo-yo?), dropping the *자매가* with a direct translation of "Do you have siblings?"

To say that you have a number of siblings, you can say **형제 자매가 있어요** (Hyeong-je ja-me-ga is-seo-yo.) which means "I have brothers and sisters.

Let's have a look at a number of example phrases:

1. 언니 한 명이 있어요.

   Eon-ni han myeo-ngi is-seo-yo.
   I have an older sister.

2. 남동생 두 명이 있어요.

   Nam-dong-seng du myeo-ngi is-seo-yo.
   I have two younger brothers.

3. 언니 한 명과 오빠 한 명이 있어요.

   Eon-ni han myeong-gwa op-pa han myeo-ngi is-seo-yo.
   I have an older sister and an older brother.

4. 저는 외동딸이에요.

   Jeo-neun we-dong-tta-ri-yeyo.
   I am an only child (girl).

More examples:

저는 장남이에요.

Jeo-neun jang-na-mi-yeyo.
I am the oldest son.

저는 둘째예요.

Jeo-neun dul-jje-yeyo
I am the second oldest.

저는 막내예요.

Jeo-neun mang-ne-yeyo.
I am the youngest.

10.4 Talking Spouse and Children

Make sure to study these Korean family words and the relevant phrases, so that it would be easy for you to talk about your loved ones.

1- "I have a husband/wife." and "I have a daughter/son."

If you are married with a family, you need to undertand how to say how many kids you have as well. There are many words to describe your own children. The most common words to say *son* -아들 (a-deul)and *daughter* -딸 (ttal).

To say "I have a son," you can say 저는 아들 한 명이 있습니다. (Jeo-neun a-deul han myeo-ngi i-seum-nida).

For "I have a daughter," say 저는 딸 한 명이 있습니다 (Jeo-neun ttal han myeo-ngi i-seum-nida).

Let's have a look at different phrases:

1. .저는 아들 한 명하고 딸 한 명이 있습니다.

Jeo-neun a-deul han myeong-hago ttal han mye-ongi i-seum-nida.

I have a son and a daughter.

2. 2.아들과 딸이 있습니다.

A-deul-gwa ttari i-seum-nida.

I have a son and a daughter.

3. 3.자식은 없습니다.

Ja-shi-geun op-seum-nida.

I have no children.

1. A: 결혼 하셨어요?
   Gyeor-hon ha-shos-soyo?
   Are you married?
2. B: 네, 결혼했어요. 집에 아들과 딸이 있어요.
   Ne, gyeor-hon-hes-soyo. ji-be a-deul-gwa ttari is-soyo.
   Yes, I am married. I have a son and a daughter.

Other vocabularies for married couples:

남편/애기 아빠/아이아빠/서방님/오빠	Husband
아내 부인 마누라 집사람 와이프	wife
아이	child
피앙세	fiance

안내/부인 is actually not commonly used by many people in Korea even though it's the official definition word for wife. It also sounds a bit too formal and generally people do not call their own wife '아내'. It is more commonly used to refer to someone else's wife.

마누라/집사람 are quite old-fashioned and only used by married men who are probably over 50 years old. 집사람 is especially old-fashioned. Its literal meaning is "home person" or "person who stays at home", so using this is not recommended. It can also be seen as rude to use 마누라/집사람 in referring to someone else's wife as this is only used between couples.

와이프 is just 'wife' sounded out using Hangul. Over the years, this word's usage has increased more and more. It has probably seen this trend due to the increase in exposure to foreign movies and TV shows from the West. This has a comfortable vibe and is the most commonly used by married men.

아이아빠/아이엄마. Korean people call their spouse as (child name)'s dad/mom. Although this form is not commonly used nowadays, there are still some couples who are comfortable using this phrase.

Example: 윤경아빠/윤경엄마

2- "I have a boyfriend/girlfriend."

Question:

지금 만나고 있는 사람 있니?

(Ji-geum man-na-go in-neun sa-ram in-ni?)

Are you seeing anyone at the moment?

Question:

남자친구/여자친구 있니?

(Nam-ja-chin-gu/yeo-ja-chingu in-ni?)

Do you have a boyfriend/girlfriend?

To respond that you are seeing someone, follow the grammatical order of *I have a daughter* (shown above).

Answers:

남자친구 있어요

(nam-ja-chin-gu is-soyo)

I have a boyfriend.

만나고 있는 사람 없어요

(Man-na-go in-neun sa-ram op-soyo)

I'm not seeing anyone.

아니요, 없어요

(A-niyo, op-soyo)

No, I don't.

A general conversation can go like this:

아버지: 지금 만나고 있는 남자 있나?

Abeoji: Jigeum mannago inneun saram innya?

Father: Are you seeing any guy at the moment?

수미: 아니요. 없어요.

Sumi: Aniyo. Eopseoyo.

Sumi: No, I'm not.

Other vocabularies for Girlfriends and Boyfriends

애인 = lover

남친 = bf

여친= gf

Endearment Terms between Couples:

자기야 = sweetie/baby

내 사랑 = my love

오빠 = honey (if bf is older)

여보 = darling (only for married couples)

10.5 Levels of Formality

At a fundamental level, Korean recognizes three primary levels of formality: formal, polite, and informal. Each level serves its purpose, ensuring that interactions remain appropriate and contextual. The decision to use one formality level over another depends on various factors, including the relationship between speakers, their respective ages, and the setting of the conversation.

1. Honorific (존댓말 - jon-den-mal)

This level exudes the utmost respect. It's typically reserved for addressing elders, superiors, or strangers. They come into play when addressing someone of higher status or when speaking about a third person deserving respect. The presence or absence of an honorific can completely change the tone and meaning of a sentence.

Here, the conversation steers clear of colloquialisms, adopting a tone of deference and respect.

Example:

연세가 어떻게 되십니까?
yon-sega eot-toke dwe-shim-nikka?
How old are you?

연세 means age. The question above is the version of
몇 살이에요 with highest level of respect.

These are special versions of common **nouns** intended for honorific use. By changing a noun to its honorific form, the speaker shows respect to the person they are talking about.

Example:

이름 (ireum) - name (normal form)

성함 (seongham) - name (honorific form)

Here are some more examples of nouns with equivalent honorific form:

Normal Form	Honorific Form
집 (house)	댁
생일 (birthday)	생신
생일 축하합니다 (happy birthday)	생신 축하 드립니다

Verbs can also be transformed into their honorific counterparts by adding specific endings or altering the verb stem. This modification elevates the status of the action, making it more respectful.

Example:

잡다 (japda) - to hold (normal form)

잡으시다 (ja-peu-shida) - to hold (honorific form)

Normal Form	Honorific Form
먹다 (to eat)	드시다
말하다 (to speak)	말씀하시다
주다 (to give)	드리다
있다 (to be/to have)	계시다
가다 (to go)	가시다
오다 (to come)	오시다

하다 (to do)	하시다
모르다 (to not know)	모르시다

Title Honorifics:

These are formal titles added before names to signify respect. They are often used in professional settings.

Examples:

선생님 (seon-seng-nim) - teacher or sir/madam

선배님 (seon-be-nim) - Senior

부장님 (bu-jang-nim) - Head of Department

대리님 (dae-ri-nim) - Assistant Manager

팀장님 (tim-jang-nim) - Team Leader

목사님 (mok-ssa-nim) - Pastor

기사님 (gi-sa-nim) - Driver

오라버니 (o-ra-bo-ni) - Older brother to a female

형님 (hyung-nim) - Older brother to a male

누님 (nu-nim) - Oolder sister to a male

어머님 (o-mo-nim) - Mother

아버님 (a-bo-nim) - Father

할아버님 (ha-ra-bo-nim) - Grandfather

할머님 (hal-mo-nim) - Grandmother

사장님 (sa-jang-nim) - Business owner

1. Casual Polite (해요체 - he-yo-che)

A step down from the formal level, this is the most commonly used form in daily interactions, especially among adults. It strikes a balance, being respectful yet not overly formal.

Example:

몇 살이에요?
(myeot-sa-ri-ye-yo)
How old are you?

2. Informal Level (반말 - ban-mal)

This is the most casual form, often used among close friends, peers, or those younger than the speaker. It's a relaxed mode of communication, devoid of the trappings of formality.

Example:

몇 살이야?
(myeot-sa-ri-ya)
How old are you?

Navigating the Levels

Selecting the appropriate formality level requires a keen understanding of the context. For instance, while it's common to use the informal level with close friends, switching to a more formal tone might be necessary in the presence of elders or in official settings.

For instance, using informal language with an elder or superior might be perceived as rude or dismissive. Conversely, being overly formal with peers might create a sense of distance or aloofness.

The Cultural Significance

Korea's emphasis on Confucian values, which prioritize respect for elders and adherence to social norms, is evident in these formality levels. They serve as a constant reminder of one's position in the societal fabric, fostering a sense of community and mutual respect.

While the traditional levels of formality remain intact, there's a noticeable shift in modern Korean society. With the influence of Western culture and the changing dynamics of Korean youth, the lines separating these levels are becoming increasingly blurred, especially in urban settings.

The levels of formality in the Korean language are more than mere linguistic tools. By understanding and adeptly navigating these levels, one not only becomes proficient in the language but also gains a deeper appreciation for the nuances and subtleties of Korean society.

When to Use Which Level

In the dynamic dance of the Korean language, choosing the appropriate level of formality or honorifics is akin to selecting the right dance move. One misstep can change the tone of an entire conversation, making it essential to understand when and where to use each level. While the rules may seem intricate, a closer look reveals a system deeply intertwined with Korean culture and societal norms.

Factors Influencing the Choice

Several factors determine which level of formality or honorific to use. These factors act as guiding lights, ensuring that every interaction is respectful and appropriate.

1. **Relationship Dynamics:**

The nature of the relationship between speakers plays a pivotal role. Close friends might opt for informal speech, while acquaintances or strangers would typically use polite or formal levels.

2. Age Differences:

Age is more than just a number in Korean society. It dictates the level of respect and formality in interactions. When addressing elders or those even slightly older, it's customary to use a more respectful tone.

3. Setting and Context:

A casual chat in a café would differ vastly from a business meeting or a formal event. The setting dictates the tone, with formal events necessitating more respectful language.

Exercises

10.1 Family Members Exercises

Complete the conversations based on the provided pictures. The answer should include how many members are there and who they are.

1. (Wife, Son)

A: 가족이 몇 명이에요?

B.

2. (Grandmother, older brother)

A: 가족이 몇 명이에요?

B.

3. (Father, Mother, Older Sister)

A: 가족이 몇 명이에요?

B.

4. (Father, Mother)

A: 가족이 몇 명이에요?

B.

10.2 Choose the best word to fill in the blank.

1. 가: 여동생이 있어요? (Do you have a younger sister?)

나: 아니요, _____. (No, I don't.)

a.   예뻐요   b. 작아요   c. 없어요   d. 있어요

2. 가: 가족이 어디에 살아요? (Where does your family live?)

나: 아버지___어머니는 필리핀에 살아요.

(My father __ mother live in the Philippines.)

a.　　에　　　　　b. 에서　　　　c. 가　　　　　d. 하고

3.　가:_____.

나: 아니요, 없어요. (No, I do not.)

a.누구예요?　　　　　　b. 누나가 있어요?

c. 몇 살이에요?　　　　d. 가족이 몇 명이에요?

4.　**가**: 수피카 씨는 수루 씨하고 같이 살아요?

(Does Supika live together with Suru?)

나: 아니요, 수루 씨는 지금 기숙사 _____ 살아요.

(No, Suru lives in the dorm now.)

a.　　가　　　　　b. 에　　　　　c. 는　　　　　d. 하고

5.　**가**: 투안 씨는 형이 있어요?

(Does Tuan have an older brother?)

나: 아니요. 그런데___은/는 한 명 있어요.

(No, but he has one ___.)

가: 몇 살이에요? (How old is he?)

나: 스무 살이에요. (He is twenty years old.)

a.　　가족　　　　b. 부모　　　　c. 오빠　　　　d. 동생

10.3 Composition Practice

Answer the following sentences in Korean introducing details about your family. Write each sentences in 3 different level of politeness (informal, casual polite and honorific)

　　1.　How many are you in the family?

2. Where do you live?

3. How many brothers and sisters do you have?

4. Are you married?/Do you have a boyfriend/girlfriend?

5. Do you have a child?

6. How many kids do you have?

Fun Fact Breather Section

National Flower

Meet the Mugunghwa, also known as the Rose of Sharon—South Korea's national flower.

Sun Dodging

Koreans have mastered the art of avoiding the sun. Umbrellas aren't just for rain here!

Black Day

April 14th is Black Day, a day for singles to get together and 'mourn' their status by eating jjajangmyeon.

Chapter Eleven
Negative Sentences

In the symphony of human communication, **negative sentences** play a distinct role. They help express refusal, contradiction, or the absence of something. The Korean language, with its rich grammatical structures, offers systematic ways to convey negative meanings, enabling speakers to articulate these sentiments clearly and effectively.

11.1 Present Tense Negation

Let's take a look first at particles that are added before the verb or adverb.

안 (an) / 못 (mot)

The negative particle 안 (an) is a shortened version of 아니 (ani), which means no. The negative particle 못 (mot) means cannot. You can easily make a negative sentence or phrase by placing either 안 (an) or 못 (mot) in front of the verb or adverb.

못 (mot) means one's inability to do something so you should not confuse it with the negative particle 안 (an).

To help you better understand the difference of these two negative particles, let's look at this example: 아파요 (a-pa-yo) which means painful. It would be wrong to say 못 아파요 (mot apayo), 안 아파요 (an a-pa-yo) is the correct way form.

Examples:

안 (an) + Verb

안 + 가요 = 안 가요

(an ga-yo) – not going

안 + 마셔요 = 안 마셔요

(an ma-sheo-yo) – not drinking

안 + 자요 = 안 자요

(an ja-yo) – not sleeping

안 (an) + Adjective

안 + 아파요 = 안 아파요

(an apa-yo) – not painful

안 + 예뻐요 = 안 예뻐요

(an yep-po-yo) – not pretty

안 + 바빠요 = 안 바빠요

(an bap-pa-yo) – not busy

못 (mot) + Verb

못 + 가요 = 못 가요

(mot ga-yo) – cannot go

못 + 마셔요 = 못 마셔요

(mot ma-sheo-yo) – cannot drink

못 + 자요 = 못 자요

(mot ja-yo) – cannot sleep

Now, it's time to take a look at the most common negative particles placed after the verb or adverb.

1. -지 않다/-못 하다

The purpose and meaning of -지 않아요/-지 못해요 is the same with 안 (an) / 못 (mot), the only difference is that, this particle is placed after the verb or adjective.

The conjugation works the same for verbs, adverbs and adjectives.

We start by dropping 다, then we add the 지 않다/-못 하다 conjugated particle.

Here is a clearer formula:

-지 않다

Informal:

verb + 않아

가다 ➞ 가지 않아

(I) don't go – (gaji a-na)

Casual Polite:

verb + 않아요

가다 ➞ 가지 않아요

(I) don't go – (gaji a-na-yo)

Honorific:

verb + 않습니다

먹다 (meokda) = 먹지 않습니다

(I) don't eat = (meok-ji an-sum-nida).

Again, we apply the same rule for 지 못 하다 (ji mot hada).

-지 못 하다

Informal:

팔다 = 팔지 못 해

(I) am unable to sell – (pa-ji mot-he)

Casual Polite:

뛰다 ➞ 뛰지 못 해요

(I) am unable to run – (ttwi-ji mot-heyo)

Honorific:

읽다 ➞ 읽지 못 했습니다

(I) am unable to read – (ik-ji mot-hes-sumnida)

2. -지 말다

This is what you add to the verb or adverb if you want to say please don't do/please don't. For this imperative particle, the same format is used.

Examples:

하지마 = don't..

하지 말아요 = please don't do..

-지 말다

Informal:

팔다 = 팔지 마

Don't sell – (pal-ji ma)

Casual Polite:

뛰다 → 뛰지 마요

(I) Please don't run – (ttwi-ji ma-yo)

Honorific:

읽다 → 읽지 말아요

(I) am unable to read – (ik-ji mal-la-yo)

---

3. 없다

없다 (eop-ta) is a negative particle is added after any noun and adjective to indicate that you or the subject don't have something. It is the opposite of 있다 which means to have.

Examples:

시간이 없어요

(Shi-gani eop-soyo)

I don't have time

돈이 없어요

Do-ni eop-soyo

I don't have money

친구 없어요

Chin-gu eop-so-yo

I don't have a friend/friends

없다 can also be used to mean that *something/someone was not present at a particular location.*

Example:

수미는 지금 집에 없어요.

Su-mi-neun ji-geum ji-be eop-so-yo

4. 싫어하다

싫어하다 (shi-ro-hada) is a verb that's used to say that one does not like something or hate something. The opposite of 싫어하다 (shi-ro-hada) is 좋아하다 (jo-wa-ha-da), which means to like something.

Example:

나 김치를 **싫어해**.

Na kim-chi-reul shi-ro-he.

I don't like kimchi.

저는 여름을 싫어해요.

Jeo-neun yeo-reu-meul shi-ro-heyo.

I hate summer.

5. -기 싫다

기 싫다 (gi shil-ta) is used to express that somebody *doesn't want to (or like to) do something.* To construct this type of sentence, the rule of conjugation is the same -지 않다 which is as follows:

Verb 기 (gi) + 싫다 (silta)

걷기 **싫어**

(geot-gi shi-ro)

I dislike walking.

가기 **싫어요**

(geot-gi shi-ro-yo)

I dislike walking.

11.2 Answering a question negatively

By using -아니다 (anida)

아니다 (anida) means not to be. Like most Korean verbs, this one is conjugated by dropping 다 to get the verb stem 아니 (ani).

Examples:

Informal:

A: 그릇 누가 깼어? 너야?

(Geu-reut nu-ga kkes-so? Noh-ya?)
Who broke the bowl? Is it you?

B: 아니, 나 아니야.

(Ani, na aniya.)
No, it's not me.

Casual Polite:

A: 혹시 민재 씨?

Hoksi min-je shi?
Are you Min Je?

B: 아니요, 민재 아니예요.

(Aniyo, min-je ani-yeyo.)
No, I'm not Min Jae.

Honorific:

저는 학생이 아닙니다.

(Jeoneun haksengi animnida.)
I am not a student.

11. 3 Negative Prefixes

-비 / 무

Some Korean words can be negated using the prefixes 비 and 무. These prefixes are analogous to the English "un-" or "in-."

Examples:

Original	Negated
효과 (effect)	비효과 (ineffectiveness)
색 (color)	무색 (colorless)

11. 4 Past Tense Negation

To negate verbs in the past tense, you can use "지 않았다" after the verb stem.

Example:

먹지 않았다 (did not eat)

Informal: 먹지 **않았어**.

Casual Polite: **않았어요**.

Honorific: 먹지 **않았습니다**.

11.5 Future Tense Negation

For future tense negation, the structure "지 않을 것이다" is applied.

Example:

가지 않을 것이다 (will not go)

Informal: 가지 않을 거야.

Casual Polite: 가지 않을 거예요.

Honorific: 가지 않을 것입니다.

Challenges and Considerations

Forming negative sentences in Korean requires attention to context, politeness levels, and the specific message one wants to convey. While the rules and structures provide a framework, real-life conversations might see variations based on regional dialects, individual preferences, or evolving language trends.

Negative sentences are a critical component of the Korean language, allowing speakers to convey a wide range of **emotions, refusals, or contradictions.** Understanding the various ways to form these sentences, and the nuances that come with them, enriches one's Korean repertoire. As with all aspects of language learning, immersion, practice, and real-life application will solidify these concepts, enabling more nuanced and effective communication

Exercises

11.1 Complete the sentences based on the pictures provided.

1. 가: 남자 입니까?

나: _____. (No, I am a woman)

2. 가: 간호사 ____?

나: _____. (No, I am a doctor)

3. 가:요리사 _____?

나: _____. (No, I am a carpenter)

11.2. Writing Practice

Write the negative equivalent of the provided words/phrase in each level of politeness. Each sentence would require a total of 3 answers.

1. 아파요

2. 마시다

3. 집에 가요

4. 남자친구 있어요

5. 저는 치즈를 좋아해요

11.3 Composition Practice

Write the following sentences in Korean using the honorific negative negation format.

I am not a singer.

I am unable to go to school today.

I do not like cooking.

I did not not see the car.

I hate that guy!

Fun Fact Breather Section

Bowl Returns

Ordered food delivery? Don't forget, they'll come back for the bowls! Make sure to leave your bowls in front of your door after eating

Piggy Dreams

Dreaming of pigs? That's a Korean sign of good fortune coming your way.

Jinro Soju

Jinro Soju is not just popular; it's the world's best-selling liquor for over a decade.

Answers Key

CHAPTER 1

1.1 Korean Alphabets

1. c.
2. c
3. a
4. c
5. d

1.2

1. Gom, Gong
2. Dal, Dap
3. Mok, Mom
4. Bang, Bal
5. Sam, San
6. Nun, San, Pyeon-ji
7. Bam, Ma-eum, Mom-mu-ge
8. Gong, Yang, Kang-a-ji
9. Jib, ip, su-eop

10. ot, nat, kot

1.3

1. 한국
2. 사람
3. 밥
4. 한강
5. 대한민국
6. 우리 나라
7. 새우
8. 치마
9. 아버지
10. 반친구

CHAPTER 2

1.1

1. b
2. c
3. c
4. b
5. d

1.2

1.   들

2.   와
3.   까지
4.   에서
5.   를
6.   를
7.   이
8.   이

9. 하고

10. 만

CHAPTER 3

3.1

1. A
2. C
3. B
4. False

3.2

1. 저는 수지예요.
2. 그녀는 민아예요.
3. 그들은 한국팀이에요.
4. 그는 배고파요.
5. 저는 학생입니다.

CHAPTER 4

4.1

1. B
2. C
3. D
4. a

4.2

1. 텔레비전을 봐요. I am watching tv.
2. 일해요. I am working.
3. 커피를 마셔요. I am drinking coffee.

4. 운동해요. I am exercising.
5. 장을 봐요. I am grocery shopping.

4.3

6. 쉽니다
7. 도착합니다
8. 돌아옵니다
9. 집에 옵니다
10. 회사에 갑니다

CHAPTER 5

5.1

1. A
2. D
3. D
4. C
5. d

CHAPTER 6

6.1

1. C
2. A
3. d

6.2

1. 너 어디 살아?

2. 언제 베트남 왔어?

3. 뭐 먹어?

6.3

1. 가장 좋아하는 음식은 뭐예요?

2. 지금 식사하러 가시나요?

3. 어디 가세요?

CHAPTER 7

7.1

1. B
2. C
3. D
4. a

7.2

1. (재미있어, 재미있어요, 재미있습니다)

2. (통통해, 통통해요, 통통합니다)

3. (행복해, 행복해요, 행복합니다)

4. (아름다워, 아름다워요, 아름답습니다)

5. (드물어, 드물어요, 드뭅니다)

7.3

1. 완벽하게 (wan-byeok-ha-ge)

2. 깨끗하게 (kke-keut-ha-ge)

3. 촉촉하게 (cheok-cheok-ha-ge)

4. 특별하게 (teuk-byeol-ha-ge)

5. 가만하게 (ga-man-ha-ge)

CHAPTER 8

8.1

1. 앞

2. 뒤

3. 안

4. 옆

8.2

1. b, c, e

CHAPTER 9

9.1

1. 오전 한 시

2. 오전 열한 시

3. 오후 한 시

4. 오전 열 시

9.2

1. 1967 년 7 월 15 일

2. 1992 년 3 월 27 일

3. 2015 년 2 월 12 일

4. 1950 년 11 월 19 일

5. 1972 년 5 월 27 일

CHAPTER 10

10. 1

1. 아내하고 아들, 세명이에요.

2. 할머니하고 형, 세명이에요.

3. 네명이에요. 아버지하고 어머니 누나가 있어요.

4. 아버지하고 어머니, 세명이에요.

10.2

1.	C
2.	D
3.	B
4.	B
5.	d

CHAPTER 11

11.1

1. 아니요, 여자입니다.

2. 간호사 입니까? - 아니요, 의사입니다.

3. 요리사 입니까? - 아니요, 목수입니다.

11. 3

1. 저는 가수 아닙니다.

2. 저는 오늘 학교에 갈 수 없습니다.

3. 저는 요리를 좋아하지 않습니다.

4. 저는 차를 보지 못했습니다.

5. 저는 그 사람을 좋아하지 않습니다.

Conclusion

Learning the basics of any language is difficult, and the Korean language can especially feel daunting for many newcomers. With that being said, if you were able to finish all of the lessons in this book, you have built a solid foundation in Korean grammar.

However, learning a language is a long process that rewards consistency. Even just listening and watching Korean shows for 30 minutes a day can go a long way in improving your Korean skills. We sincerely hope that you continue your Korean language journey with the foundation you have built up and reach your goals, whether that be to understand the basics or speak like a native.

Thank you for choosing our book along your path to Korean mastery and we hope that you obtained a lot of useful information! If you have any questions, comments, or even suggestions we would love to hear from you by email at Contact@worldwidenomadbooks.com. We greatly appreciate the feedback and this allows us to improve our books and provide the best language learning experience we can.

Thank you,

Worldwide Nomad Team

Learn Conversational Korean for
Adult Beginners

All the Essential Phrases in Context with In-Depth
Explanations Needed To Visit Korea and
Understand the Culture

Worldwide Nomad

Introduction

Language is the road map of a culture. It tells you where its people come from and where they are going –

- Rita Mae Brown

In the vibrant tapestry of languages spoken across our globe, few are as captivating and enigmatic as the Korean language. With its melodious rhythm, intricate characters, and rich cultural heritage, Korean is a language that not only bridges communication but also unveils the essence of a nation deeply rooted in tradition and innovation.

Welcome to *Learn Conversational Korean*, a journey through the heart and soul of this extraordinary language. Whether you're an aspiring traveler, a businessperson looking to expand your horizons, or simply someone eager to explore the beauty of Korean culture, this book is your key to unlocking the door to understanding and speaking conversational Korean.

This book aims to empower you with the essential skills and knowledge to engage in meaningful conversations in Korean. It is designed for learners of all levels, from absolute beginners to those seeking to enhance their existing Korean language skills. By the end of this book, you will have not only a solid grasp of conversational Korean but also a deeper appreciation of Korean culture and customs.

Have you ever dreamed of wandering the bustling streets of Seoul, savoring mouthwatering street food, or simply immersing yourself in the rich cultural heritage of Korea? Conversational Korean is your passport to such experiences. This book is created with a clear purpose in mind.

Firstly, it aims to provide you with the skills for practical communication. Whether you find yourself ordering your favorite Korean dish at a local restaurant, seeking directions, or engaging in casual conversations with locals, this book equips you with the ability to communicate effectively in everyday situations.

Secondly, this book offers cultural insight. It delves into the intricacies of Korean culture, values, and customs, enriching your interactions and fostering meaningful connections with native speakers. Understanding the cultural context of the language will not only enhance your proficiency but also deepen your appreciation of Korean culture.

This book is also designed to boost your confidence in speaking Korean. It achieves this by gradually introducing you to the language's fundamentals and guiding you through practical exercises and real-life dialogues. As you progress through the chapters, you will find yourself becoming more comfortable and proficient in expressing yourself in Korean.

When it comes to Korean, a language renowned for its unique script, Hangul, the initial intimidation can be daunting. However, fear not, this book is meticulously written to transform your language-learning journey into an enjoyable and highly effective experience.

In addition to linguistic proficiency, we will offer invaluable cultural insights. By exploring the customs, traditions, and etiquette that shape both the language and its native speakers, you will gain a deeper appreciation of Korean culture. This cultural understanding will not only enrich your interactions but also foster a sense of respect and connection with the people you communicate with.

The ability to navigate real-life scenarios is an essential component of language learning. This book equips you with the necessary tools to excel in practical situations by providing dialogues and vocabulary tailored to everyday conversations. Whether you're ordering your favorite Korean dish at a restaurant or seeking directions on the bustling streets of Korea, you'll be well-prepared for your interactions, ensuring that your experiences in Korea are both enjoyable and enriching.

Now that you possess the essential linguistic tools from the Korean Grammar book, it's time to apply them to real-world situations. From ordering delectable dishes at a local restaurant to seeking directions through unfamiliar streets and engaging in casual chit-chat, we will prepare you for the myriad of everyday scenarios you may encounter while exploring Korea.

Language and culture are inextricably intertwined, forming the essence of a nation's identity. You'll gain profound insights into Korean customs, traditions, and social etiquette. This cultural understanding ensures that your conversations not only maintain linguistic accuracy but also reflect a deep respect for the rich tapestry of Korean culture.

Building upon the sturdy foundation established earlier, you'll be introduced to an expansive array of vocabulary. You'll acquire words and phrases spanning various topics, empowering you to engage in diverse conversations and express your thoughts and emotions with precision.

Throughout this book, you'll find that the Korean language is not just a means of communication; it's a key that opens doors to a rich and vibrant culture. So, let's embark on this adventure together. Ready your Hangul characters, sharpen your curiosity, and let's set sail into the world of Conversational Korean!

Chapter One
Numbers and Money

Numbers are the foundation of any language and play an integral role in our daily lives. From counting and telling time to expressing quantities and discussing prices, numbers and money-related vocabulary are vital components of effective communication. Whether you're planning a shopping spree in bustling markets, dining out at a local restaurant, or simply conversing with Korean-speaking friends, having a firm grasp of numbers and currency will greatly enhance your ability to communicate.

Here we'll start by exploring the Korean number system, which is unique and different from the Western numerical system you may be familiar with. Understanding how to count, tell time, and express dates will be our initial focus.

Once we have a solid foundation in numbers, we will delve into the world of money, where we'll learn how to discuss prices, make transactions, and handle financial exchanges confidently. You'll discover key vocabulary and phrases that will empower you to shop with ease, negotiate effectively, and manage your finances while in a Korean-speaking environment.

Here we will provide clear explanations and practical examples to reinforce your learning. Remember, mastering numbers and money in Korean is not only about acquiring the language but also about gaining cultural insights that will enrich your experiences in Korea and with Korean-speaking communities worldwide.

At the end you'll be well-prepared to handle everyday situations with confidence and ease, enhancing your overall language proficiency and cultural appreciation. Let's get started!

Numbers and money are ubiquitous in our daily lives, and understanding them is crucial for effective communication and seamless transactions. Whether you're shopping at a bustling market, dining at a local restaurant, or even just conversing with Korean-speaking friends, mastering the concepts of numbers and money is indispensable. Let's explore why these skills are vital for all your interactions involving transactions and amounts.

Navigating Everyday Transactions

Numbers and money are the language of transactions. Whether you're buying groceries, paying for transportation, or splitting a bill with friends, you'll need to understand and use numbers and currency. Without this knowledge, everyday tasks can become challenging, and miscommunication may lead to misunderstandings or overpayments.

Expressing Quantities

When discussing quantities or amounts in Korean, understanding the numerical system is essential. Whether you're specifying the number of items you want to purchase, describing the size or weight of a product, or indicating the time of day, numbers play a pivotal role in conveying accurate information.

Shopping and Bargaining

If you enjoy shopping, you'll appreciate how numbers and money become essential tools for getting the best deals. Understanding prices, discounts, and the ability to negotiate effectively can save you money and enhance your shopping experience.

Currency Conversion

If you're traveling to South Korea or engaging in international trade, understanding the Korean Won (₩) and its exchange rates becomes crucial. Knowing how to convert currency and manage finances while in Korea or dealing with Korean businesses is essential for travelers and business professionals alike.

Cultural Sensitivity

Understanding how numbers and money are viewed in Korean culture is equally important. Some numbers are considered lucky, while others are avoided because they are associated with bad luck. Being aware of these cultural nuances can help you navigate social interactions and avoid unintentional cultural insensitivity.

But before diving into these aspects, we'll start by exploring the Korean numerical system, which differs from the Western system you may be familiar with.

Whether you plan to visit South Korea, engage in business dealings, or simply have an interest in the Korean language, grasping the concepts of numbers is vital. We'll start by introducing the Korean numeral system, which is quite distinct from the Western system, and then delve into practical advice for effectively handling money and safeguarding yourself from potential scams.

Korean Numbers

To comprehend numbers in the Korean language, it's important to understand that there are two primary sets of numbers: native Korean numbers and Sino-Korean numbers. Native Korean numbers are used for counting items, while Sino-Korean numbers are commonly employed in formal or complex situations, such as counting money, minute of time(while hour of time will be in Native Korean numbers) or expressing dates.

Native Korean Numbers

Unlike English, there are two numerical systems in Korean: Sino-Korean and native Korean. Each of these groups of numbers is used to count and talk about different things, so when learning to count in Korean, we have to learn these two number systems.

I know it may seem very confusing, but don't worry, once I explain below how they work and when to use them, you will be counting in Korean in less time than you imagine.

- 하나(hana) - One

- 둘(dul) - Two

- 셋(set) - Three

- 넷(net) - Four

- 다섯(daseot) - Five

- 여섯(yeoseot) - Six

- 일곱(ilgop) - Seven

- 여덟(yeodeol) - Eight

- 아홉(ahop) - Nine

- 열(yeol) - Ten

Sino-Korean Numbers

This system is influenced by the Chinese language, a language that influenced the way of communicating in Korea before the Korean alphabet, Hangul, was created in 1443.

Sino-Korean numbers are used to talk about specific things, such as:

- Dates

- Telephone numbers

- Addresses

- Count days

- Money

Since Sino-Korean numbers are the ones used to count money, and money can have huge figures, this is the system used when large figures need to be mentioned, specifically beyond 99.

- 일(il) - One

- 이(i) - Two

- 삼(sam) - Three

- 사(sa) - Four

- 오(o) - Five

- 육(yuk) - Six

- 칠(chil) - Seven

- 팔(pal) - Eight

- 구(gu) - Nine

- 십(sip) - Ten

When counting items or people, you generally use native Korean numbers. For instance, counting from one to five would be: "하나 둘 셋 넷 다섯" (hana, dul, set, net, daseot). When combining numbers with units, like counting objects or people, you add the unit following the number. For instance, "three apples" would be "사과 세 개" (sagwa se gae).

Korean Numbers From 11 to 99

The general rule for forming a two-digit Korean number is ↓

number + 십(ship) + number

For example, to form the Korean number 30 it would be:

30: 3(sam) + 10(ship) → samship

To form the Korean number 77 it would be:

77: 7(chil) + 10(ship) + 7(chil) → chilshipchil

To form the Korean number 15 it would be:

15: 10(ship) + 5(o) → ship-o

*Note that for 11 to 19, 일(il) will be excluded, for example, 17 is ship-chil, not a ilship-chil.

Do you see it?

It is as if to say 77 you say "7 times ten plus 7", that is why the number 10 (ship) generally goes second in order. We also apply this same rule with numbers from 100 onwards.

Korean Numbers From 100 and Up

Now that you've learned how to form the Korean numbers from 1 to 99, let's move on to the larger figures. To do this we will learn the number 100 and the multiples of 1000. With the help of them and the numbers 1-10 we can form any figure.

100 → 백(baek)

1000 → 천(cheon)

10,000 → 만(man)

100,000 → 십만(shipman)

1,000,000 → 백만(baekman)

10,000,000 → 천만(cheonman)

100,000,000 → 억(eok)

1,000,000,000 → 십억(shipeok)

Korean Numbers From 100 to 999

To form any number between 100 and 199 the general rule is ↓

백+ number+ 십+ number

And to form any number between 200~999, the general rule is ↓

number + 백+ number+ 십+ number

For example:

250 → 이백 오십(ibaek oship)

Korean Numbers From 1000 to 9999

To form any number between 1000 and 1999 the rule is ↓

천+ number + 백+ number + 십+ number

And to form any number between 2000 and 9999 the general rule is ↓

number + 천 + number + 백 + number + 십 + number

1500 → 천오백 (cheon obaek)

Korean Numbers 10000 and 99999

To form any number between 10,000 and 19,999 the rule is:

만 + number + 천 + number + 백 + number + 십 + number

And to form any number between 20,000 and 99,999 the general rule is:

number + 만 + number + 천 + number + 백 + number + 십 + number

For example:

30,700 삼만 칠백 (samman chilbaek)

Practical Advice for Handling Money and Avoiding Scams

Before delving into the nuances of handling money and avoiding scams in South Korea, it's essential to acquaint yourself with the local currency.

Basic money-related vocabulary includes:

- 돈 (don) - Money

- 지폐 (jipye) - Bill (banknote)

- 동전 (dongjeon) - Coin

- 환전 (hwanjeon) - Currency exchange

- 계산 (gyesan) - Bill or check (at a restaurant or mart)

Here are some valuable tips for effectively handling money and staying safe from potential scams in South Korea

- **Counting money:** When giving or receiving money, it is customary to use polite language and handle the transaction with both hands, which signifies respect.

- **Currency exchange:** If you need to exchange currency, opt for reputable exchange offices or banks. Avoid street vendors who may offer better rates but could be involved in scams.

- **Scams to watch out for:** South Korea is generally a safe country, but it's wise to exercise caution. Be vigilant for scams involving counterfeit money, overcharging by taxi drivers, and unauthorized credit card charges. Stick to official businesses and always request a receipt.

- **Tipping:** Tipping is not common in South Korea and, in some cases, may even be declined. However, in more international or tourist-oriented areas, a small tip might be appreciated.

- **Using cards:** Credit and debit cards are widely accepted, but it's advisable to carry some cash for smaller purchases or for use in places that do not accept cards.

- **Digital payments:** It is getting common to pay with digital payment like Kakaopay, Naverpay at restaurants or small shops. Kakao and Naver is Korea's biggest service provider for searching engine and messenger app then they have payment function so Koreans are also using kakaopay to transfer money to friend or break bills for their ease.(More than 90% of Korean population uses Kakaotalk as their messenger app.)

Practice these concepts, and you'll be well-prepared to navigate the Korean-speaking world as a savvy traveler or businessperson.

General Price Ranges and Basic Korean Numbers for Shopping and Dining

Understanding general price ranges to ensure fair transactions and learning basic Korean numbers for shopping and dining.

Navigating prices in a foreign country can be a challenge, but having a sense of general price ranges will help you make informed decisions and avoid overpaying for goods and services in South Korea. While prices may vary depending on the location and type of establishment, here are some approximate price ranges for common items:

- **Street Food:** ₩1,000 - ₩5,000

- **Coffee:** ₩3,000 - ₩6,000

- **Public Transportation (Single Fare):** ₩1,250 - ₩2,500

- **Restaurant Meals (Per Person):** ₩7,000 - ₩20,000 (varies widely)

- **Groceries:** Prices vary; expect to pay around ₩40,000 - ₩60,000 per week for essentials.

- **Clothing:** Prices vary significantly based on the type of clothing and location.

These price ranges are approximate and can fluctuate depending on factors like the region, quality, and local economic conditions. It's advisable to do some research on specific costs in the area you plan to visit for a more accurate understanding.

When shopping or dining out in South Korea, knowing basic Korean numbers and phrases is invaluable for effective communication. Here are some essential numbers and expressions to help you in these situations:

Asking About Prices

- "이거 얼마에요?" (Igeo eolmaeyo?) - How much is this?

Numbers for Quantities

- "한 개" (Han gae), "두 개" (Du gae), "세 개" (Se gae)- One, two, three (items)

Ordering in Restaurants

- "메뉴판 주세요." (Menyupan juseyo) - Please give me the menu.

Paying and Receiving Change

- "계산 해 주세요." (Gyesan hae juseyo) - Please calculate the bill.

Learning these basic numbers and phrases will enable you to engage with locals more comfortably and handle everyday shopping and dining situations with confidence.

Using Numbers to Negotiate Prices

Negotiating prices can be a valuable skill, whether you're shopping for souvenirs in bustling markets or looking to secure a better deal in South Korea.

This is a common practice in South Korea, especially in traditional markets, street stalls, and smaller shops. It's a way of engaging with local vendors and often results in better deals for shoppers. Here are some key phrases and strategies to use numbers to your advantage when negotiating prices:

Starting the Negotiation

- "할인해 주세요." (Harin hae juseyo.) or "깎아 주세요" (Kkaka juseyo) - Please give me a discount.

Making Counteroffers

- "₩10,000 원으로 되요?" (manwon-euro due-yo?) - Is ₩10,000 okay?

Negotiating Politeness

- "아쉽지만 이 가격으로는 안돼요." (Ashipjiman i gagg-euronun andwaeyo.) - I wish I could, but not at this price.

Sealing the Deal

- "그럼, 팔천원에 팔 수 있어요?" (Geuleom, ₩8,000 palcheon won-e pal su iss-eoyo?) - Can you sell it for ₩8,000 then?

- "네, 좋아요." (Ne, joh-a-yo.) - Yes, that's fine.

Remember that politeness is essential in negotiations. Even if you are trying to haggle for a better price, maintaining a respectful tone and demeanor is appreciated. Also using proper appellation helps as it make vedor feel more happy and generous. For example, 아줌마(Ajuma) which is for married / middle-aged woman is not recommended in restaurants, shops. Instead you can use '이모'(Emo) – aunt, or '언니/누나'(Unni/Nuna).

Currency and Denominations in South Korea

Understanding the local currency and its denominations is vital when shopping or negotiating prices in South Korea. The official currency is the Korean Won, represented by the symbol ₩. Commonly used banknotes include ₩1,000, ₩5,000, ₩10,000, and ₩50,000. Coins come in ₩10, ₩50, ₩100, and ₩500 denominations.

Now, armed with the ability to understand and use numbers effectively, you can explore local markets, haggle for deals, and make informed purchasing decisions. Whether you're bargaining for a traditional souvenir, ordering delicious street food, or shopping for clothing, numerical fluency enhances your shopping experiences and allows you to engage more deeply with local culture. With this knowledge, you can shop confidently and engage in meaningful interactions with local vendors.

When managing your expenses or making purchases in South Korea, it's crucial to convey your budget clearly and effectively. Here are some phrases to help you communicate your budget to others

Setting a Budget

- "제 예산은 ₩50,000 원입니다." (Je yesaneun ₩50,000 wonimnida.) - My budget is ₩50,000.

- "예산이 얼마에요?" (Yesani eolmaeyo?) – How much is your budget?

- "한 달에 얼마를 쓸 수 있어요?" (Han dal-e eolmaleul sseul su iss-eoyo?) - How much can I spend per month?

Seeking Affordable Options

- "제 예산에 맞는 것을 추천해 주세요." (Je yesan-e majneun geos-eul chucheonhae juseyo.) - Please recommend something within my budget.

- "싸고 좋은 가격인 것을 찾고 있어요." (Ssago joh-eun gageogin geos-eul chajgo iss-eoyo.) - I'm looking for something cheap and good value.

Negotiating Based on Budget

- "이 가격으로 깎아주실 수 있어요?" (I gagg-eulo kkakkajusil su iss-eoyo?) - Can you lower the price to this amount?

- "물건을 저의 예산에 맞게 할인해 주실 수 있나요?" (Mulgeon-eul jeo-ui yesan-e majge halinhae jusilsu iitnayo?) - Can you offer a discount to match my budget?

These phrases allow you to communicate your financial limits politely and effectively, ensuring that you stay within your budget while making purchases or engaging in financial discussions.

When it comes to tipping in South Korea, the customs and expectations differ significantly from many Western countries. In fact, tipping is not considered a standard practice in most situations. South Korea has a strong culture of hospitality and service, and tipping can sometimes be seen as unnecessary or even inappropriate.

Understanding Tax and Additional Charges

Understanding tax and additional charges is essential for making informed financial decisions in South Korea. Here are some important points:

Value-Added Tax (VAT)

South Korea has a Value-Added Tax (VAT) system, which is included in the price of most goods and services. The standard VAT rate is 10%. You'll see this tax applied to various items when you shop or dine out.

Service Charges

Some high-end restaurants and international hotels may add a service charge to your bill. This charge typically ranges from 10% to 15%, and it is intended as compensation for the service staff.

Additional Charges

In some cases, you might encounter additional charges, such as corkage fees in restaurants if you bring your own alcohol or service fees for certain activities or amenities in hotels. Always check your bill for any extra charges.

Credit Card Use

Credit cards are widely accepted in South Korea, but it's a good practice to check whether there are any surcharges for using a credit card, especially for small purchases. Some businesses may prefer cash for smaller transactions.

Duty-Free Shopping

South Korea offers duty-free shopping for tourists, allowing you to get tax refunds on eligible purchases. Be sure to keep your receipts and follow the necessary procedures at the airport before departure. Also you can visit 'Duty-free shop' in the city (such as Lotte duty free shop, Shilla duty free shop) that prices are already applied excluding tax.

Understanding the local tax system, service charges, and additional fees will help you manage your budget effectively and make informed financial choices during your stay in South Korea.

Now you've explored a diverse array of topics, from understanding Korean currency and mastering the art of negotiation to comprehending tipping customs and embracing money-saving strategies.

As we conclude, it's vital to recognize that these skills not only serve practical purposes but also serve as cultural bridges, facilitating deeper connections and meaningful interactions.

These newly acquired abilities will not only enhance your financial acumen but also enrich your engagement with local culture. As you continue your journey to learn conversational Korean, always remember that practice and immersion are key to mastery in these essential facets of language and culture.

Now, for the next chapter, it's time for you to learn how to greet others warmly, navigate social customs gracefully, and introduce yourself confidently. These skills will not only help you initiate conversations but also foster positive connections with locals.

Chapter Two
Korean Greetings/ Etiquette/ Introducing Yourself

Korea, with its rich history and dynamic contemporary society, places great emphasis on courtesy and respect in interpersonal interactions. Whether you are planning a trip to this beautiful land or fostering friendships, understanding Korean greetings and etiquette is essential.

It's time to explore several key aspects of Korean greetings and etiquette, each providing a valuable insight into the intricate tapestry of Korean culture and social interactions.

Formal Introductions

When introducing yourself in a formal context, it's important to use polite language. Start by saying "저는" (jeoneun), which means "I am." Then, state your name. For example, "저는 마이클입니다" (jeoneun Michael imnida) means "I am Michael." You can also mention your nationality by saying "저는 미국인이에요" (jeoneun migug-in-ieyo), which means "I am from U.S.."

Informal Introductions

In more casual situations, you can use a simpler form of introduction. Instead of "저는" (jeoneun), you can say "나는" (naneun), which means "I am" as well but in casual way. For example, "나는 마이클이에요" (naneun Michael-ieyo) means "I am Michael." Remember to use this form only with close friends or peers of a similar age.

In Korean culture, age is an important factor in social interactions. It's common to ask someone's age as a way to determine the appropriate level of politeness. To state your age, you can say "나는 스물다섯 살이에요" (naneun seumuldaseot sari-eyo), which means "I am 25 years old."

Remember to practice these phrases and adapt them to your own personal details. Introducing yourself in Korean will open doors to meaningful connections and cultural understanding.

Essential Korean Greetings and Their Meanings

Greetings in Korean culture are much more than mere words; they are the keys to unlocking meaningful interactions and connections. In this section, we will explore some essential Korean greetings, each brimming with its unique significance and cultural depth.

안녕하세요 (Annyeonghaseyo) - Hello

Starting with this versatile greeting, which is the cornerstone of Korean salutations. It is suitable for both formal and informal settings, reflecting warmth and friendliness. Use it when meeting someone for the first time, in professional contexts, or when addressing your elders.

안녕 (Annyeong!) - Hi/Hey or Bye

This is more casual and informal version of "안녕하세요," "안녕" is perfect for interactions with friends, peers, or those younger than you. It maintains a friendly and approachable tone. This can be "Bye" in casual way with your friends or peers.

안녕히 가세요! (Annyeonghi gaseyo!) - Goodbye (to someone leaving)

When someone is departing, 안녕히 가세요 is the phrase to use. It conveys your well-wishes for their safe journey and is a polite way to bid farewell. The response is typically "안녕히 계세요" (Annyeonghi gyeseyo!), meaning "Please stay safely."

안녕히 가십시오! (Annyeonghi gasibsio!) - Goodbye (more formal)

In formal or professional settings, a more formal farewell is appropriate. "안녕히 가십시오" is the phrase to use to bid someone goodbye respectfully. You can use this when you are at work specially to your bosses.

잘 지냈어요? (Jal jinaess-eoyo?) - How have you been?

This caring inquiry about someone's well-being reflects genuine concern. By asking "잘 지냈어요?" you show that you care about their welfare and are interested in their life. A common response is "네, 잘 지냈어요" (Ne, jal jinaess-eoyo), meaning "Yes, I've been well."

감사합니다 (Gamsahamnida) - Thank you

Expressing gratitude is essential in any culture, and in Korean, "감사합니다" is the most common way to say thank you, being this phrase a respectful way to acknowledge kindness. In another way, you can use "고맙습니다(Gomapseumnida)" as well.

These essential Korean greetings serve as the foundation for courteous and meaningful interactions in Korean society. Understanding not only the words but also the cultural nuances behind these greetings will enable you to connect more deeply with Koreans and embrace the rich tapestry of their culture. Remember that greetings are more than just words; they are the keys to open doors to new friendships and experiences.

In Korean culture, there is also a gesture that is a deeply ingrained tradition that transcends mere politeness — bowing; it symbolizes respect, humility, and acknowledgment of another person's presence. Mastering the art of bowing is crucial for understanding and participating in Korean greetings and etiquette effectively. Here are some essential tips to guide you in this fascinating practice:

Bowing Angle

The depth and angle of your bow convey various messages. For casual situations or when meeting peers, a slight nod of the head is appropriate, with your eyes still making contact with the other person. In formal or solemn settings, a deeper and more pronounced bow is customary, accompanied by a lowered gaze. Deeper the bow, the bigger the respect.

Eye Contact

Maintaining eye contact is crucial while bowing in Korean culture. It signifies sincerity and respect. Failing to meet someone's gaze during a bow can be perceived as insincere or disrespectful. Therefore, always make an effort to maintain eye contact, especially in formal situations.

Hands and Arms

Keep your hands at your sides or in front of you when bowing in casual situations. In more formal contexts, you can place your hands together in a slight prayer-like position, near your chest. The specific hand placement may vary based on the formality of the occasion.

Bowing Frequency

When meeting someone for the first time or in formal settings, a bow is customary. However, subsequent bows may be less formal, especially in casual or familiar settings. Always follow the lead of the person you are interacting with, adapting the depth and frequency of your bow accordingly.

Return the Bow

If someone initiates a bow toward you, it is courteous to reciprocate with a bow of similar depth and formality, especially if they are older or hold a higher position of authority. This reciprocal bowing is a sign of respect and acknowledgment.

Handshakes

Handshakes are common in Korea using their right hand mostly. To show respect, support right forearm with left hand and handshakes are more common between men. Elder/higher position can suggest handshake first, in case yonger/employee want to suggest handshake, bow need to come first then handshake with two hands.

The Significance

Beyond the physical act, bowing signifies the acknowledgment of hierarchy, age, and social roles in Korean society. It is a non-verbal way of showing respect, expressing gratitude, and apologizing. The practice of bowing fosters harmony and demonstrates proper etiquette in interpersonal interactions.

Understanding the significance of bowing and practicing it correctly is integral to respecting Korean customs and building meaningful connections. Whether you're greeting someone, expressing gratitude, or offering condolences, bowing plays a pivotal role in conveying your intentions and maintaining social harmony.

In the realm of conversational Korean, making a positive impression hinges not only on what you say but also on how you say it. Respectful language, known as "honorifics" or "존댓말" (jondestmal) in Korean, is a pivotal element of Korean etiquette. It reflects your respect for others, acknowledges social hierarchies, and fosters harmonious interactions. In this section, we will delve into how to use respectful language to leave a lasting and favorable impression.

Using Formal Endings

In Korean, adding formal endings to verbs and adjectives is a fundamental way to show respect. Here are some common formal endings:

- **-요 (-yo):** This polite ending is versatile and can be used in various situations. It's suitable for addressing strangers, colleagues, or people you want to show respect to.

- **-습니다/-니다 (-seumnida/-nida):** This is an even more formal version of -요 and is often used in written or formal contexts, such as business emails or official documents. But also can be used in spoken language.

Using Honorific Titles

Addressing someone by their appropriate title is another way to demonstrate respect. Common honorific titles include:

- **선생님 (seonsaengnim):** This title is used for teachers, doctors, and other professionals.

- **아버님 (abeonim) / 어머님 (eomeonim):** These titles are used to address someone else's parents respectfully.

- **님 (nim):** Adding "님" after a person's name or title is a common way to show respect. For example, "좋은 아침이에요" (joheun achimieyo) means "Good morning," but adding "님" to the end when addressing someone respectfully, it becomes "좋은 아침이에요, 선생님" (joheun achimieyo, seonsaengnim) or "Good morning, teacher."

- **씨 (ssi):** In workplaces or with someone not close, add "씨" after one's name is common in Korea. Seldom calls only name and this is considered very rude specially when you are calling elders.

Using Polite Verbs

Korean verbs can be conjugated to show politeness and respect. Here are two common polite verb forms:

- **하십시오체 (hasipsioche):** This form is used in formal and polite contexts. For example, instead of saying "먹어" (meok-eo) for "eat," you would say "드세요" (deuseyo) to show respect.

- **하게체 (hageche):** This form is more informal than 하십시오체 but still polite. It's suitable for everyday interactions with people you want to show respect to.

Using Polite Language Particles

In addition to verb endings, Korean has special particles that add politeness to sentences. For instance:

- **좀 (jom):** This particle is often used to make a polite request. For example, "물 좀 주세요" (mul jom juseyo) means "Please give me some water," where "주세요" (juseyo) adds politeness.

This not only showcases your courtesy but also helps you navigate social hierarchies and establish rapport with people of all ages and backgrounds. Remember that respect is the cornerstone of meaningful and harmonious interactions, making your language skills all the more powerful.

Casual Politeness (Informal)

- **v-어/-아요 (-eo/-ayo):** This is the least formal politeness level and is used among close friends, family members, or people of the same age. It adds a friendly and relaxed tone to greetings.

- **뭐해? (Mwohae?)** - A very informal way to ask "What are you doing?" suitable for close friends.

Respectful Politeness (Honorific)

- **안녕하십니까? (Annyeong hasimnikka?):** A very formal and respectful way to say "Hello" or "How are you?" this can be used for addressing elders or superiors.

- **뭐 하십니까? (Mwo hasimnikka?):** A highly formal way to ask "What are you doing?" appropriate for formal settings.

Understanding the nuances of politeness levels in Korean greetings is essential for navigating social hierarchies and relationships effectively. It demonstrates your cultural sensitivity and respect for others, fostering harmonious interactions in various contexts.

Matching the Situation with the Greeting

Understanding the appropriate greeting for different situations is crucial for effective communication.

In formal settings, like a business meeting or meeting someone in a position of authority, "안녕하세요 (Annyeonghaseyo)" is always appropriate.

In casual settings or with friends, a simple and relaxed "안녕 (Annyeong!)" suffices.

Adding a Personal Touch

Incorporate personal details in your greeting based on your relationship with the person. Using their name or a suitable honorific, or referencing a recent event or context can make the greeting more personalized and thoughtful.

Example: "안녕하세요, 민지님 (Annyeonghaseyo, Minji min.)" - "Hello, Minji."

Greetings are the foundation of meaningful relationships, setting the stage for a fruitful and engaging conversation.

Hierarchy and Age

Korean society places significant emphasis on age and social hierarchy. When exchanging pleasantries, it's essential to consider the age and status of the person you are addressing.

Elders

Always show respect to elders by using formal language and honorific titles like "선생님 (seonsaengnim)" for teachers or "아버님 (abeonim)" for someone else's father. You don't call their name if they are older than you.

Peers

Among peers or those of similar age, casual language and informal greetings like "안녕 (Annyeong!)" are acceptable.

Superiors

In professional settings, use formal language and address superiors with titles or honorifics.

By understanding and embracing these customs, you not only show respect for Korean culture but also open the door to meaningful connections with Koreans. Remember, a warm smile, a simple "안녕하세요" (Annyeonghaseyo), and a respectful bow can go a long way in building positive relationships.

In the next chapter we will guide you through the essential Korean phrases and customs you'll need to navigate your arrival or departure from Korea seamlessly. From understanding airport signage and announcements to interacting with airport personnel, we'll ensure you're well-prepared for your Korean travel adventure.

Chapter Three
Airport

Common Phrases	Translation
안녕하세요. (Annyeonghaseyo.)	Hello.
감사합니다. (Gamsahamnida.)	Thank you.
어서오세요. (Eoseo oseyo.)	Welcome.
여권을 보여주세요. (Yeogwon-eul boyeojuseyo.)	Please show your passport.
어디로 가시나요? (Eodiro gasinayo?)	Where is your destination?
영어를 할 수 있나요? (Yeongeoreul hal su innayo?)	Can you speak English?
비행기 표를 예약했어요. (Bihaenggi pyo-leul yeyakhaesseoyo.)	I have a flight reservation.
어디에서 수하물을 찾을 수 있나요? (Eodieseo Suhamul-eul chajeul su innayo?)	Where can I find my luggage?

출구는 어디에 있나요? (Chulgu-neun eodie innayo?)	Where is the exit?
환전소가 어디에 있나요? (Hwanjeonso-ga eodie innayo?)	Where is the currency exchange?
와이파이 비밀번호가 뭐에요? (Wi-Fi bimilbeonho-ga mwoeyo?)	What is the Wi-Fi password?
식당은 어디에 있나요? (Sikdang-eun eodie innayo?)	Where is the restaurant?
화장실은 어디에 있나요? (Hwajangsil-eun eodie innayo?)	Where is the restroom?
이용 안내를 받을 수 있을까요? (Iyong annae-leul badeul su isseulkkayo?)	Can I get some assistance?
비행기가 언제 출발하나요? (Bihaenggi-ga eonje chulbalhanayo?)	When does the flight depart?
여권 신고를 해야 하나요? (Yeogwon singo-leul haeya hanayo?)	Do I need to report my passport?
수하물은 어디에서 찾을 수 있나요? (Suhamul-eun eodieseo chajeul su innayo?)	Where can I claim my baggage?
이곳에서 전화를 걸 수 있나요? (Igot-eseo jeonhwa-leul geol su innayo?)	Can I make a phone call here?
비상구는 어디에 있나요? (Bisanggu-neun eodie innayo?)	Where is the emergency exit?
이곳에서 무료 셔틀 버스를 탈 수 있나요? (Igot-eseo muryo shuttle bus-leul tal su innayo?)	Can I take a free shuttle bus from here?
이곳에서 호텔 예약을 할 수 있나요? (Igot-eseo hotel yeyak-eul hal su innayo?)	Can I make a hotel reservation here?

비자 신청을 어디에서 할 수 있나요? (Visa sincheong-eul eodieseo hal su innayo?)	Where can I apply for a visa?
이곳에서 휴대폰 충전기를 빌릴 수 있나요? (Igot-eseo hyudae-phone chungjeon-gi-leul billil su innayo?)	Can I borrow a mobile phone charger here?
이곳에서 세관 신고를 해야 하나요? (Igot-eseo segwan singo-leul haeya hanayo?)	Do I need to declare at customs here?
이곳에서 관광 안내지를 얻을 수 있나요? (Igot-eseo gwan gwang annaeji-leul eodeul su innayo?)	Can I get a tourist guide here?
이곳에서 무료 와이파이를 사용할 수 있나요? (Igot-eseo muryo Wi-Fi-leul sayonghal su innayo?)	Can I use free Wi-Fi here?
수하물은 어디에서 받나요? (Suhamul-eun eodieso batnayo?)	Where is the baggage claim area?
출입국 심사대는 어떻게 가나요? (Churipguk simsadae-neun eotteoke ganayo?)	How do I get to the immigration counter?
여기에 환전소가 있나요? (Yeogie hwanjeonsol-ga innayo?)	Is there a currency exchange counter here?
SIM 카드를 어디서 구입할 수 있나요? (SIM card-leul eodiseo guibiphal su innayo?)	Where can I buy a SIM card?
공항 내 면세점이 있나요? (Gonghang nae myeonsejeom-i innayo?)	Are there any duty-free shops in the airport?
여기서 도심으로 가는 방법이 무엇인가요? (Yeogiseo dosimeuro ganeun bangbeob-i mueosingayo?)	How can I get to the city center from here?
수하물 카트를 어디서 구할 수 있나요? (Suhamul cart-leul eodiseo	"Where can I find a luggage cart?"

guhal su innayo?)	
분실물 센터가 있나요? (Bunsilmul center-ga innayo?)	"Is there a lost and found office in the airport?"
터미널에 ATM 이 있나요? (Terminal-e ATM-i innayo?)	"Are there any ATMs in the terminal?"
신용카드로 결제할 수 있나요? (Sinyong-card-ro gyeoljehal su innayo?)	"Can I use my credit card to pay for purchases?"
무료 Wi-Fi 를 사용할 수 있나요? (Muryo Wi-Fi-leul sayonghal su innayo?)	"Is there free Wi-Fi available?"
화장실은 어디에 있나요? (Hwajangshil-eun eodie innayo?)	"Where can I find a restroom?"
공항 내 음식점이나 카페가 있나요? (Gonghang nae eumsikjeom-ina cafe-ga innayo?)	"Are there any restaurants or cafes in the airport?"
비행기 탑승을 위해 얼마나 일찍 도착해야 하나요? (Bihaenggi topseong-eul wihae eolmana iljjik dochakhaeya hanayo?)	How early should I arrive for my flight?
공항 내 흡연 구역이 있나요? (Gonghang nae heubyeon guyeogi innayo?)	Is there a smoking area in the airport?
교통 수단에 대한 정보는 어디에서 얻을 수 있나요? (Gyotong sudan-e daehan jeongbo-neun eodieseo eodeul su innayo?)	Where can I find information about transportation options?
교통 수단에 대한 정보는 어디에서 얻을 수 있나요? (Gyotong sudan-e daehan jeongbo-neun eodieseo eodeul su innayo?)	Where can I find information about transportation options?
탑승객용 라운지가 있나요? (Tapseunggaek-yong longe ga innayo?)	Are there any lounges for passengers?

비행기 안에 음식과 음료를 가져갈 수 있나요? (Bihaenggi ane eumsikgwa eumryo-leul gajyeogal su innayo?)	Can I bring food and drinks on the plane?
공항 내 약국이 있나요? (Gonghang nae yakguki innayo?)	Is there a pharmacy in the airport?
전자기기 충전 스테이션은 어디에 있나요? (Jeonjagigi chungjeon station-eun eodie innayo?)	Where can I find a charging station for my electronic devices?
어린이를 위한 시설이 있나요? 예를 들어 놀이터 같은거요 (Eorini-leul wihan siseori innayo?, yeleul deureo noliteo gateungeoyo.)	Are there any facilities for children, like play areas?
공항 셔틀 서비스를 어떻게 이용하나요? (Gonghang shuttle service-leul eotteoke iyonghanayo?)	How can I access the airport's shuttle service?
수하물을 임시로 보관할 수 있는 곳이 있나요? (Suhamul-eul imsiro bogwanhal su inneun gosi innayo?)	Is there a place to store my luggage temporarily?
공항 지도는 어디에서 얻을 수 있나요? (Gonghang jido-neun eodieseo eodeul su innayo?)	Where can I find a map of the airport?
기내 수하물로 액체를 가지고 들어갈 때 제한이 있나요? (Ginae suhamul-ro aekche-leul gajigo deureogal ttae jehan-i innayo?)	Are there any restrictions on carrying liquids in my hand luggage?
이동에 불편을 겪는 사람을 위한 지원 서비스를 어떻게 요청하나요? (Idong-e bulpyeon-eul geokneun sarameul wihan jiwon service-leul eotteoke yocheonghanayo?)	How can I request special assistance for someone with mobility issues?
간단한 간식이나 커피를 먹을 수 있는 곳이 있나요? (Gandanhan gansik-ina coffee-leul meokeul su inneun gosi innayo?)	Is there a place to get a quick snack or coffee?
비행기 지연이나 취소에 대한 정보는 어디에서 얻을 수 있나요? (Bihaenggi jiyeon-ina chwiso-e daehan jeongbo-neun eodieseo eodeul su	Where can I find information about flight delays or cancellations?

innayo?)	
문제가 발생했을 때 항공사에 어떻게 연락할 수 있나요? (Munje-ga balsenghaesseul ttae hanggongsa-e eotteoke yeollakhal su innayo?)	How can I contact my airline if I have a problem?

Common Vocabulary at the Airport

Vocabulary	Translation
터미널 (Terminal)	Terminal
출발 (Chulbal)	Departure
도착 (Dochak)	Arrival
탑승구 (Tapseunggu)	Gate
탑승권 (Tapseunggwon)	Boarding pass
보안 검사 (Boan geomsa)	Security check
수하물 수취 (Suhamul suchwi)	Baggage claim
세관 (Segwan)	Customs
이민 (Imin)	Immigration
여권 (Yeogwon)	Passport

비자 (Visa)	Visa
항공편 (Hanggongpyeon)	Flight
지연 (Jiyeon)	Delayed
취소 (Chwiso)	Cancelled
체크인 카운터 (Check-in counter)	Check-in counter
기내 수하물 (Ginae suhamul)	Carry-on luggage
위탁 수하물 (Witak suhamul)	Checked baggage
수하물 태그 (Suhamul tag)	Baggage tag
(통합 보안 검색소) (TSA (tonghap boan geomsaek so))	TSA (Transportation Security Administration)
엑스레이 기계 (X-ray gigye)	X-ray machine
금속 탐지기 (Geumsok tamjigi)	Metal detector
면세점 (Myeonsejeom)	Duty-free shop
연결 항공편 (Yeongyeol hanggongpyeon)	Connecting flight
경유 (Gyeong-yu)	Layover

항공사 (Hanggongsa)	Airline
승무원 (Seungmuwon)	Cabin crew
조종사 (Jojongsa)	Pilot
활주로 (Hwaljuro)	Runway
수하물 회전대 (Suhamul hoejeondae)	Baggage carousel
분실물 센터 (Bunsilmul center)	Lost and found

Chapter Four
Taxis

Taxis play a role in the daily lives of its inhabitants, that's why it's essential to understand the significance of taxis in Korean culture.

Taxis in Korea are known for their safety, cleanliness, and punctuality. In a culture that values respect for others and adherence to schedules, these qualities are highly prized. Korean taxi drivers take their profession seriously, often striving to provide a comfortable and pleasant experience for their passengers.

Getting a taxi in Korea is a straightforward process. You'll find them at designated taxi stands, but if you're on a busy street, simply raise your hand to signal an available taxi. The iconic orange or silver color of Korean taxis is hard to miss. Keep in mind that there are different types of taxis, each with its own fare structure, so it's essential to choose the right one for your needs. You can see many other Koreans call a taxi by an app called Kakao Taxi. If you have a Korean phone number, it's recommended to download Kakaomap app then you can call a taxi. Uber is not available in Korea while the most used taxi app is Kakaotaxi.

Korean taxis accept various payment methods, making it convenient for passengers. You can pay with cash, credit cards, or mobile payment apps like KakaoPay or T-money. It's always a good idea to check with the driver about their preferred payment method before starting your journey. These days most of the payments are with credit card or some sort of digital payment in Korea. Taxis are the same so sometimes taxi drivers might not have some change for your cash payment.

Korean taxi drivers are generally polite and professional. While some may not speak English fluently, they often go out of their way to assist foreigners. You can open your map on your phone and show them where you want to go. Kakaomap or Navermap is mostly used in Korea rather than Google map. Learning some basic Korean phrases for communication can be helpful and greatly appreciated. Let's learn some of them.

Common Phrases and Questions for Korean Taxis

Common Phrases	Translation
어디로 가세요? (Eodiro gaseyo?)	Where are you going?

목적지가 어디세요? (Mokjeokji-ga eodiseyo?)	What's your destination?
이 곳에서 택시를 잡기 어려워요. (I got-eseo taeksi-reul japgi eoryeowoyo.)	It's difficult to catch a taxi here.
차가 많이 막혀요. (Cha-ga mani makhyeoyo.)	There's a lot of traffic.
어떻게 운전하면 좋을까요? (Eotteoke unjeonhamyeon joheulkkayo?)	How should I drive?
거스름돈이 없어요. (Geosureumdon-i Ubsseoyo.)	I don't have exact change.
감사합니다. (Gamsahamnida.)	Thank you.
안녕히 가세요. (Annyeonghi gaseyo.)	Goodbye (when leaving the taxi).
[Location]로 가주세요. ([Location] ro gajuseyo.)	Please take me to [location].
여기에서 얼마나 걸릴까요? (Yeogieseo eolmana geollilkkayo?)	How long will it take from here?
빨리 가주세요. (Ppalli gajuseyo.)	Please go quickly.
천천히 가주세요. (Cheoncheonhi gajuseyo.)	Please go slowly.
이 길로 가주세요. (Igil-ro gajuseyo.)	Please take this route.
네비게이션을 사용해 주세요. (Navigagion-eul sayonghaejuseyo.)	Please use the GPS.
라디오를 켜주세요. (Radio-reul kyeojuseyo.)	Please turn on the radio.
라디오를 꺼주세요. (Radio-reul kkeujuseyo.)	Please turn off the radio.

창문을 열어주세요. (Changmun-eul yeoleojuseyo.)	Please open the window.
창문을 닫아주세요. (Changmun-eul dadajuseyo.)	Please close the window.
짐을 실을 공간이 필요해요. (Jim-eul sileul gonggan-i pillyohaeyo.)	I need space for luggage.
트렁크를 열어 주세요. (Trunk-reul yeoleo juseyo.)	Please open the trunk.
영수증을 주세요. (Yeongsujeung-eul juseyo.)	Please give me a receipt.
카드로 결제할게요. (Card-ro gyeoljehalgaeyo.)	I'll pay with a card.
현금으로 결제할게요. (Hyungeum-euro gyeoljehalgaeyo.)	I'll pay with cash.
어떤 음악을 좋아하세요? (Eotteon eumageul joahaseyo?)	What kind of music do you like?
소리를 크게 해주세요. (Sori-leul keuge haejuseyo.)	Please turn up the volume.
소리를 작게 해주세요. (Sori-leul jakge haejuseyo.)	Please turn down the volume.
다리에서 내려주세요. (Darieseo naeryeojuseyo.)	Please drop me off at the bridge.
터미널까지 가주세요. (Termal-kkaji gajuseyo.)	Please take me to the terminal.
주유소에 들려주세요. (Juyuso-e deullyeojuseyo.)	Please stop at the gas station.
도움이 필요해요. (Doum-i piryohaeyo.)	I need help.
주변에 음식점이 어디 있어요? (Jubyeon-e eumsikjeom-i eodiisseoyo?)	Where are the restaurants nearby?

요금이 얼마에요? (Yogeum-i eolmaeyo?)	How much is the fare?
여기서 내릴게요. (Yeogieseo naerilgeyo.)	I'll get off here.
미안합니다, 잠시만 기다려주세요. (Mianhamnida, jamsiman gidaryeojuseyo.)	I'm sorry, please wait for a moment.
여행지를 추천해주세요. (Yeohaengji-leul chucheonhaejuseyo.)	Please recommend a tourist destination.
어디서 택시를 잡을 수 있어요? (Eodiseo taxii-leul jabul su isseoyo?)	Where can I catch a taxi?
목적지까지 얼마나 걸릴까요? (Mokjeokjikkaji eolmana geollilkkayo?)	How long will it take to get to my destination?
여기에서 어떻게 [location]로 갈 수 있어요? (Yeogieseo eotteoke [location]-ro gal su isseoyo?)	How can I get to [location] from here?
이 길은 어때요? (Ii gireun eottaeyo?)	How's this route?
출퇴근 시간에는 교통이 어떤가요? (Chultaeguen sigan-eneun gyotong-i eotteogayo?)	What's traffic like during rush hour?
이 주변에 주요 관광지가 어디 있나요? (Ii jubyeone juyo gwangwangjiga eodi iitnayo?)	Where are the major tourist attractions around here?
이 택시는 카드 결제가 가능한가요? (Ii taxi-neun card gyeolje-ga ganeunghangayo?)	Can I pay with a card in this taxi?
지금 얼마에요? (Jigeum eolmaeyo?)	How much is it now?
가는 길에 마트에 들려주실 수 있어요? (Ganeun gile mart-e deullyeojusil su isseoyo?)	Can you stop by the supermarket on the way?

운전기사님, 길을 건너주세요. (Unjeon gisanim, gil-eul geonneojuseyo.)	Driver, please cross the street.
[호텔/숙소]로 가려고 하는데, 어떻게 가야 해요? ([Hotel/sukso]-ro garyeogo haneunde, eotteoke gaya haeyo?)	I want to go to [hotel/accommodation], how should I go there?
가는 길에 음식점이 어디 있나요? (Ganeun gil-e eumsikjeom-i eodi-iitnayo?)	Where are the restaurants on the way?
언제까지 하세요? (Eonjekkaji haseyo?)	Until what time do you operate?
고속도로를 타야 하나요? (Gosokdoro-reul taya hanayo?)	Do I need to take the expressway?
여기 근처에 휴게소가 어디 있나요? (Yeogi geuncheoe hyugeso-ga eodi iitnayo?)	Where is the rest area near here?
내릴 수 있을 때 알려주세요. (Naeril su isseul ttae allyeojuseyo.)	Let me know when I can get off.
이 동네는 안전한가요? (Ii dongnae-neun anjeonhankayo?)	Is this area safe?
여기 주위에 병원이 어디 있나요? (Yeogi juwi-e byeongwon-i eodi itnayo?)	Where is the hospital around here?
밤 늦게까지 운행하나요? (Bam neutgekkaji unhaenghanayo?)	Do you operate late into the night?
이 주위에 주차장이 어디 있어요? (Ii juwie juchajang-i eodie isseoyo?)	Where is the parking lot around here?
공항으로 가야 돼요. (Gonghang-euro gaya dwaeyo.)	I need to go to the airport.
핸드폰 충전기 있으세요? (Handphone chungjeongi isseuseyo?)	Do you have a phone charger?

환전할 수 있는 곳이 어디에요? (Hwanjeonhal su itneun got-i eodieyo?)	Where can I exchange currency?
시내 버스 터미널로 가주세요. (Sinae bus terminal-ro gajuseyo.)	Please take me to the downtown bus terminal.
고속버스 터미널로 가주세요. (Gosokbus terminal-ro gajuseyo.)	Please take me to the intercity bus terminal.
다리를 건너주세요. (Dari-leul geonneojuseyo.)	Please cross the bridge.
이 자리에 물병이 있어요? (Ii jari-e mulbyeong-i isseoyo?)	Is there a water bottle in this seat?
다음 주유소에 들려주세요. (Daeum juyuso-e deullyeojuseyo.)	Please stop at the next gas station.
여기서 내려 주세요. (Yeogieseo naeryeo juseyo)	Please drop me off here.
가까운 ATM 이 어디에요? (Gakkawoon ATM-i eodieyo?)	Where is the nearest ATM?
편의점에 잠시 들려주실 수 있어요? (Pyeonuijeome jamsi deullyeojusil su isseoyo?)	Can you stop at a convenience store?

Vocabulary

Vocabulary	Translation
택시 (Taxi)	Taxi
기사님 (Gisanim)	Driver
손님 (Sonnim)	Guest (Driver calls you in this way)

목적지 (Mokjeokji)	Destination
요금 (Yogeum)	Fare
미터 (Meter)	Meter
계산 (Gyesan) / 결제 (Gyeolje)	Payment
주행거리 (Juhaenggeori)	Distance traveled
속도 (Sokdo)	Speed
시간 (Sigan)	Time
길 (Gil)	Road
교통 (Gyotong)	Traffic
주차 (Jucha)	Parking
요금 표 (Yogeum pyo)	Fare chart
빨리 (Ppalli)	Quickly
천천히 (Cheoncheonhi)	Slowly
여기 (Yeogi)	Here
저기 (Jeogi)	There
앞 (Ap)	Front

뒤 (Dwi)	Back
왼쪽 (Wenjjok)	Left
오른쪽 (Oreunjjok)	Right
주유소 (Juyuso)	Gas station
공항 (Gonghang)	Airport
터미널 (Terminal)	Terminal
버스 정류장 (Bus jeongryujang)	Bus stop
다리 (Dari)	Bridge
도로 (Doro)	Roadway
고속도로 (Gosokdoro)	Expressway
창문 (Changmun)	Window
승객 (Seunggaek)	Passenger
현금 (Hyungeum)	Cash
카드 (Card)	Card
지도 (Jido)	Map
휴대폰 (Hyudae-phone)	Mobile phone

승객 좌석 (Seunggaek jwaseok)	Passenger seat
운전석 (Unjeonseok)	Driver's seat
예약 (Yeyak)	Reservation
물병 (Mulbyeong)	Water bottle
고객 서비스 (Gogaek service)	Customer service
커피숍 (Coffee shop)	Cafe
음악 (Eum-ak)	Music
라디오 (Radio)	Radio
휴게소 (Hyugeso)	Rest area
도움 (Doum)	Help
안전 (Anjeon)	Safety
표시된 (Pyosideon)	Displayed
음식점 (Eumsikjeom)	Restaurant
병원 (Byeongwon)	Hospital
편의점 (Pyeonuijeom)	Convenience store
숙소 (Sukso)	Accommodation

네비게이션 (Navigation)	GPS map for car
영수증 (Yeongsujeung)	Receipt

Chapter Five
Subway/ Buses/ Transportation in Korea

Public transportation in South Korea is more than a functional necessity; it reflects the nation's unwavering commitment to efficiency, convenience and environmental sustainability. This extensive network of subways and buses not only eases traffic congestion but also contributes to cleaner and more sustainable urban environments. Korean cities, known for their sprawling metropolises, rely on these systems as the lifeblood that keeps them moving.

How Korean Subway and Bus Systems Work

Navigating Korean subways and buses may initially seem complex, but it becomes straightforward with a basic understanding.

Subway System

To begin your journey, determine your destination and find the nearest subway station. Many Koreans use smartphone apps or websites for route planning, but you can also seek assistance from locals or station attendants.

At the subway station, you can purchase a single journey card or a T-money card, a reloadable transportation card accepted on subways, buses, and taxis. The latter is convenient for frequent travelers and can be purchased at most of convenient stores. Single journey card has deposit when you purchase, so after you finish to use it, you can refund deposit at vending machines located in stations.

Korean subway stations are well-designed and feature clear signage in both Korean and English. Follow signs to your designated subway line and platform.

Subway maps are user-friendly, using color-coded lines for easy comprehension. Find your initial station and destination, then trace the line on the map. Each station is numbered for tracking progress.

Upon reaching your destination station, follow signs to the appropriate exit, as stations typically have multiple exits.

Bus System

Understanding the bus system requires knowledge of the bus number and its route. Bus stops display information about the buses serving them, including route numbers and destinations.

As your bus arrives, ensure you have your T-money card or exact fare ready. Enter through the front door and take an available seat.

Buses announce upcoming stops in Korean and English. Watch for the digital display or listen for your stop. To signal your intent to disembark, press the stop button.

Exit through the rear door, and it is customary to express gratitude to the driver as you disembark. If you are using T-money card, free transfer between bus and subway can apply within 30 minutes. You must tap T-money card when you get off from bus so that you can get discount or free transfer. Bus fare is calculated by total travel distance so it's important to tap T-money card.

In addition to these practical steps, familiarizing yourself with common Korean phrases for seeking directions and assistance can enhance your experience navigating public transportation. In the following sections, we will provide you with essential phrases and valuable tips for seeking guidance from locals and station attendants, ensuring your journey is seamless and enjoyable.

Common Phrases and Questions for Subway/ Buses/ Transportation in Korea

Common Phrases	Translation
안녕하세요. (Annyeonghaseyo)	Hello.
감사합니다. (Gamsahamnida.)	Thank you.
죄송합니다./실례합니다. (Joesonghamnida/ Sillyehamnida.)	I'm sorry./excuse me.
네. (Ne.)	Yes.

아니요. (Aniyo.)	No.
얼마에요? (Eolmaeyo?)	How much is it?
도움이 필요해요. (Dowum-i pilyo haeyo)	I need help.
이거 어디로 가나요? (Igeo eodiro ganayo?)	Where does this go?
여기에서 내리세요. (Yeogi-eso naeriseyo)	Get off here.
T-money 카드 주세요. (T-money card juseyo)	Please give me a T-money card.
한국어 못해요. (Hangugeo motheyo)	I can't speak Korean.
어디에서 내려야 돼요? (Eeodieseo naeryeoya dwaeyo?)	Where do I get off?
이 버스 어디로 가나요? (I bus-ga eodiro ganayo?)	Where does this bus go?
지하철역이 어디에요? (Jihacheolyeok-i eodieyo?)	Where is the station?
이 역에서 갈아타야 돼요. (I yeokeseo galataya dwaeyo)	You need to transfer at this station.
몇 번 출구로 가야 돼요? (Myeot beon chulguro gaya dwaeyo?)	Which exit should I take?

몇 시에요? (Meot sieyo?)	What time is it?
길을 좀 알려주세요. (Gireul jom alryeojuseyo)	Please give me directions.
지금 여기가 어디에요? (Jigeum yeogiga eodieyo?)	Where are we right now?
다음 역이 언제에요? (Daeum yeok-i eonjeyo?)	When is the next station?
언제 내려야 돼요? (Eonje naeryeoya dwaeyo?)	When do I get off?
자리 좀 양보해주세요. (Jari jom yangbohejuseyo)	Please help to vacate the seat.
이 좌석 비어 있어요. (I jwaseok bieo isseoyo)	This seat is available.
여기 앉으세요. (Yeogi anjeuseyo)	Seat here.
도와주세요. (Dowajuseyo)	Help!
응급 상황이에요. (Eunggeup sanghwangi eyo)	It's an emergency.
소방서가 어디에요? (Sobangseo-ga eodieyo?)	Where is the fire station?
병원이 어디에요? (Byeongwon-i eodieyo?)	Where is the hospital?

경찰서가 어디에요? (Gyeongchalseo-ga eodieyo?)	Where is the police station?
출구로 나가는 방향이 어디에요? (Chulguro naganeun banghyang-i eodieyo?)	Which way is the exit?
역에서 가장 가까운 출구는 어디에요? (Yeokeseo gajang gakkauun chulgu-neun eodieyo?)	Where is the nearest exit from the station?
지하철 노선도를 보여주세요. (Jihacheol noseondo-reul boyeojuseyo)	Please show me the subway map.
지하철역 화장실이 어디에요? (Jihacheolyeok hwajangsil-i eodieyo?)	Where is the restroom in the station?
조용히 해주세요. (Joyonghi hejuseyo)	Please lower the volume.
시끄럽게하지 마세요. (Sikkeureobge hajimaseyo)	Please don't be loud.
버스 정류장이 어디에요? (Bus jeongryujang-i eodieyo?)	Where is the bus stop?
버스가 언제와요? (Bus ga eonjewayo?)	When does the bus arrive?
역까지 어떻게 가나요? (Yeok-kkaji eotteoke ganayo?)	How do I get to the station?
이 버스는 어디로 가나요? (I bus-neun eodiro ganayo?)	Where does this bus go?

몇 번 버스에요? (Myeot beon bus eyo?)	What bus number is this?
어디서 내려야 돼요? (Eodieseo naeryeoya dwaeyo?)	Where should I get off for this?
지금 몇 시에요? (Jigeum myeot shieyo?)	What time is it now?
다음 역은 어디에요? (Daeum yeok-eun eodieyo?)	Where is the next station?
몇 시에 이용 가능해요? (Myeot shie iyong ganeunghaeyo?)	What time does it operate?
표는 어떻게 사나요? (Pyo-neun eotteoke sannayo?)	How do I buy a ticket?
요금이 얼마에요? (Yogeum-I eolmaeyo?)	How much is the fare ticket?
T-money 카드는 어떻게 사용하나요? (T-money card-neun eotteoke sayonghanayo?)	How do I use a T-money card?
어디서 T-money 카드를 충전할 수 있어요? (Eodieseo T-money card-reul chungjeonhal su isseoyo?)	Where can I recharge my T-money card?
이 역에서 환승 가능한가요? (Ii yeokeseo hwanseung ganeunghangayo?)	Can I transfer at this station?
이 역에서 정기권을 살 수 있어요? (Ii yeokeseo jeonggigweon-eul sal su isseoyo?)	Can I buy a monthly pass at this station?
얼마에요? (Eolmaeyo?)	How much is it?

현금만 받아요? (Hyungeomman badayo?)	Do you accept cash only?
신용카드로 결제할 수 있어요? (Sinyong-card-ro gyeoljehal su isseoyo?)	Can I pay with a credit card?
학생 할인이 있어요? (Haksaeng halin-i isseoyo?)	Is there a student discount?
어떻게 [Destination]으로 갈 수 있어요? (Eotteoke [Destination]ero gal su isseoyo?)	How can I get to [Destination]?
이 버스는 [Destination]로 가요? (I bus-neun [Destination] ro gayo?)	Does this bus go to [Destination]?
몇 번 출구로 가야 돼요? (Myeot beon chulguro gaya dwaeyo?)	Which exit should I take?
여기에서 가장 가까운 출구 어디에요? (Yeogieseo gajang gakkauun chulguro eodieyo?)	Where is the nearest exit from here?
이 역에서 어떻게 [Landmark]로 가요? (I yeokeseo eotteoke [Landmark]ro gayo?)	How do I get to [Landmark] from this station?
[Landmakr]로 연결되는 출구는 몇 번이에요? ([landmark]ro yeongyeoldweneun chulguneun meot beon ieyo?)	Which exit is connected to [landmakr]?
[Landmark]가 어디에요? ([Landmark]ga eodieyo?)	Where is [Landmark] located?
주변에 음식점이 어디있어요? (Jubyeon-e eumsikjeom-i eodiissoyo?)	Where are the restaurants around here?

이 근처에 편의점이 어디있어요? (I geuncheo-ejiyeoge pyeonuigeom-i eodiissoyo?)	Where is the convenience store in this area?
이 곳에서 주요 관광지로 어떻게 갈 수 있어요? (I goteseo juyo gwangwangji-ro eotteoke gal su isseoyo?)	How can I get to major tourist attractions from here?
가방이 없어졌어요, 어떡해야 돼요? (Gabangi eopssojesseoyo, eotteokhaeya dwaeyo?)	My bag is missing, what should I do?
지갑을 잃어버렸어요, 도와주세요. (Jigabeul ilheobeolyeotsseoyo, dowajuseyo.)	I lost my wallet, please help.
승강기가 고장났어요, 누구에게 말해야 돼요? (Seunganggi-ga gojangnasseoyo, nuguege malhaeya dwaeyo?)	The elevator is broken, should I inform someone?
어떻게 구급차를 부를 수 있어요? (Eotteoke gugeumcha-reul bureul su isseoyo?)	How can I call an ambulance?
무엇이길래 급하게 가야 돼요? (Mueos-igillae geuphage gayadwaeyo?)	What's so urgent that you need to hurry?
밀지 마세요. (Milji maseyo.)	Don't push.
여기에 자전거 대여소가 있어요? (Yeogie jajeongeo daeyeosoga isseoyo?)	Is there a bike rental station here?
여기에 짐을 보관할 수 있는 곳이 있어요? (Yeogie jimeul bogwanhal su itneun gosi isseoyo?)	Is there a locker to put my luggage?

Vocabulary

Vocabulary	Translation
지하철 (Jihacheol)	Subway
버스 (Bus)	Bus
역 (Yeok)	Station
정류장 (Jeongryujang)	Bus stop
환승 (Hwanseung)	Transfer
티켓 (Ticket)	Ticket
T-money 카드 (T-money card)	T-money card (rechargeable transportation card)
출구 (Chulgu)	Exit
플랫폼 (Platform)	Platform
시간표 (Siganpyo)	Timetable
노선도 (Noseondo)	Route map
유료 (Yuryo)	Paid
무료 (Muryo)	Free
열차 (Yeolcha)	Train

방향 (Banghyang)	Direction
출발 (Chulbal)	Departure
도착 (Dochak)	Arrival
지하 (Jiha)	Underground
지상 (Jisang)	Above ground
승강기 (Seunganggi)	Elevator
남쪽 (Namjjok)	South
북쪽 (Bukjjok)	North
동쪽 (Dongjjok)	East
서쪽 (Seojjok)	West
주변 (Jubyeon)	Around
근처 (Geuncheo)	Near
멀리 (Meolli)	Far
중심 (Jungsim)	Center
공항 (Gonghang)	Airport
역사적 장소 (Yeoksajeok jangso)	Historical site

관광지 (Gwangwangji)	Tourist attraction
자동차 (Jadongcha)	Car
자전거 (Jajeongeo)	Bicycle
기차 (Gicha)	Train
항공편 (Hanggongpyeon)	Flight
지하철 역 (Jihacheol yeok)	Subway station
버스 정류장 (Bus jeongryujang)	Bus stop
성인 (Seong-in)	Adult
어린이 (Eorin-i)	Child
청소년 (Cheongsonyeon)	Teenager
무료 이용 (Muryo iyong)	Free admission
할인 (Hal-in)	Discount
현금 (Hyungeum)	Cash
신용카드 (Sinyong card)	Credit card

Chapter Six
Hotel/ Airbnb in Korea

Korea's hospitality industry is renowned for its warm and attentive service, making your stay memorable and comfortable. As you step into the realm of Korean accommodations, it's crucial to be mindful of cultural nuances and etiquettes that govern interactions. Respect and courtesy are paramount in Korean culture, and adhering to these values will help you foster positive relationships with hotel staff, hosts, and fellow guests. Here we'll provide you with phrases, questions, and vocabulary specific to the world of hotels and Airbnb stays so by the end of this chapter, you'll possess the knowledge and language skills necessary to navigate the world of accommodations in Korea with confidence and respect.

Common Phrases and Question for Hotel/ Airbnb in Korea

Common phrases	Translation
예약자 성함이 어떻게 되십니까? (Yeyakja seongham-I eottoke dweosimnikka?)	May I know name for your reservation?
예약한 이름은 [Your Name] 입니다. (Yeyakhan ireum-eun [Your Name] imnida.)	My reservation is under [Your Name].
체크인 할게요. (Check-in halgeyo.)	I'm here to check in.
예약 확인해 주세요. (Yeyak hwaginhae juseyo.)	Please confirm my reservation.

방 번호가 뭐에요? (Bang beonho-ga mwoeyo?)	What is my room number?
방 키를 주세요. (Bang key-leul juseyo.)	Please give me the room key.
Wi-Fi 비밀번호가 뭐에요? (Wi-Fi bimilbeonho-ga mwoeyo?)	What is the Wi-Fi password?
조식이 포함되어 있나요? (Josik-i pohamdwoeeo innayo?)	Is breakfast included?
룸 서비스가 있나요? (Room service-ga innayo?)	Do you have room service?
수건이 더 필요해요. (Sugeon-I deo piryohaeyo.)	I need more towels.
이불을 교체해 주세요. (Ibul-eul gyochaehae juseyo.)	Please change the bedding.
에어컨을 켜 주세요. (Aircon-eul kyeo juseyo.)	Please turn on the air conditioning.
방에 물이 있나요? (Bang-e mul-i innayo?)	Is there water in the room?
주차장은 어디에요? (Juchajang-eun eodieyo?)	Where is the parking lot?
체크아웃 시간은 언제에요? (Check-out shigan-eun eonjeeyo?)	What time is checkout?
알람콜을 해주실 수 있나요? (Alarm call-eul hejusil su innayo?)	Can you give me a alarm call?

부엌이 있나요? (Bueogi innayo?)	Is there a kitchen?
냉장고가 있나요? (Naengjanggo-ga innayo?)	Is there a refrigerator?
화장실은 어디에요? (Hwajangshil-eun eodieyo?)	Where is the bathroom?
샴푸와 비누가 있나요? (Shampoo wa binu-ga innayo?)	Do you have shampoo and soap?
헤어 드라이어가 있나요? (Hair dryer-ga innayo?)	Is there a hair dryer?
아침식사 시간은 어떻게 되나요? (Achim-siksa sigan-eun eotteoke dwoennayo?)	What are the breakfast hours?
미리 체크아웃을 할 수 있나요? (Miri check-out-eul hal su innayo?)	Can I check out early?
주변에 음식점이 어디 있나요? (Jubyeone eumsikjeom-i eodi innayo?)	Where are the restaurants nearby?
비상 상황이 있을 때 어떻게 연락하나요? (Bisang sanghwangi isseul ttae eotteoke yeollakhanayo?)	How do I contact you in case of an emergency?
이 호텔에서 [tourist attraction]로 어떻게 가나요? (I hotel-eseo [tourist attractions]ro eotteoke ganayo?)	How do I get to the [tourist attractions] from this hotel?
주변에 ATM 이 어디 있나요? (Jubyeone ATM-i eodi innayo?)	Where is the nearest ATM?
현금으로 결제할 수 있나요? (Hyungeum-euro gyeolje-	Can I pay in cash?

hal su innayo?)	
신용 카드로 결제할 수 있나요? (Sinyong card-ro gyelje-hal su innayo?)	Do you accept credit cards?
투숙 중에 문제가 생기면 어떻게 도와주실 수 있나요? (Toosuk jung-e munje-ga saenggimyeon eotteoke dohwajusil su innayo?)	How can you assist if any issues arise during my stay?
수영장은 언제 오픈하나요? (Suyeongjang-eun eonje open-hanayo?)	When does the swimming pool open?
주차 요금이 얼마에요? (Juchayogeum-i eolmaeyo?)	How much is the parking fee?
TV 채널을 변경할 수 있나요? (TV channel-eul byeongyeonghal su innayo?)	Can I change the TV channels?
투숙 기간 중에 룸 클리닝이 언제 이루어지나요? (Toosuk gigan jung-e room cleaning-i eonje irueojinayo?)	When is room cleaning done during my stay?
방 안에 커피 머신이 있나요? (Bang an-e coffee machine-i innayo?)	Is there a coffee machine in the room?
룸 서비스로 음식을 주문할 수 있나요? (room service-ro eum-sik-eul jumoonhal su innayo?)	Can I order food through room service?
관광 팜플렛을 얻을 수 있나요? (Gwangwang pampeulret-eul eodeul su innayo?)	Can I get tourist brochures at this hotel?
엘리베이터는 어디에 있나요? (Elevator-neun eodie innayo?)	Where is the elevator?

이제 수건이 필요하지 않아요. (Ije sugeon-i piryohaji anayo.)	I don't need any more towels.
이 호텔은 금연이에요, 맞죠? (I hotel-eun geumyeon-ieyo, matjyo?)	This hotel is non-smoking, right?
퇴실할 때 어디에 키를 놓아야 하나요? (Twoesilhal ttae eodie key-leul noaya hanayo?)	Where should I leave the key when checking out?
예약을 변경하려고 합니다. (Yeyak-eul byeongyeong haryeogo hamnida.)	I'd like to modify my reservation.
이 호텔에 미니 바가 있나요? (I hotel-e mini bar-ga innayo?)	Does this hotel have a minibar?
체크아웃 시간을 연장하고 싶어요. (Check-out shigan-eul yeonjanghago sipeoyo.)	I would like to extend my checkout time.
저녁 식사 예약을 하려고 합니다. (Jeonyeok sigsa yeyak-eul haryeogo hamnida.)	I'd like to make a dinner reservation.
호텔 주변에 가볼만 한 곳은 어디인가요? (Hotel jubyeone gabolmanhan got-euneodi ingayo?)	What are some places worth visiting around the hotel?
호텔에서 택시를 부를 수 있나요? (hotel-eso taxi-leul buleul su innayo?)	Can I call a taxi from this hotel?
조용한 방으로 옮겨 주세요. (Joyonghan bang-euro omgyeo juseyo.)	Please move me to a quieter room.
아침에 여기서 조식을 먹을 수 있나요? (Achim-e yeogiseo josig-eul meogeul su innayo?)	Can I have breakfast here in the morning?

다음에 다시 여기에 묵을 거예요. (Daeum-e dasi yeogi-e muk-eul geoyeyo.)	I'll stay here again next time.
주변에 대형 쇼핑 몰이 어디 있나요? (Jubyeon-e daehyeong shopping mall-i eodi innayo?)	Where is the nearest large shopping mall?
주변에 있는 주요 관광지로 가려면 어떤 대중 교통 수단을 이용할 수 있나요? (Jubyeon-e itneun juyo gwangwangji-ro garyeomyeon etteon daejung gyotong sudan-eul iyong hal su innayo?)	What public transportation options are available to major tourist attractions nearby?
어메니티를 좀 더 가져다 주실 수 있을까요? (Amenity-leul jom deo gajeoda jusil su isseulkkayo?)	Could you bring more amenities?
바베큐 시설을 제공하나요? (Barbecue siseol-eul jegonghanayo?)	Do you provide barbecue facilities?
이 호텔/에어비앤비에서 세미나나 회의를 할 수 있나요? (I hotel/airbnb-eseo seminar-na hoeui-leul halsu innayo?)	Can I hold seminars or meetings at this hotel/Airbnb?
주변에 산책하기 좋은 곳은 어디인가요? (Jubyeon-e sanchaeghagi joeun got-eun eodi ingayo?)	Where are good places for a stroll nearby?
이 호텔/에어비앤비에 아이들을 위한 시설이 있나요? (I hotel/airbnb-e aideul-eul wihan siseol-i innayo?)	Does this hotel/Airbnb have facilities for children?
주변에 미술관이나 박물관이 어디있나요? (Jubyeon-e misulgwan-ina bakmulgwan-i eoi innayo?)	Where are the art galleries or museums nearby?
이 호텔/에어비앤비는 할인이 가능한가요? (I	Is bargaining possible at this hotel/Airbnb?

hotel/airbnb-neun halin-I ganeung hangayo?)	
주변에 안전한 산책로가 있나요? (Jubyeon-e anjeonhan sanchaeglo-ga innayo?)	Are there safe walking paths around?
무료 아침 식사는 어떤 종류인가요? (Muryo achim siksa-neun eotteon jonglyuingayo?)	What type of complimentary breakfast is offered at this hotel/Airbnb?
주변에 유명한 레스토랑이 어디에요? (Jubyeon-e yumyeonghan restaurant-i eodieyo?)	Where are the famous restaurants nearby?
출입 시간 제한이 있나요? (Chulip shigan jehan-I innayo?)	Are there any restrictions on entry and exit times at this hotel/Airbnb?
이 호텔/에어비앤비는 조용해야 하는 시간이 있나요?(I hotel/airbnb-neun choyong heaya haneun shigan-I innayo?)	Does this hotel/Airbnb have quiet hours?
주변에 적당한 쇼핑 지역이 어디에요? (Jubyeon-e jeokdanghan shopping jiyeok-i eodieyo?)	Where is a suitable shopping district nearby?
이 호텔/에어비앤비는 현금으로 예약할 수 있나요? (I hotel/airbnb-neun hyeongeum-euro yeyakhal su innayo?)	Can I make a cash reservation at this hotel/Airbnb?
주변에 가장 가까운 지하철 역은 어디에요? (Jubyeon-e gajang gakkaun jihacheol yeok-eun eodieyo?)	Where is the nearest subway station?
이 호텔/에어비앤는 무료 주차 가능한가요? (I hotel/airbnb-neun muryo jucha ganeunghangayo?)	Is there free parking at this hotel/Airbnb?
이 호텔/에어비앤비에서 스파 서비스를 제공하나요? (I hotel/airbnb-eseo spa service-leul jegonghanayo?)	Does this hotel/Airbnb offer spa services?

주변에 쉬기 좋은 공원이 어디에요? (Jubyeon-e shigii joeun gongwon-i eodieyo?)	Where are nice parks to relax nearby?
이 호텔/에어비앤비는 출입 카드를 사용하나요? (I hotel/airbnb-neun chulip card-leul sayonghanayo?)	Do you use access cards at this hotel/Airbnb?
이 호텔/에어비앤비에서는 특별한 이벤트를 개최하나요? (I hotel/airbnb-eseoneun teukbyeolhan event-leul gaechoehanayo?)	Does this hotel/Airbnb host special events?
주변에 바다나 호수가 어디에요? (Jubyeon-e badana hosuga eodieyo?)	Where is the sea or lake nearby?
이 호텔/에어비앤비에서는 렌터카 서비스를 제공하나요? (I hotel/airbnb-eseonuen rent car service-leul jegonghanayo?)	Does this hotel/Airbnb offer car rental services?
이 호텔/에어비앤비에서는 장애인 편의 시설을 제공하나요? (I hotel/airbnb-eseoneun jangaein pyeonui siseol-eul jegonghana-yo?)	Does this hotel/Airbnb provide facilities for people with disabilities?
주변에 자전거 대여 서비스가 어디 있나요? (Jubyeon-e jajeongeo daeyeo service-ga eodi innayo?)	Where is the bicycle rental service nearby?
이 호텔/에어비앤비에서 스키용 장비 대여 서비스를 제공하나요? (I hotel/airbnb-eseo ski-yong jangbi daeyeo service-leul jegonghanayo?)	Does this hotel/Airbnb offer ski equipment rental services?
주변에 어린이 놀이터가 어디에요? (Jubyeon-e eorini noliteo-ga eodieyo?)	Where is the children's playground nearby?

이 호텔/에어비앤비에서는 숙박 중에 추가 게스트를 허용하나요? (I hotel/airbnb-eseoneun sukbak jung-e chuga guest-leul heoyonghanayo?)	Does this hotel/Airbnb allow additional guests during the stay?
주변에 해변이 어디 있어요? (Jubyeon-e haebeon-i eodi isseoyo?)	Where is the beach nearby?
이 호텔/에어비앤비에 수영장이 있나요? (I hotel/airbnb-e suyeongjang-i innayo?)	Does this hotel/Airbnb have a swimming pool?
주변에 테니스 코트가 어디 있나요? (Jubyeon-e tennis court-ga eodi innayo?)	Where is the tennis court nearby?
이 호텔/에어비앤비에서 주차장을 예약할 수 있나요? (I hotel/airbnb-eseo juchajang-eul yeyakhal su innayo?)	Can I make a reservation for car parking at this hotel/Airbnb?
이 호텔/에어비앤비에서는 수영복을 빌릴 수 있나요? (I hotel/airbnb-eseonuen suyeongbok-eul bilil u innayo?)	Does this hotel/Airbnb offer swimsuit rental services?
주변에 골프 코스가 어디에요? (Jubyeon-e golfcourse-ga eodieyo?)	Where is the golf course nearby?
이 호텔/에어비앤비에 기념품 가게가 있나요? (I hotel/airbnb-e ginyeompum gage-ga innayo?)	Does this hotel/Airbnb have a souvenir shop?
이 호텔/에어비앤비에서 무료 셔틀 서비스를 제공하나요? (I hotel/airbnb- eseo muryo shuttle bus service-leul jegonghanayo?)	Does this hotel/Airbnb offer free shuttle service?

주변에 생태 공원이 어디에요? (Jubyeon-e saengtae gongwon-i eodieyo?)	Where is the eco-park nearby?
이 호텔/에어비앤비에서는 금고를 제공하나요? (I hotel/airbnb-eseoneun geumgo-leul jegonghanayo?)	Does this hotel/Airbnb provide a safe?
주변에 스노우보드 장비 대여 서비스가 어디 있나요? (Jubyeon-e snow board-jangbi daeyeo service-ga eodi innayo?)	Where is the snowboard equipment rental service nearby?
이 호텔/에어비앤비에서는 야외 활동을 연결해 주나요? (I hotel/airbnb-eseonuen yaweo hwaldong-eul yeongyeol hejunayo?)	Does this hotel/Airbnb arrange outdoor activities?
주변에 문화 센터나 예술 공간이 어디에요? (Jubyeon-e munhwa center-na yesul gonggan-i eodieyo?)	Where are the cultural centers or art spaces nearby?
이 호텔/에어비앤비는 무료 물병을 제공하나요? (I hotel/airbnb-neun muryo mulbyeong-eul jegonghanayo?)	Does this hotel/Airbnb provide complimentary water bottles?
이 호텔/에어비앤비의 편의 시설은 어떤 것이 있나요? (I hotel/airbnb-ui pyeonui siseol-eun eotteon geot-I innayo?)	What amenities are available at this hotel/Airbnb?
주변에 카페나 커피숍이 어디에요? (Jubyeon-e cafe-na coffeeshop-i eodieyo?)	Where are the cafes or coffee shops nearby?
이 호텔/에어비앤비에서는 공항 셔틀 서비스를 제공하나요? (I hotel/airbnb-eseoneun gonghang shuttle service-leul jegonghanayo?)	Does this hotel/Airbnb offer airport shuttle service?

Vocabulary

Vocabulary	Translation
호텔 (Hotel)	Hotel
에어비앤비 (Airbnb)	Airbnb
예약 (Yeyak)	Reservation
체크인 (Check-in)	Check-in
체크아웃 (Check-out)	Check-out
방 (Bang)	Room
방 번호 (Bang beonho)	Room number
수건 (Sugeon)	Towel
이불 (Ibul)	Bedding
냉장고 (Naengjanggo)	Refrigerator
무선 인터넷 (Museon internet)	Wireless internet
아침식사 (Achim siksa)	Breakfast
룸 서비스 (Room service)	Room service
애완동물 (Aewan-dongmul)	Pet

에어컨 (Air-con)	Air conditioning
난방 (Nanbang)	Heating
샤워 (Shower)	Shower
화장실 (Hwajangsil)	Bathroom
주차장 (Juchajang)	Parking lot
주차 요금 (Jucha yogeum)	Parking fee
로비 (Lobby)	Lobby
엘리베이터 (Elevator)	Elevator
로비 바 (Lobby bar)	Lobby bar
레스토랑 (Restaurant)	Restaurant
바 (Bar)	Bar
수영장 (Suyeongjang)	Swimming pool
피트니스 센터 (Fitness center)	Fitness center
사우나 (Sauna)	Sauna
비밀번호 (Bimilbeonho)	Password
텔레비전 (Television)	Television

커피 머신 (Coffee machine)	Coffee machine
물병 (Mulbyeong)	Water bottle
신용카드 (Sinyong card)	Credit card
현금 (Hyeongeum)	Cash
슬리퍼 (Slipper)	Slippers
소파 (Sofa)	Sofa
전화 (Jeonhwa)	Telephone
금고 (Geumgo)	Safe
헤어 드라이어 (Hair dryer)	Hair dryer
리셉션 (Reception)	Reception
디포짓 (Deposit)	Deposit
미니바 (Mini-bar)	Mini-bar
발코니 (Balcony)	Balcony
조식 (Josik)	Breakfast (meal)
무료 (Muryo)	Free
흡연 (Heubyeon)	Smoking

금연 (Geumyeon)	Non-smoking
소음 (Soeum)	Noise
주차 가능 (Jucha ganeung)	Parking available

Chapter Seven
Food/ Restaurants/ Convenience Stores in Korea

Food is at the heart of Korean culture, and sharing meals with friends and family is a cherished tradition. Whether you're an avid food enthusiast or simply seeking to navigate the culinary landscape while visiting South Korea, we'll equip you with the language skills needed to confidently communicate in restaurants, order your favorite dishes, and fully immerse yourself in the delightful world of Korean cuisine.

Throughout this chapter, we will cover a wide range of topics related to food and dining in Korea. Here's a glimpse of what you can expect:

- **Basic food vocabulary:** We'll give you a solid foundation of Korean food-related vocabulary, allowing you to identify ingredients, dishes, and flavors with ease.

- **Ordering food:** Whether you find yourself at a traditional Korean eatery, a trendy fusion restaurant, or enjoying street food from a vendor, you'll master the art of placing orders in Korean restaurants.

- **Expressing preferences:** You'll discover how to confidently convey your food preferences, allergies, and dietary restrictions, ensuring that you enjoy your meal exactly the way you want it.

- **Asking questions:** Equipping yourself with the ability to ask questions about the menu, ingredients, and preparation methods will enable you to make informed choices when dining out.

By the time you reach the end of this chapter, you'll be well-prepared to savor the diverse and delectable dishes that Korea has to offer, engage in meaningful conversations with locals, and navigate the world of food and dining in South Korea with ease. Together, we will build your conversational skills and explore the tantalizing world of Korean food! Bon appétit, or 맛있게 드세요 (Masitge deuseyo)!

Common Phrases and Questions for Food/ Restaurants/ Convenience Stores in Korea

Common phrases	Translation
메뉴판 주세요. (Menupan juseyo.)	Can I have the menu, please?
물 주세요. (Mul juseyo.)	Water, please.
주문할게요. (Jumun halgeyo.)	I would like to order.
이거 뭐에요? (Igeo mwoeyo?)	What is this?
추천 메뉴가 뭐에요? (Chucheon menu-ga mwoeyo?)	What do you recommend on the menu?
매운 음식은 어디 있어요? (Maewoon eumsig-eun eodi isseoyo?)	Where can I find spicy food?
조금 덜 맵게 해 주세요. (Jogeum deol maepge hejuseyo.)	Can you make it less spicy?
매우 맵게 해주세요. (Maewoo maepge hejuseyo.)	Make it very spicy, please.
이거 포장해 주세요. (Igeo pojanghe juseyo.)	Please pack this to go.
계산할게요. (Gyesan halgeyo.)	I would like to pay.
신용 카드 되나요? (Sinyong card dweonayo?)	Do you accept credit cards?

현금만 받아요. (Hyungeumman badayo.)	We only accept cash.
식사 맛있었어요. (Siksa masisseosseoyo.)	The meal was delicious.
계산서 주세요. (Gyesanseo juseyo.) / 계산해 주세요. (Gyesanhae juseyo.)	Can I have the bill, please?
저는 채식주의자에요. (Jeoneun chaesikjuuija-eo.)	I am a vegetarian.
육류를 먹지 않아요. (Yukryu-leul meokji anayo.)	I don't eat meat.
알러지가 있어요. (Allergy-ga isseoyo.)	I have allergies.
물 좀 더 주세요. (Mul jom deo juseyo.)	Can I have more water?
냄새가 좋아요. (Naemsae-ga joayo.)	It smells good.
소스 좀 주세요. (Sauce jom juseyo.)	Please give me some sauce.
소금이 필요해요. (Sogeum-i piryohaeyo.)	I need salt.
차가운 물 좀 주세요. (Chagawun mul jom juseyo.)	Can I have cold water?
어떤 음식을 추천하세요? (Eotteon eumsik-eul chucheon haseyo?)	What food do you recommend?
물 한 병 주세요. (Mul han byeong juseyo.)	One bottle of water, please.

아메리카노 주세요. (Americano juseyo.)	Can I have an Americano, please?
이거 얼마에요? (Igeo eolmaeyo?)	How much is this?
아이스크림이 어디 있어요? (Ice cream-i eodi isseyo?)	Where is the ice cream?
김밥 한 줄 주세요. (Kimbap han jul juseyo.)	Can I have one kimbap, please?
죄송합니다. (Joesonghamnida.)	I'm sorry.
괜찮아요. (Gwaenchanayo.)	It's okay.
천천히 말해 주세요. (Cheoncheonhi malhae juseyo.)	Please speak slowly.
이거 좀 더 주세요. (Igeo jom deo juseyo.)	Please give me more of this.
매장에서 먹을래요. (Maejangeseo meogeullae yo.)	I want to eat in the restaurant.
포장해 주세요. (Pojanghe juseyo.)	Please pack this to go.
여기서 먹을게요. (Yeogiseo meogeulgeyo.)	I'll eat here.
도시락 주세요. (Dosirak juseyo.)	Can I have a lunchbox, please?
맛있어요. (Masisseoyo.)	It's delicious.
더 필요하신 게 있나요? (Deo piryohasin ge innayo?)	Do you need anything else?

조금 더 기다려주실 수 있어요? (Jogeum deo gidaryeo jusil su isseoyo?)	Can you wait a little longer?
어제 뭐 드셨어요? (Eoje mwo deussiotsseoyo?)	What did you eat yesterday?
이 음식은 어떻게 만들어요? (I eumsig-eun eotteoke mandeuleoyo?)	How is this dish prepared?
메뉴 추천 좀 해 주세요. (Menyu chucheon jom hae juseyo.)	Please recommend a menu item.
밥 주세요. (Bap juseyo.)	Rice, please.
음식이 언제 나와요? (Eumsigi eonje nawayo?)	When will the food be ready?
이런 음식 처음 먹어 봐요. (Ireon eumsik cheoeum meogeo bwayo.)	I'm trying this kind of food for the first time.
너무 맛있어요! (Neomu masisseoyo!)	It's so delicious!
냉면주세요. (Naengmyeon juseyo.)	Can I have cold noodles, please?
어떤 음식을 추천해 주시겠어요? (Eotteon eumsigeul chucheonhae jusigesseoyo?)	What food do you recommend?
이 음식은 매워요? (I eumsig-eun maewoyo?)	Is this dish spicy?
어떤 종류의 빵이 있어요? (Eotteon jongryuui bbangi isseoyo?)	What types of bread do you have?

카페인이 들어가 있어요? (Caffein-i deureoga isseoyo?)	Does it contain caffeine?
저는 초콜릿을 좋아해요. (Jeoneun chocolate-eul joahaeyo.)	I like chocolate.
피자는 어디서 주문해요? (Pizza-neun eodiseo jumonhaeyo?)	Where can I order pizza?
이 음식은 건강에 좋아요. (I eumsig-eun geongange joayo.)	This dish is good for your health.
달콤한 디저트를 주문하고 싶어요. (Dalkomhan dejuteu-leul jumonhago sipeoyo.)	I'd like to order a sweet dessert.
저는 유제품을 먹을 수 없어요. (Jeoneun yujepum-eul meogeul su eobsseoyo.)	I can't eat dairy products.
샐러드 주세요. (Salad juseyo.)	Can I have a salad, please?
치즈 더 주세요. (Cheese deo juseyo.)	Please add more cheese.
라면은 어디 있어요? (Ramyeon-eun eodi issoyo?)	Where is the instant ramen?
음료수는 어디에 있어요? (Eumryosu-neun eodie issoyo?)	Where are the beverages?
라면 한 개 주세요. (Ramyeon han gae juseyo.)	One instant ramen, please.
더 필요한 게 있어요? (Deo pillyohan ge isseoyo?)	Is there anything else you need?

미안해요, 실수했어요. (Mianhaeyo, silsuhaesseoyo.)	I'm sorry, I made a mistake.
나중에 다시 오겠습니다. (Najunge dasi ogesseumnida.)	I'll come back later.
음식을 포장해 주세요. (Eumsigeul pojanghe juseyo.)	Please pack the food to go.
안녕히 계세요. (Annyeonghi gyeseyo.)	Goodbye (said when you are leaving place).

Vocabulary

Vocabulary	Translation
음식 (Eumsik)	Food
밥 (Bap)	Rice
고기 (Gogi)	Meat
생선 (Saengseon)	Fish
야채 (Yachae)	Vegetables
고추 (Gochu)	Chili pepper
치즈 (Cheese)	Cheese
계란 (Gyeran)	Egg
빵 (Bbang)	Bread

과일 (Gwa-il)	Fruit
된장 (Dwenjang)	Bean paste (for miso soup)
국수 (Guksu)	Noodles
소금 (Sogeum)	Salt
설탕 (Seoltang)	Sugar
양념 (Yangnyeom)	Seasoning
버터 (Butter)	Butter
오일 (Oil)	Oil
식초 (Sikcho)	Vinegar
양파 (Yangpa)	Onion
마늘 (Maneul)	Garlic
향신료 (Hyangsinryo)	Spice
조미료 (Jomiryo)	Seasoning (MSG)
음식 메뉴 (Eumsik menu)	Food menu
아침 (Achim)	Breakfast
점심 (Jeomsim)	Lunch

저녁 (Jeonyeok)	Dinner
후식(Husik) /디저트 (Dissert)	Dessert
주문 (Jumun)	Order
메뉴판 (Menupan)	Menu
반찬 (Banchan)	Side dishes
냉면 (Naengmyeon)	Cold noodles
김밥 (Gimbap)	Korean rice rolls
비빔밥 (Bibimbap)	Mixed rice with vegetables and sauce
불고기 (Bulgogi)	Marinated and grilled meat
국밥 (Gukbap)	Soup with rice
찌개 (Jjigae)	Stew
초밥 (Chobap)	Sushi
토스트 (Toast)	Toast
햄버거 (Hamburger)	Hamburger
레스토랑 (Restaurant) / 식당(Sikdang)	Restaurant
주방 (Jubang)	Kitchen

접시 (Jeopshi)	Plate
숟가락 (Sutgarak)	Spoon
젓가락 (Jeotgarak)	Chopsticks
주류 (Juryu)	Alcohol
수저 (Sujeo)	Utensils (spoon and chopsticks)
샐러드 (Salad)	Salad

Chapter Eight
Shopping in Korea

In Korea, shopping is not just a transaction; it's an adventure. From fashion enthusiasts seeking the latest trends to souvenir collectors yearning for unique treasures, there's something for everyone. Whether you're navigating the bustling traditional markets, exploring charming boutiques, or wandering through modern shopping malls, we will empower you to interact confidently with locals and shopkeepers alike.

Korea offers an array of shopping experiences, from the historic alleyways of Insadong to the upscale boutiques of Gangnam. You'll learn how to greet and engage with shopkeepers and fellow shoppers, inquire about product details, sizes, and prices, skillfully negotiate and bargain, express your preferences, make informed purchasing decisions, seek assistance in navigating sprawling shopping complexes, and grasp the common vocabulary used in shopping scenarios.

Whether you're on the hunt for the latest fashion trends, traditional Korean handicrafts, or simply wish to immerse yourself in the vibrant market culture.

Common Phrases and Question for Shopping in Korea

Common Phrases	Translation
할인해 주실 수 있나요? (Halinhae jusil su innayo?)	Can you give me a discount?
사이즈가 어떻게 되요? (Size-ga eotteoke dweoyo?)	What size is this?
다른 색깔이 있나요? (Dareun saegkkari innayo?)	Do you have this in a different color?

현금으로 계산할 수 있어요? (Hyungeum-euro gyesanhal su isseoyo?)	Can I pay in cash?
카드로 결제할 수 있어요? (Card-ro gyeoljehal su isseoyo?)	Can I pay with a card?
영수증 주세요. (Yeongsujeung juseyo.)	Can I have a receipt, please?
이거 세일 가격이에요? (Igeo sale gagyeok-ieyo?)	Is this the sale price?
이거 입어 볼 수 있어요? (Igeo ibeo bol su isseoyo?)	Can I try this on?
더 큰 사이즈로 바꿔 주실 수 있어요? (Deo keun size-ro bakkkwo jusil su isseoyo?)	Can I exchange this for a larger size?
환불 가능해요? (Hwanbul ganeunghaeyo?)	Is it possible to return this?
언제까지 할인해요? (Eonjekkaji halin-heyo?)	How long is the sale going on?
이 상품은 어떻게 사용해요? (I sangpum-eun eotteoke sayonghaeyo?)	How do you use this product?
어떤 브랜드가 제일 인기 있어요? (Eotteon brand-ga jeil ingi isseoyo?)	Which brand is the most popular?
이 가방은 어떤 소재로 만들어졌어요? (I gabang-eun eotteon sojaero mandeuleo jyeosseoyo?)	What material is this bag made of?
저기 있는 거 보여 주세요. (Jeogi inneun geo boyeo	Can you show me that item over there?

juseyo.)	
이거 할인되는 거 맞아요? (Igeo halin-doeneun geo majayo?)	Is this item on sale?
이게 최저 가격이에요? (Ige choejoe gagyeok- ieoyo?)	Is this the lowest price?
이거 다른 매장에서 파나요? (Igeo dareun maejangeseo panayo?)	Can I find this item in other stores?
좀 더 싸게 해 주세요. (Jom deo ssage hae juseyo.)	Can you give me a better discount?
이거 선물용으로 적합해요? (Igeo seonmul-yong-euro jeokhaphaeyo?)	Is this suitable for a gift?
얼만큼 사면 무료 배송이 되요? (Eolmankeum samyeon muryo baesong-I dweoyo?)	Is there free shipping if I buy this amount?
이 가게의 주요 브랜드는 뭐에요? (I gageui juyo brand-neun mwoeyo?)	What are the main brands in this store?
이거 언제까지 파세요? (Igeo eonjekkaji paseyo?)	Until when is this item available?
보증 기간이 얼마에요? (Bojeung gigan-I eolmaeyo?)	How long is the warranty period?
추천해 주실 수 있나요? (Chucheonhae jusil su innayo?)	Can you recommend?
이 가게의 영업 시간은 어떻게 되나요? (I gageui	What are the store's opening hours?

yeongeop sigan-eun eotteoke dweonayo?)	
세일 기간 중에 얼마나 할인돼요? (Sale gigan junge eolmana halindweoyo?)	How much is the discount during the sale period?
가격이 괜찮네요. (Gagyeok-I gwenchanneyo.)	This is at a reasonable price.
이거 마음에 들어요. (Igeo maeume deuleoyo.)	I like this.
이거 예쁘네요. (Igeo yeppeuneyo.)	This is pretty.
이거 신발 사이즈가 어떻게 돼요? (Igeo sinbal size-ga eotteoke dweoyo?)	What is the shoe size for this?
이거 어떤 디자인이에요? (Igeo eotteon design-ieyo?)	What's the design of this?
이거 한 번 입어봐도 되요? (Igeo han beon ibeobwado doeyo?)	May I try this on once?
이거 저희 나라로 배송해 주실 수 있어요? (Igeo jeohui nararo baesonghae jusil su isseoyo?)	Can you ship this to my country?
어떤 히스토리가 있어요? (Eotteon history-ga isseoyo?)	Does this have any history?
무게가 어떻게 돼요? (Mugae-ga eotteoke doeyo?)	What is the weight of this?
이거 어디에서 만들었어요? (Igeo eodi-eseo mandeureosseoyo?)	Where is this made?

다른 패턴이 있어요? (Dareun pattern-i isseoyo?)	Do you have this in a different pattern?
어떻게 관리하면 좋아요? (Eotteoke gwanrihamyeon joayo?)	How should I take care of this?
이거 먼저 확인해 볼 수 있어요? (Igeo meonjeo hwaginhae bol su isseoyo?)	Can I check this out first?
환불 정책이 어떻게 되요? (Hwanbul jeongchaegi eotteoke dweoyo?)	What is the refund policy for this?
이거 가격이 어떻게 되나요? (Igeo gagyeok-i eotteoke dweonayo?)	How much does this cost?
이거 어떤 소리가 나나요? (Igeo eotteon soriga nanayo?)	What kind of sound does it make?
이거 세일 중에만 팔아요? (Igeo sale jungeman parayo?)	Is this only available during the sale?
이거 품절되었어요? (Igeo pumjol dweoeosseoyo?)	Is this sold out?
어떤 특별한 기능이 있어요? (Eotteon teukbyeolhan gineungi isseoyo?)	Does this have any special features?
이거 신상품이에요? (Igeo sinsangpum-ieyo?)	Is this a new arrival?
이거 최신 유행이에요? (Igeo choesin yuhaeng-ieyo?)	Is this the latest trend?

무료로 선물 포장 가능할까요? (Muryolo seonmul pojang ganeunghalggayo?)	Can you gift wrap this for free?
더 싸게 주실 수 있어요? (Deo ssage jusil su isseoyo?)	Can you sell this for a lower price?
이거 어떤 재료로 만들어져 있어요? (Igeo eotteon jaeryo-ro mandeuleo jyeo isseoyo?)	What is this made of?
이거 어떤 스타일인가요? (Igeo eotteon style-ingayo?)	What style is this?
이거 여러 개 사면 더 싸게 해주시나요? (Igeo yeoreo gae samyeon deo ssage haejusinayo?)	Can you give me a better deal if I buy more than one?
어떤 기능이 있어요? (Eotteon gineungi isseoyo?)	What functions does this have?
이거 어떻게 관리해요? (Igeo eotteoke gwanliheyo?)	What kind of maintenance does it require?
이거 특별 할인이 있어요? (Igeo teukbyeol halin-i isseoyo?)	Is there a special discount on this?
이거 예약해 놓을 수 있어요? (Igeo yeyakhae noeul su isseoyo?)	Can I reserve this in advance?
이거 화장품이에요? (Igeo hwajangpum-ieyo?)	Is this cosmetics?
이거 어떻게 포장돼요? (Igeo eotteoke pojangdweoyo?)	How is this packaged?
이거 어떤 향이 나요? (Igeo eotteon hyangi nayo?)	What does this smell like?

이거 손님용 맞아요? (Igeo sonnimyong majayo?)	Is this for guests?
이거 미리 주문할 수 있어요? (Igeo miri jumunhal su isseoyo?)	Can I place an order in advance?
어떤 색깔이 더 인기 있어요? (Eotteon saegkkali deo ingi isseoyo?)	Which color is more popular?
어떤 액세서리가 포함돼 있어요? (Eotteon accessory-ga pohamdweo isseoyo?)	What accessories are included with this?
어떤 배송 옵션이 가능한가요? (Eotteon baesong option-i ganeung hangayo?)	What shipping options are available for this?
가격을 깎아 주실 수 있어요? (Gagyeok-eul ggakka jusil su isseoyo?)	Can you lower the price for me?
이거 무게가 얼마나 나가나요? (Igeo mugega eolmana naganayo?)	What is the weight of this?
이거 세일 가격으로 주세요. (Igeo sale gagyeok-euro juseyo.)	Please give me the sale price.
이거 프로모션 중이에요? (Igeo promotion jung-ieyo?)	Is this part of a promotion?
이거 어떤 브랜드의 제품이에요? (Igeo eotteon brand-ui jepum-ieyo?)	Which brand is this product from?
배송료가 얼마에요? (Baesongryo-ga eolmaeyo?)	How much is the shipping fee?

결제는 어떻게 하나요? (Gyeolje-neun eotteoke hanayo?)	What payment methods are accepted?
세금 포함 가격이에요? (Segeum poham gagyeok-ieyo?)	Is this price inclusive of taxes?
이거 할인 쿠폰을 사용할 수 있어요? (Igeo halin coupon-eul sayonghal su isseoyo?)	Can I use a discount coupon for this?
배송은 얼마나 걸려요? (Baesong-eun eolmana geollyeoyo?)	How long does delivery take?
이거 리필용으로 팔아요? (Igeo refill-yong-euro palayo?)	Do you sell refills for this?
이거 온라인으로도 구매 가능해요? (Igeo online-eurodo gume ganeunghaeyo?)	Can I purchase this online as well?
이거 선물 포장해 주실 수 있어요? (Igeo seonmul pojang hae jusil su isseoyo?)	Can you gift-wrap this for me?
이거 어떤 인증을 받았나요? (Igeo eotteon injeung-eul badatnayo?)	Does this have any certifications?
어떤 결제 방식을 사용하세요? (Eotteon gyeolje bangsik-eul sayonghaseyo?)	What payment system do you use?
이거 어떤 종류의 원단으로 만들어져 있어요? (Igeo eotteon jonglyu-ui wondan-euro mandeureo jyeo isseoyo?)	What type of fabric is this made of?
이거 어떤 알레르기 반응이 있을 수 있어요? (Igeo eotteon allereugi ban-eung-i isseul su isseoyo?)	Are there any possible allergic reactions to this?

어떤 장식이 들어가 있어요? (Eotteon jangsig-i deuleoga isseoyo?)	What kind of decorations are included?
이거 다른 사이즈로 주문할 수 있어요? (Igeo dareun size-ro jumunhal su isseoyo?)	Can I order this in a different size?
이거 보증 내용이 어떻게 되요? (Igeo bojeung neyong-I eotteoke doeyo?)	What warranty is applicable to this?
이거 어떤 디자인으로 변경이 가능해요? (Igeo eotteon design-euro byeongyeong-i ganeunghaeyo?)	What design customizations are possible?
이거 교환 정책이 어떻게 되요? (Igeo gyohwan jeongchaek-i eotteoke doeyo?)	What is the exchange policy for this?
이거 사이즈가 작아요? (Igeo size-ga jagayo?)	Is this size small?
좋은 선물이 될거에요. (Joen sunmul-I doelgeo-eyo.)	This would make a suitable gift.
어떤 추가 서비스가 포함돼 있어요? (Eotteon chuga service-ga pohamdweo isseoyo?)	What additional services are included?
이거 특별 행사로 파는 중인가요? (Igeo teukbyeol hengsaro paneun geongayo?)	Is this being sold as part of a special event?
여기에 어울리는 액세서리를 함께 추천해 주세요. (Yeogie eoulineun accessory-leul hamkke chucheonhae juseyo.)	Please recommend some accessories to go with this.
사용법을 알려주세요. (Sayongbeob-eul allyeojuseyo.)	Please explain how to use this.

어떤 고유한 특징이 있어요? (Eotteon goyuhan teukjing-i isseoyo?)	What unique features does this have?

Vocabulary

Vocabulary	Translation
쇼핑 (Shopping)	Shopping
상점 (Sangjeom)	Store
가게 (Gagae)	Shop
물건 (Mulgeon)	Item
가격 (Gagyeok)	Price
할인 (Halin)	Discount
판매 (Panme)	Sale
구매 (Gume)	Purchase
결제 (Gyeolje)	Payment
현금 (Hyeongeum)	Cash
카드 (Card)	Card
영수증 (Yeongsujeung)	Receipt
환불 (Hwanbul)	Refund

크기 (Keugi)	Size
색깔 (Saegkkal)	Color
디자인 (Design)	Design
브랜드 (Brand)	Brand
소재 (Sojae)	Material
스타일 (Style)	Style
액세서리 (Accessory)	Accessories
패턴 (Pattern)	Pattern
모델 (Model)	Model
인기 (Ingi)	Popularity
세탁 (Setak)	Laundry
배송 (Baesong)	Shipping
마감일 (Magam-il)	Deadline
입어 보다 (Ibeo boda)	To try on
사이즈 (Size)	Size (clothing)
거래 (Geolae)	Transaction

관리 (Gwanli)	Maintenance
특별한 기능 (Teukbyeolhan gineung)	Special features
할부 (Halbu)	Installment payment
예약 (Yeyak)	Reservation
포장 (Pojang)	Packaging
손님 (Sonnim)	Guest
원단 (Wondan)	Fabric
무게 (Muge)	Weight
배송료 (Baesongryo)	Shipping fee
결제 방법 (Gyeolje bangbeob)	Payment method
소비자 (Sobija)	Consumer
이벤트 (Event)	Event
가격표 (Gagyeokpyo)	Price tag
할인 쿠폰 (Halin coupon)	Discount coupon
세금 (Segeum)	Tax
구매력 (Gumeryeok)	Purchasing power

리필 (Refill)	Refill
배송 시간 (Baesong sigan)	Delivery time
선입금 (Seonipgeum)	Deposit
판매자 (Panmeja)	Seller
교환 (Gyohwan)	Exchange
알레르기 (Allereugi)	Allergy
다양성 (Dayangseong)	Variety
상품 (Sangpum)	Product
개봉 (Gaebong)	Unboxing
착용 (Chakyong)	Wearing
대금 (Daegum)	Payment (sum of money)
환전 (Hwanjeon)	Currency exchange
현지 통화 (Hyeonji tonghwa)	Local currency
할인율 (Halin-yul)	Discount rate
가게 주인 (Gagae juin)	Shop owner
포인트 (Point)	Loyalty points

반품 (Banpum)	Return (of goods)
소매 (Some)	Sleeve
솔기 (Solgi)	Seam
장바구니 (Jangbaguni)	Shopping cart
ATM (ATM)	ATM (Cash withdrawal machine)
환율 (Hwanyul)	Exchange rate
손목 시계 (Sonmok sigye)	Wristwatch
신발 끈 (Sinbal kkeun)	Shoelace
손수건 (Sonsugeon)	Handkerchief
목걸이 (Mokgeori)	Necklace
팔찌 (Paljji)	Bracelet
반지 (Banji)	Ring
귀걸이 (Gwigeori)	Earrings
모자 (Moja)	Hat
가방 (Gabang)	Bag
지갑 (Jigab)	Wallet

스카프 (Scarf)	Scarf
양말 (Yangmal)	Socks
티셔츠 (T-shirts)	T-shirt
원피스 (Wonpiseu)	Dress
스커트 (Skirt)	Skirt
바지 (Baji)	Pants
코트 (Coat)	Coat
재킷 (Jacket)	Jacket
슈트 (Suit)	Suit
양복 (Yangbok)	Formal wear
비치웨어 (Beachwear)	Beachwear
야구 모자 (Yagu moja)	Baseball cap
헤드폰 (Headphone)	Headphones
스피커 (Speaker)	Speaker
스마트폰 (Smartphone)	Smartphone
태블릿 (Tablet)	Tablet

노트북 (Notebook)	Laptop
가전제품 (Gajeonjepum)	Home appliances
스타일리시 (Stylish)	Stylish
오프라인 (Offline)	Offline (brick-and-mortar)
온라인 (Online)	Online
재고 (Jaego)	Inventory
구매자 (Gumeja)	Buyer
고객 만족도 (Gogaek manjokdo)	Customer satisfaction
패션 트렌드 (Fashion trend)	Fashion trend
시장 조사 (Sijang josa)	Market research
상품평 (Sangpum pyeong)	Product review
리뷰 (Review)	Review
주문서 (Jumunseo)	Order form
매출 (Maechul)	Revenue
판매량 (Panmae-ryang)	Sales volume
주문번호 (Jumun beonho)	Order number

수령 (Sureong)	Receipt (of goods)
홈페이지 (Homepage)	Homepage
품질 (Pumjil)	Quality
교환 정책 (Gyohwan jeongchaek)	Exchange policy
신용카드 (Sinyong card)	Credit card
영수증 확인 (Yeongsujeung hwagin)	Receipt verification
재고 소진 (Jaego sojin)	Inventory depletion
구매 결정 (Gume gyeoljeong)	Purchase decision
상품 정보 (Sangpum jeongbo)	Product information
구매력 증진 (Gumeryeok jeungjin)	Boosting purchasing power
가격 대비 (Gagyeok daebi)	Value for money
시즌 세일 (Season sale)	Seasonal sale
브랜드 로고 (Brand logo)	Brand logo
가격 대조 (Gagyeok daejo)	Price comparison
피팅 룸 (Fitting room)	Fitting room
배송 지연 (Baesong jiyeon)	Shipping delay

반품 정책 (Banpum jeongchaeg)	Return policy
재고 관리 (Jaego gwangli)	Inventory management
판매원 (Panmewon)	Sales clerk
소비 행동 (Sobi haengdong)	Consumer behavior
소비자 보호 (Sobija boho)	Consumer protection
환경 친화적 (Hwangyeong chinhwajeok)	Environmentally friendly
구매 의도 (Guma uido)	Purchase intent
가격 조정 (Gagyeok jojeong)	Price adjustment
고객 서비스 센터 (Gogaek service center)	Customer service center
무료 체험 (Muryo chehum)	Free trial
프로모션 (Promotion)	Promotion
인기 상품 (Ingi sangpum)	Bestseller
광고 (Gwanggo)	Advertisement
리워드 프로그램 (Rewards program)	Rewards program
주문 확인 (Jumun hwagin)	Order confirmation
세일 가격표 (Sale gagyeokpyo)	Sale price tag

현금 인출 (Hyeongeum inchul)	Cash withdrawal
비용 (Biyong)	Cost

Chapter Nine
Hospital/Pharmacy/Hangover Medicine in Korea

South Korea, renowned for its rich history, vibrant cuisine, and breathtaking landscapes, also boasts a thriving drinking culture that plays a significant role in the social fabric of the nation. Koreans are known for their strong sense of community and propensity for bonding over a shared meal or a round of drinks. Whether it's over a bottle of soju, makgeolli, or the beloved Korean barbecue, these communal gatherings provide opportunities for connection, celebration, and unwinding from the rigors of daily life. However, a night of revelry can sometimes lead to the infamous Korean "hangover," an experience that can be challenging for newcomers who aren't aware of the many hangover medicines and cures that exist.

Navigating a hospital or pharmacy in a foreign country can be a daunting task, especially when you're feeling unwell. With these questions and phrases, you'll gain the confidence to express your needs, symptoms, and concerns effectively in Korean, ensuring a good experience during medical visits.

Common Phrases	Translation
병원에 가야 해요. (Byeong-won-e gaya haeyo.)	I need to go to the hospital.
의사를 불러주세요. (Uisareul bulleojuseyo.)	Please call a doctor.
어디 아파요? (Eodi apayo?)	Where does it hurt?

열이 있어요. (Yeoli isseoyo.)	I have a fever.
통증이 있어요. (Tongjeung-i isseoyo.)	I have pain.
약을 처방해 주세요. (Yageul cheobanghae juseyo.)	Please prescribe medication.
토해요. (Tohaeyo.)	I'm vomiting.
설사해요. (Seolsahaeyo.)	I have diarrhea.
기침이 있어요. (Gichimi isseoyo.)	I have a cough.
콧물이 나요. (Cotmul-I nayo.)	I have running nose.
몸이 아파서 움직일 수 없어요. (Momi apaseo umjigil su eopseoyo.)	I'm in too much pain to move.
혈압을 측정해 볼게요. (Hyeolabeul cheukjeonghae bolgeyo.)	I'll check your blood pressure.
피부에 발진이 나서 걱정돼요. (Pibu-e baljin-i naseo geokjeongdwaeoyo.)	I'm worried about a skin rash.
피가 나요. (Piga nayo.)	I'm bleeding.
체온계가 필요해요. (Cheongyeonge-ga piryohaeyo.)	I need a thermometer.

처방전을 써주실 수 있어요? (Cheobangjeon-eul sseojusil su isseoyo?)	Can you write a prescription?
약을 사러 왔어요. (Yageul sareo wasseoyo.)	I've come to buy medicine.
이 약은 어떻게 먹어야 해요? (I yageun eotteoke meogeoya haeyo?)	How should I take this medicine?
복용량은 어떻게 되나요? (Bogyongryang-eun eotteoke dweonayo?)	How do I follow the dosage?
이 약에 부작용이 있을까요? (I yage bujakyong-i isseulkka?)	Does this medicine have any side effects?
이 약은 식사 전에 드셔야 해요. (I yageun sigsa jeone deusheoya haeyo.)	You should take this medicine before a meal.
이 약은 식사 후에 드셔야 해요. (I yageun sigsa hue deusheoya haeyo.)	You should take this medicine after a meal.
알러지가 있으면 주의해야 해요. (Allerjiga issmyeon juuihaeya haeyo.)	Be cautious if you have allergies.
이 약은 수면제예요. (I yageun sumyeonje-yeyo.)	This medicine is a sleeping pill.
약국에 재고가 남아 있나요? (Yakguge jaego ga nama innayo?)	Do you have this medicine in stock?
이 약을 주실 수 있어요? (I yageul jusil su isseoyo?)	Can you give me this medicine?
숙취가 심해요. (Sukchwi ga simhaeyo.)	I have a bad hangover.

숙취해소제를 추천해 주세요. (Sukchwihesoje-leul chucheonhae juseyo.)	Please recommend a hangover remedy.
머리가 아파요. (Meoriga apayo.)	I have a headache.
물을 한 잔 주세요. (Mul-eul han jan juseyo.)	Please give me a glass of water.
비타민을 복용해야 해요. (Vitamin-eul bogyonghaeya haeyo.)	You should take vitamins.
탄산음료가 도움이 돼요. (Tansan-eumryo-ga doum-i dwaeoyo.)	Carbonated drinks can help.
치료법이 뭐에요? (Chiryobeob-I mwoeyo?)	Wha''s the treatment?
가벼운 운동이 좋아요. (Gabyeoun undong-i joayo.)	Light exercise is good.
약을 몇 번이나 먹어야 돼요? (Yageul myeot beon-ina meogeoya dwaeoyo?)	How many times should I take the medicine?
빨리 회복하고 싶어요. (Ppalli hoebokhago sipeoyo.)	I want to recover quickly.
제 몸에 무슨 문제가 있을까요? (Je mom-e museun munje-ga isseulkkayo?)	What could be wrong with my body?
환자 등록을 해야 하나요? (Hwanja deunglok-eul haeya hanayo?)	Do I need to register as a patient?
처방전이 필요해요. (Cheobangjeon-i piryohaeyo.)	I need a prescription.

병실을 어떻게 찾아가요? (Byeongsil-eul eotteoke chajagayo?)	How do I find the hospital room?
의사 선생님을 기다려야 해요. (Uisa seonsaengnim-eul gidalyeoya haeyo.)	I need to wait for the doctor.
이 병원은 24 시간 운영해요. (I byeongwon-eun isipsa sigan unyeonghaeyo.)	This hospital operates 24 hours.
입원이 필요해요. (Ibwon-i piryohaeyo.)	I need to be hospitalized.
입원 일정을 어떻게 정하나요? (Ibwon iljeong-eul eotteoke jeonghanayo?)	How is the hospitalization schedule determined?
퇴원일은 언제인가요? (Tweowon-il-eun eonjeingayo?)	When is the discharge date?
의사와 상담하고 싶어요. (Uisa-wa sangdamhago sipeoyo.)	I want to consult with a doctor.
환자 정보를 확인하려면 어떻게 해야 하나요? (Hwanja jeongbo-leul hwaginharyeomyeon eotteoke haeya hanayo?)	How do I verify patient information?
의료보험이 있어요. (Uilyoboheom-I isseoyo.)	I have medical insurance.
진료비는 어떻게 지불하나요? (Jinlyobi-neun eotteoke jibulhanayo?)	How do I pay for medical expenses?
혈액검사를 받아야 해요. (Hyeol-aeg-geomsa-leul badaya haeyo.)	I need to get a blood test.
입원실은 어떻게 예약하나요? (Ibwonsil-eun eotteoke	How do I make a reservation for a hospital room?

yeyaghanayo?)	
이 약은 일주일 동안 복용하세요. (I yageun iljuil dongan bogyong haseyo.)	Take this medicine for one week.
이 약은 식후에 드세요. (I yageun sikhue deuseyo.)	Take this medicine after a meal.
어떤 약을 추천해 주실 수 있어요? (Eotteon yageul chucheonhae jusil su isseoyo?)	What medicine do you recommend?
약국에 얼마나 머물러야 해요? (Yakgug-e eolmana meomulleoya haeyo?)	How long do I need to stay at the pharmacy?
약 가격이 얼마에요? (Yak gagyeok-i eolmaeyo?)	How much does the medicine cost?
이 약은 처방전 없이 살 수 있나요? (I yageun cheobangjeon eobsi sal su innayo?)	Can I buy this medicine without a prescription?
약은 언제 복용해야 해요? (Yageun eonje bogyonghaeya haeyo?)	When should I take the medicine?
약을 잘못 복용했어요. (Yageul jalmot bogyongheasseoyo.)	I took the medicine incorrectly.
약을 먹기 전에 식사를 하지 말아야 해요. (Yageul meoggi jeon-e sigsa-leul haji malaya haeyo.)	Don't eat before taking the medicine.
약을 어떻게 보관해야 해요? (Yageul eotteoke bogwanhaeya haeyo?)	How should I store the medicine?
오늘 아침에 숙취 때문에 힘들어요. (Oneul achim-e sukchwi	I'm having a hard time this morning because of the hangover.

ttaemune himdeuleoyo.)	
어떤 숙취해소제가 좋을가요? (Eotteon sukchwihaesoje-ga joeulkkayo?)	What hangover remedy do you recommend?
물을 먹고 얼마나 기다려야 돼요? (Muleul meokgo eolmana gidaryeoya dwaeoyo?)	How long should I wait after drinking water?
머리가 너무 아픈데 어떻게 해야 해요? (Meoriga neomu apeunde eotteoke haeya haeyo?)	My head hurts a lot, what should I do?
숙취해소제는 어떻게 복용해야 돼요? (Sukchwihaesoje-neun eotteoke bogyonghaeya dwaeoyo?)	How should I take the hangover remedy?
오늘 밤에 또 술을 마실 거예요. (Oneul bame tto sul-eul masil geoyeyo.)	I'll drink again tonight.
알코올을 줄이는 방법이 뭐에요? (Alcohol-eul julineun bangbeob-i mwoeyo?)	What are some ways to reduce alcohol consumption?
물을 마시면 숙취에 도움이 될까요? (Mul-eul masimyeon sukchwi-e doum-i dweolkkayo?)	Will drinking water help with the hangover?
숙취 때문에 두통이 있어요. (Sukchwi ttaemun-e dutong-i isseoyo.)	I have a headache because of the hangover.
술을 너무 많이 마셨어요. (Sul-eul neomu mani masseotsseoyo.)	I drank too much alcohol.
의사 선생님이 언제 오시나요? (Uisa seonsaengnim-i eonje osinayo?)	When will the doctor arrive?

혈액 검사 결과가 나왔어요. (Hyeol-aeg geomsa gyeolgwa-ga nawasseoyo.)	The blood test results are out.
약을 언제까지 복용해야 해요? (Yageul eonjekkaji bogyonghaeya haeyo?)	How long should I take the medicine?
환자 기록을 열람하려면 어떻게 해야 하나요? (Hwanja gilok-eul yeollamharyeomyeon eotteoke haeya hanayo?)	How can I access my medical records?
무슨 검사를 해야 할까요? (Museun geomsa-leul haeya halkkayo?)	What tests should I have?
보험으로 처리할 수 있나요? (Boheom-euro cheolihal su innayo?)	Can this be covered by insurance?
병원비가 얼마나 나와요? (Byeongwon-bi ga eolmana nawayo?)	How much is the hospital bill?
제 상태를 설명해볼게요. (Je sangtae-leul seolmyeonghae bolgeyo.)	Let me describe my condition.
약을 먹고 나서 어떤 증상이 있을 수 있나요? (Yageul meokgo naseo eotteon jeungsang-i isseul su innayo?)	What symptoms can occur after taking the medicine?
병원 내 식당은 어디에요? (Byeongwon nae sikdang-eun eodieyo?)	Where is the hospital cafeteria?
이 병원은 어떤 분야에 전문이에요? (I byeongwon-eun eotteon bunya-e jeonmunieyo?)	What specialties does this hospital have?
환자 대기 시간이 얼마나 걸려요? (Hwanja daegi sigan-i eolmana geolryeoyo?)	How long is the patient waiting time?

진료비를 신용카드로 낼 수 있어요? (Jinlyobi-leul sinyong card-ro nael su isseoyo?)	Can I pay for the medical expenses with a credit card?
치료 계획을 설명해 주세요. (Chiryo gyehweok-eul seolmyeonghae juseyo.)	Please explain the treatment plan.
이 약은 수면제인가요? (I yageun sumyeonjeingayo?)	Is this medicine a sleep aid?
이 약은 종류가 뭐에요? (I yageun jonglyuga mwoeyo?)	What type of medicine is this?
약을 어떻게 받나요? (Yageul eotteoke batnayo?)	How should I take the medicine?
약을 먹어도 되요. (Yageul meogeodo dweoyo.)	It's okay to take the medicine.
아이에게 약을 어떻게 주어야 해요? (Aiege yageul eotteoke jueoya haeyo?)	How should I give medicine to a child?
이 약은 부작용이 있을까요? (I yageun bujakyong-i isseulkkayo?)	Does this medicine have any side effects?
약을 정확하게 어떻게 복용해야 해요? (Yageul jeonghwakhage eotteoke bogyonghaeya haeyo?)	How should I take the medicine correctly?
약을 먹고 효과를 느낄 때까지 얼마나 걸려요? (Yageul meoggo hyogwa-leul neukkil ttaekkaji eolmana geolryeoyo?)	How long does it take to feel the effects of the medicine?
눈에 이 약을 넣어야 해요. (Nun-e i yageul neoeoya haeyo.)	You should put this medicine in your eye.
이 약은 아침에 먹어야 해요. (I yageun achime meogeoya	Take this medicine in the morning.

haeyo.)	
이 약을 물과 함께 복용해야 해요. (I yageun mulgwa hamkke bogyonghaeya haeyo.)	Take this medicine with water.
숙취해소제를 어떻게 사용해야 하나요? (Sukchwihaesoje-leul eotteoke sayonghaeya hanayo?)	How should I use the hangover remedy?
술을 많이 마셨어요. (Sul-eul manhi masyeosseoyo.)	I drank a lot of alcohol.
숙취해소제를 언제 먹어야 돼요? (Sukchwihaesoje-leul eonje meogeoya dwaeoyo?)	When should I take the hangover remedy?
숙취가 꽤 심해요. (Sukchwi-ga kkwae simhaeyo.)	The hangover is quite severe.
술을 조금 마셨는데도 숙취가 있어요. (Sul-eul jogeum masyeotneundedo sukchwi-ga isseoyo.)	I have a hangover even though I drank a little.

Vocabulary

Vocabulary	Translation
병원 (Byeong-won)	Hospital
의사 (Uisa)	Doctor
간호사 (Ganhosa)	Nurse
환자 (Hwanja)	Patient

입원 (Ibwon)	Hospitalization
진료 (Jinryo)	Medical examination
검사 (Geomsa)	Test
처방전 (Cheobangjeon)	Prescription
수술 (Susul)	Surgery
상담 (Sangdam)	Consultation
병실 (Byeongsil)	Hospital room
약국 (Yakguk)	Pharmacy
약 (Yak)	Medication, Medicine
진단 (Jindan)	Diagnosis
진통제 (Jintongje)	Painkiller
발진 (Baljin)	Rash
수면제 (Sumyeonje)	Sleeping pill
체온계 (Chae-ongye)	Thermometer
혈압기계 (Hyeolabgigye)	Blood pressure monitor
의료보험 (Uiryoboheom)	Health insurance

비타민 (Vitamin)	Vitamin
종류 (Jonglyu)	Type
복용 (Bogyong)	Dosage
부작용 (Bujakyong)	Side effects
먹는 방법 (Meogneun bangbeop)	How to take
식후 (Sikhu)	After a meal
식전 (Sikjeon)	Before a meal
효과 (Hyogwa)	Effect
약사 (Yaksa)	Pharmacist
유효기간 (Yuhyogigan)	Expiration date
경고 (Gyeonggo)	Warning
저장 방법 (Jeojang bangbeop)	Storage instructions
숙취 (Sukchwi)	Hangover
숙취해소제 (Sukchwihaesoje)	Hangover remedy
물 (Mul)	Water
통증 (Tongjeung)	Pain

두통 (Dutong)	Headache
구토 (Guto)	Vomiting
설사 (Seolsa)	Diarrhea
식욕 (Sikyok)	Appetite
음료수 (Eumryosu)	Beverage
치료 (Chiryo)	Treatment
마시다 (Masida)	To drink
아프다 (Apeuda)	To be in pain
회복 (Hoebok)	Recovery
수면 (Sumyeon)	Sleep
탄산음료 (Tansan-eumryo)	Carbonated drink
스캔 (Scan)	Scan
병력 (Byeonglyeok)	Medical history
알약 (Alyak)	Pill
주사 (Jusa)	Injection
마취 (Machi)	Anesthesia

국민건강보험 (Gungmin geongangboheom)	National health insurance
퇴원 (Tweowon)	Discharge
수술실 (Susulsil)	Operating room
응급실 (Eunggeupsil)	Emergency room
병력 조사 (Byeonglyeok josa)	Medical history assessment
의료진 (Uiryojin)	Medical staff
치과 (Chigwa)	Dentistry
마취제 (Machije)	Anesthetic
산부인과 (Sanbuingwa)	Obstetrics and gynecology
정신과 (Jeongsingwa)	Psychiatry
교통사고 (Gyotongsago)	Traffic accident
알레르기 반응 (Allereogi baneung)	Allergic reaction
병실 요금 (Byeongsil yogeum)	Room charge
진료비 영수증 (Jinryobi yeongsujeung)	Medical receipt
혈액형 (Hyeol-aeghyeong)	Blood type
종이 처방전 (Jong-i cheobangjeon)	Paper prescription

약효 (Yakhyo)	Medicinal effect
약봉투 (Yakbongtu)	Medication pouch
일일 투여량 (Il-il tuyeorang)	Daily dosage
액체 (Aegche)	Liquid
약물 상호 작용 (Yakmul sangho jakyong)	Drug interaction
의사 처방 (Uisa cheobang)	Doctor's prescription
일회용 주사기 (Ilhoeyong jusagi)	Disposable syringe
처방전 재발급 (Cheobangjeon jaebalgeub)	Prescription reissue
건강 보조제 (Geongang bojoje)	Dietary supplement
약물 오용 (Yakmul oyong)	Medication misuse
이상 반응 (Isang baneung)	Adverse reaction
약물 남용 (Yakmul namyong)	Medication abuse
숙취해소제 (Sukchwi haesoje)	Hangover relief
알코올 중독 (Alcohol jungdok)	Alcohol addiction
음주량 (Eumjuryang)	Alcohol consumption
숙취 증상 (Sukchwi jeungsang)	Hangover symptoms

탈수 (Talsu)	Dehydration
음주 후 두통 (Eumju hu dutong)	Post-drinking headache
미지근한 물 (Mijigeunhan mul)	Lukewarm water
해독 음료 (Haedok eumryo)	Detox drink
식욕 상실 (Sikyok sangsil)	Loss of appetite
어지러움 (Eojireoum)	Dizziness
식욕 회복 (Sikyok hweobok)	Appetite recovery
음주 후 메스꺼움 (Eumju hu meseuggeoum)	Nausea after drinking
복통 (Boktong)	Stomachache
과음 (Gwaum)	Heavy drinking
숙취 예방 (Sukchwi yebang)	Hangover prevention

Chapter Ten
What Not to Do in Korea Common Cultural Mistakes to Avoid in Korea

It is imperative to recognize and respect the cultural nuances that significantly influence communication and daily life in South Korea. Exploring common cultural mistakes ensures respectful and mindful interactions with the local population.

Tips on Being Respectful and Mindful of Local Customs

As it was mentioned in previous chapters, bowing is a customary greeting and a symbol of respect. The depth of the bow may vary depending on the level of formality and the person's social status. However, even a slight bow, accompanied by a warm smile, is generally well-received and appreciated.

Additionally, remember to remove your shoes before entering someone's home, traditional restaurants, or certain businesses. It is customary to leave your outdoor footwear at the door. Signs or indications usually guide you in determining whether this practice is expected.

Addressing people in Korea is an art in itself. Remember that Koreans use honorifics when addressing someone who is older or holds a higher social status. The Korean language employs specific verb endings and honorific titles to convey respect. Taking the time to learn and use these honorifics correctly will not only demonstrate your cultural awareness but also earn you respect from locals.

Moreover, in Korea, it is often preferred to communicate indirectly rather than through direct criticism. Instead of delivering a blunt "no," Koreans might use phrases like "I'll think about it" to convey their reservations or objections, maintaining harmony and avoiding confrontations. And it is also very important to listen others carefully until they finish. During discussion, Koreans seldom jump on while others are talking. This is considered as respecting others. As Korean sentence structure is different from English, verb coms last within the sentence so you need to listen until the last word to understand their meaning and nuance.

Guidelines for Behavior in Public Spaces, Like Subways

Public spaces in Korea, including subways and buses, have their own set of behavioral norms that you should be aware of. Queueing politely is a fundamental practice, and cutting in line or pushing ahead is considered extremely impolite. Koreans take pride in maintaining order and courtesy in public queues.

Maintaining a peaceful environment is highly valued in public spaces, and this extends to conversational volume. To respect this cultural norm, it is essential to keep your voices down in places like subways, buses, and libraries. Engaging in loud conversations is generally seen as disruptive and disrespectful.

Koreans also place a strong emphasis on offering seats to those in need, such as the elderly, pregnant women, or individuals with disabilities, while using public transportation. This reflects the profound respect for elders that is deeply ingrained in Korean culture. Thus, offering your seat in such situations is considered a thoughtful and considerate gesture. Most of transportations have special seats for elders, individuals with disabilities or pregnant women so you would avoid to seat there and you can notice with proper signage there.

Furthermore, public displays of affection are generally discouraged in Korean society. Hugging, kissing, or any other form of physical affection should be kept private and not displayed in public spaces. Such behavior is seen as immodest and inappropriate.

Dress Code and Appropriate Attire in Different Settings

Understanding appropriate attire in various settings is another essential aspect of cultural sensitivity in Korea. In formal business settings, conservative and professional attire is crucial. Men typically wear dark suits, while women opt for classic dresses or suits. Bright colors and flashy accessories are generally avoided, as a modest and professional appearance is highly regarded.

In more casual settings, such as restaurants and social gatherings, stylish yet modest clothing is appropriate. Avoid overly revealing or provocative outfits, as Korean culture places value on maintaining a sense of decorum and modesty.

When visiting temples or cathedrals, it is essential to dress modestly out of respect for the cultural significance of these places. People should cover their shoulders and knees. This practice is considered a sign of reverence for the spiritual and historical importance of these sites.

Lastly, it's important to note that in Korea, removing your shoes before entering certain establishments, such as traditional Korean restaurants, temples, or private homes, is a customary sign of respect and cleanliness. Koreans used to live without shoes in home so most of Koreans take off shoes before they go into home. Be attentive to signs or cues indicating whether this practice is expected.

Being respectful and mindful of local customs, behaving appropriately in public spaces, and dressing considerately in different settings are all essential elements of our cultural journey in South Korea.

Understanding Personal Space and Boundaries

Personal space is a universally recognized concept, but its nuances can vary significantly from one culture to another. In Korea, personal space tends to be narrower than in many Western cultures. It's essential to be aware of this difference to ensure respectful interactions with locals.

In crowded places don't be surprised if you find yourself in close proximity to others. It's customary to stand closely, and physical contact may occur. While this may initially feel uncomfortable for some, it's important to remain composed and understanding. Avoid displaying signs of discomfort or frustration, as Koreans value maintaining a calm and harmonious atmosphere in public spaces.

During conversations, be aware of personal space as well. While shaking hands is common, physical contact beyond that, such as hugging or kissing, is typically reserved for close friends or family. Always gauge the other person's comfort level and follow their lead regarding physical contact.

Cultural Sensitivities Related to Religion and Traditions

Korea is a nation steeped in history and tradition, and respect for these customs is integral to Korean culture. Understanding and respecting the religious and traditional sensitivities of the country is crucial to avoid unintentional offense.

Religion in Korea is diverse, with Buddhism, Christianity, and various indigenous beliefs being practiced. When discussing religious topics, it's advisable to do so with an open mind and a spirit of curiosity rather than criticism. Avoid engaging in debates about religion, as this can be seen as disrespectful.

Traditional customs and rituals are an essential part of Korean culture. When attending events like weddings or funerals, it's essential to adhere to the appropriate dress code and behavior. Bowing and offering condolences in a respectful manner are customary during funerals, while weddings may involve specific ceremonies and customs that you should observe quietly and with reverence. Black suit or dress are considered for funeral while white color dress is avoided for women for wedding.

Korea also celebrates various traditional holidays, such as Chuseok (Korean Thanksgiving) and Seollal (Lunar New Year). These holidays often involve specific customs, rituals, and ancestral memorial services. Participating in these traditions when invited can be a beautiful way to immerse yourself in Korean culture and show respect for local customs.

Furthermore, while visiting temples or other religious sites, maintain a respectful demeanor. Dress modestly and adhere to any specific rules or guidelines for visitors. Keep in mind that these places hold profound spiritual significance for many Koreans, and it's essential to be considerate of their practices and beliefs.

Respecting Elders and Authority Figures

Respect for elders and authority figures is deeply ingrained in Korean culture. Demonstrating this respect is not merely a matter of courtesy; it is a fundamental aspect of social harmony and cohesion.

In Korean society, addressing older individuals with the appropriate honorifics is essential. Use "오빠" (oppa) for older brothers if you are women, "언니" (eonni) for older sisters. If you are men, use "형" (hyeong) for older brothers, use "누나" (nuna) for older sisters. "아저씨" (ajeossi) for older men, and "아줌마" (ajumma) for older women can be used but only in close and casual situation. For example, you'd better call "이모" (imo) / "누나" (nuna) / "언니" (eonni) when you are in shop or restaurant to call staff rather than "아줌마" (ajumma). These honorifics convey respect and should be used in both formal and informal settings.

When receiving or giving something to an elder, always use both hands as a sign of respect. This gesture demonstrates your sincerity and appreciation for their wisdom and experience.

Additionally, standing when an elder enters the room and offering them your seat in public places like buses or subways is a common practice. This act of deference reflects the high regard Koreans have for their elders.

Proper Conduct During Traditional Ceremonies

Korea boasts a rich tapestry of traditions and customs, many of which are intertwined with religious and cultural significance. When invited to participate in traditional ceremonies, it's essential to approach them with a respectful and open-minded attitude.

During ancestral rites or memorial services, maintain a solemn and quiet demeanor. These events hold great importance to Koreans, as they pay homage to their ancestors and heritage. Your respectful observance of these rituals will be appreciated.

Avoiding Loud or Disruptive Behavior in Public

Korean culture values tranquility and maintaining a peaceful atmosphere in public spaces. Loud or disruptive behavior is generally frowned upon, as it disrupts the harmony that Koreans cherish.

When in public spaces such as subways, buses, or libraries, make an effort to keep your voice at a considerate volume. Engaging in loud conversations or creating unnecessary noise can be perceived as impolite.

Moreover, it's essential to be mindful of your surroundings when using electronic devices. Keep your phone on silent mode and use headphones in shared spaces to minimize disturbances to others.

Public displays of affection, such as kissing or hugging, should be reserved for private settings. Korean culture emphasizes modesty and discretion in public, so it's best to keep physical affection between friends and loved ones private.

These actions reflect a willingness to embrace local customs and uphold the values that are integral to Korean society. In doing so, you'll find yourself more warmly received and better integrated into this vibrant and respectful community.

Environmental Conservation and Eco-Friendly Practices

Environmental conservation is a global concern, and South Korea is no exception. Responsible environmental practices are crucial.

Recycle diligently by separating waste into the designated categories. Familiarize yourself with local recycling rules and guidelines.

Minimize plastic usage by carrying reusable bags and containers. Single-use plastics are a significant environmental issue, and avoiding them demonstrates your commitment to sustainability. Recently many of restaurants and coffee shops suggest to use paper or eco-friendly made straws and bring their own tumbler for cup of coffee. If you shop in big marts, you need to pack by yourself in used box that are displayed at packing corner. You can purchase paper bag, reusable bag or plastic bag if you need.

Handling Encounters with Wildlife and Animals

When interacting with wildlife and animals in Korea, it's essential to do so responsibly and ethically.

Do not feed wild animals or disturb their natural habitat. Feeding wild animals can disrupt their natural behaviors and diet, leading to unintended consequences.

If you encounter stray animals, exercise caution and avoid approaching them unless you are certain they are friendly and safe to interact with. Contact local animal control or rescue organizations if assistance is needed.

Respect the rules and guidelines at wildlife sanctuaries and animal-related attractions. These facilities often have specific regulations in place to protect both animals and visitors.

Handling Trash and Recycling Responsibly

South Korea takes environmental conservation seriously, and proper waste disposal is a significant part of this effort. To respect local customs and the environment, it's essential to handle trash and recycling responsibly.

Separate your trash into designated categories, such as recyclables, food waste, and general waste. Each category usually has its designated collection bins or bags. Familiarize yourself with the specific sorting rules in your area, as they can vary. For example, you can find various bins depending on the material of the product such as plastic (plastic containers) / pet (plastic bottles) / paper / glass / can. When you throw away, you should empty the contains especially if it is food. Food waste is separately taken care of with other bins. Other than these, there are non-recyclable waste which is not recyclable.

Dispose of your waste in the appropriate bins and follow the schedule for waste collection. Leaving trash in public areas or overfilling bins is considered inconsiderate and could result in fines.

Appropriate Gift-Giving and Gestures of Gratitude

Gift-giving is a common practice in Korean culture, but there are specific customs and etiquette to be aware of to avoid unintentional offense.

Use both hands as a sign of respect to present your gifts. Gifts are often wrapped neatly, and the presentation is as important as the gift itself.

Avoid giving gifts in sets of four, as the number four sounds similar to the word for "death" in Korean and is considered unlucky. Instead, opt for sets of three or five.

When receiving a gift, it's customary to express gratitude. Saying "감사합니다" (gamsahamnida) or "고맙습니다" (gomapseumnida) is appropriate. You may also bow slightly while expressing your thanks.

Alcohol Consumption Etiquette and Moderation

Korean social gatherings often involve alcohol, and understanding the etiquette surrounding drinking is essential

When pouring drinks for others, hold the bottle or pouring vessel with two hands as a sign of respect. If someone offers you a drink, it's polite to accept it and reciprocate with a drink in return. Also use both hand for receiving drinks in you cup, you can hold the cup with two hands or one hand with cup and other hand to support your elbow.

Never pour your own drink; instead, wait for someone to offer to pour for you. If you don't wish to drink alcohol, it's acceptable to decline politely by saying, "저는 안 마실게요" (jeo-neun an masilgeyo), meaning "I won't drink."

Or if you are not able to drink alcohol, you can say "저는 술 못 마셔요" (jeo-neun sul mot maseoyo) meaning "I don't drink."

While drinking, it's customary to turn away from elders or those of higher social status when taking a sip. This gesture demonstrates respect and humility.

Dealing with Smoking Restrictions and Designated Areas

Smoking is subject to strict regulations in Korea, and it's essential to be aware of designated smoking areas and follow the rules.

Smoking is prohibited in most indoor public spaces, including restaurants,cafes and on the street. Always look for designated smoking areas when you need to smoke.

Dispose of cigarette butts in designated containers and avoid littering. Fines for littering cigarette butts can be steep.

Be mindful of non-smoking zones near schools and government buildings, as well as public transportation areas where smoking is strictly prohibited.

Photography Etiquette and Respecting Privacy

Koreans value their privacy and personal space, and photography etiquette plays an important role in respecting these boundaries.

Ask for permission before taking any picture, especially if it's to a person. Politeness goes a long way, and a friendly smile and a simple "사진 좀 찍어도 될까요?" (sajin jom jigeodo doelkka?) meaning "May I take a photo?" should be used before you are taking specific individual in your camera.

Be mindful of people's comfort levels when taking pictures in public places. Avoid photographing individuals who appear uncomfortable or unwilling to be photographed.

Respect "no photography" signs in museums, galleries, and other designated areas. These restrictions are in place to protect valuable artifacts and artworks.

Rules and Norms at Historical and Sacred Sites

Korea boasts a rich cultural heritage, and when visiting historical or sacred sites, it's essential to observe specific rules and norms.

Dress modestly when visiting temples, palaces, and other sacred sites. Ensure that your clothing covers your shoulders and knees out of respect for the cultural significance of these places.

Remove your shoes when entering temple buildings or traditional Korean homes. This shows cleanliness and respect.

Speak quietly and avoid making loud noises. Many historical sites and temples are places of reflection and meditation, and maintaining a peaceful atmosphere is essential.

Do not touch or climb on historical artifacts, structures, or sacred objects. These items hold immense cultural and historical value, and preserving them is a collective responsibility.

By doing this, you will demonstrate respect for cultural values and environmental stewardship that are integral to Korean society. These actions reflect your commitment to being a responsible global citizen and a considerate guest in this diverse and culturally rich nation.

Cultural Sensitivity in Rural and Remote Areas

Rural and remote areas in Korea offer a unique glimpse into the nation's traditional way of life and natural beauty. However, it's crucial to approach these regions with cultural sensitivity and respect for local customs.

In rural areas, traditional customs and values often hold more prominence than in urban centers. Greetings, such as bowing, may be more common and formal. Take the time to learn these customs and use them appropriately to show respect for local traditions.

In some rural areas, dialects or regional languages are prevalent. While conversational Korean remains essential, it can be beneficial to familiarize yourself with basic phrases or expressions in the local dialect to facilitate communication and connect with the local community.

Respect private property and boundaries. Rural areas often have more closely-knit communities where privacy is highly valued. Always seek permission before entering private land or taking photographs of people's homes.

Responsible Travel and Ethical Considerations

Responsible travel is essential to preserve the natural beauty and cultural heritage of rural and remote areas in Korea.

Stay on designated paths and trails when hiking or exploring natural landscapes. Straying from marked areas can damage fragile ecosystems and disturb wildlife habitats.

Avoid littering, and carry reusable bags for trash. Many remote areas may not have proper waste disposal facilities, and it's crucial to pack out what you bring in.

Respect wildlife and refrain from feeding wild animals. Feeding animals can disrupt their natural behaviors and create dependency on human food sources, which can be harmful.

Consider the impact of your presence on the environment and local communities. Choose eco-friendly accommodation and support businesses that practice sustainable tourism.

Engaging with the Local Community

Engaging with the local community in rural and remote areas can be a rewarding experience, but it should be done thoughtfully and respectfully.

If you wish to participate in local activities or cultural events, inquire about them at community centers or with local residents. Your interest and respect for their traditions can lead to warm and enriching interactions.

When visiting local markets or buying handmade crafts, be prepared to pay a fair price for the goods. Bargaining may be common in some regions, but it's important to ensure that your negotiations are respectful and fair to the artisans.

Your respectful and responsible approach to rural and remote travel will contribute to the sustainable and harmonious development of these areas and leave a positive impression on the communities you encounter.

As we strive to master conversational Korean, it is equally vital to understand and appreciate the customs, traditions, and social norms that shape Korean society.

We've explored topics ranging from personal space and boundaries to responsible travel and ethical considerations, all with the aim of guiding you towards culturally informed and respectful interactions while in South Korea. These principles are not only integral to being a considerate guest but also open doors to deeper connections and a richer understanding of the diverse and multifaceted Korean culture.

By avoiding common mistakes, you will not only enhance your conversational Korean skills but also leave a positive impression on the people you encounter.

Korea is a nation where tradition and modernity coexist harmoniously, where respect for others and the environment are deeply rooted values. As you continue your journey to learn conversational Korean, remember that showing respect and cultural sensitivity will not only enrich your experiences but also contribute to the positive exchange between cultures.

Conclusion

What a fantastic journey it's been as we delved into the world of learning Korean together. As we wrap up this Book, let's take a moment to reflect on the invaluable lessons we've learned and the experiences that await us on this language adventure.

Throughout our journey, we've stressed the significance of understanding Korean culture. Language and culture are intertwined, and your efforts to grasp the Korean language have given you a glimpse into the hearts and minds of its people. Every phrase and word carry a cultural story, so remember to approach your learning with cultural curiosity.

But this is just the beginning! Learning a language is an ongoing pursuit, a lifelong love affair with the intricacies of communication. Don't be discouraged by the occasional bumps in the road; they are part of the thrilling language learning ride.

Connecting with the wonderful people you've met in Korea is key. Building relationships with native speakers will not only help you improve your language skills but will also provide you with a support system and lifelong friendships. Keep the lines of communication open and treasure these connections.

Let's not forget the amazing experiences you'll have in Korea, and those yet to come. From savoring mouthwatering Korean dishes to being mesmerized by the country's stunning landscapes, every moment in Korea is an opportunity for growth and discovery. Hold onto these experiences, let them inspire you, and use them as motivation to continue your language journey.

Even a basic understanding of Korean can work wonders during your travels. Locals appreciate the effort you put into learning their language, and it often leads to more meaningful and genuine interactions. Remember, it's not about being perfect; it's about trying and connecting.

As we wrap up, let's not lose sight of the true magic of travel and exploration. Korea has a lot of experiences waiting for you, from bustling cities to serene countryside, from ancient traditions to cutting-edge innovations. Keep that sense of wonder alive as you continue to explore the world.

Finally, as you prepare for future adventures, we extend our heartfelt wishes for a lifetime filled with fulfilling journeys, not just in Korea but all around the globe. Learning a language is like unlocking a treasure chest of opportunities and connections, making each trip a rich tapestry of excitement and discovery.

Thank you for joining us on this adventure. Your dedication to learning Korean and your passion for embracing new cultures are the keys to a world filled with endless wonder and enrichment. Keep learning, keep exploring, and may your journey be a lifetime of joy and fulfillment. Safe travels!

Worldwide Nomad Team

References

90 day korean. (2014, July 19). *Korean Etiquette: 11 Common Mistakes.* 90 Day Korean®. https://www.90daykorean.com/korean-etiquette/

Adventures of Awkward Amy. (2022). *22+ things to know before going to South Korea KR.* Www.youtube.com. https://www.youtube.com/watch?v=k2v3WDsDbrw

Aglibot, S. (2023a, February 9). *Your #1 Easy Guide To Korean Currency - Ling App.* https://ling-app.com/ko/korean-currency/

Aglibot, S. (2023b, April 5). *10 Basic Greetings In Korean: More Than A Greeting - Ling App.* https://ling-app.com/ko/basic-greetings-in-korean/

Agoda. (n.d.). *Seoul Travel Tips & South Korea Tourist Information.* Agoda: See the World for Less. Retrieved October 12, 2023, from https://www.agoda.com/travel-guides/south-korea/seoul/seoul-travel-tips-korea-tourist-information?cid=1844104

Alyse. (2020, October 15). *10 South Korea Travel Tips to Avoid Looking Like a Tourist.* The Invisible Tourist. https://www.theinvisibletourist.com/dos-donts-south-korea-travel-tips/

Anconitano, V. (2023). *60+ Expert South Korea Travel Tips And Complete Korean Guide 2023.* Thefoodellers.com. https://thefoodellers.com/en/south-korea-travel-tips

Asian Inspirations. (2020, April 24). *10 Basic Rules of Korean Dining Etiquette.* Asian Inspirations. https://asianinspirations.com.au/food-knowledge/10-basic-rules-of-korean-dining-etiquette/

Babe, A. (2016, February 8). *17 Things to Know Before You Go to Seoul.* Roads & Kingdoms. https://roadsandkingdoms.com/2016/17-things-to-know-before-you-go-to-seoul/

Bae, C. (2020, September 4). *8 Dos and Don'ts: Korean Dining Etiquette - Best of Korea.* Bestofkorea.com. https://bestofkorea.com/8-dos-and-donts-korean-dining-etiquette/

Berdin, K. (2018, August 8). *Food Etiquette in Korea: Eat Korean Barbecue Like a Local | Books and Bao.* https://booksandbao.com/food-etiquette-eat-korean-barbecue/

Clausen, T. S. (2022, July 25). *How to Easily Get a Taxi in South Korea as a Foreigner.* Timzer Travels. https://timzertravels.com/how-to-easily-get-a-taxi-in-south-korea/

Commisceo Global Consulting. (2016). *South Korea - Language, Culture, Customs and Etiquette.* Commisceo-Global.com. https://www.commisceo-global.com/resources/country-guides/south-korea-guide

Couple, A. F. (2021, July 26). *PLANNING YOUR TRIP TO SOUTH KOREA - ALL YOU NEED TO KNOW.* A Fun Couple - Travel Blog. https://afuncouple.com/korea-trip-planner/

Curly Tales. (2020). *15 Things You Need To Know About South Korea | Curly Tales.* Www.youtube.com. https://www.youtube.com/watch?v=rs_q4I5n8VE

Douglas, M. (2022, December 18). *South Korea Travel Tips - 46 Things to Know Before You Go [2023].* High Heels & a Backpack. https://www.highheelsandabackpack.com/korea-travel-guide/

Editor. (2022, January 20). *How to Prepare to Visit South Korea.* Out of Your Comfort Zone. https://www.outofyourcomfortzone.net/how-to-prepare-to-visit-south-korea/

Ehlion Team. (2019, September 16). *How to greet in korean? communication culture, style, etiquette and much more!* EHLION. https://ehlion.com/magazine/how-to-greet-in-korean/

Enkor. (2023). *How To Get A Taxi In Korea For Foreigners - Kakao Taxi App | Enkor Blog.* Stay.enkor.kr. https://stay.enkor.kr/blog/how-to-avoid-over-charged-using-a-taxi-in-korea-kakao-t

Enunce LLC. (n.d.). *Counting Numbers in Korean – The Korean Numbering System.* Enunce LLC. Retrieved October 12, 2023, from https://www.koreanfluent.com/cross_cultural/korean_numbers/korean_numbers.htm

Evason, N. (2016). *South Korean Culture - Greetings.* Cultural Atlas. https://culturalatlas.sbs.com.au/south-korean-culture/south-korean-culture-greetings

Expat Guide Korea. (2020, June 9). *Everything You Need to Know About Catching a Taxi in Seoul.* Expatguidekorea.com; Expat Guide Korea. https://expatguidekorea.com/article/everything-you-need-to-know-about-catching-a-taxi-in-seoul.html

Expat Guide Korea. (2022, December 18). *Reading and Saying Korean Numbers and Prices - The Meaning of Korean Money.* Expatguidekorea.com; Expat Guide Korea. https://expatguidekorea.com/article/reading-and-saying-korean-numbers-and-prices--the-meaning-of-korean-money.html

Flying Oyster. (2020, January 13). *How to Count Money in Korean (Part 1).* Korean Language Blog | Language and Culture of the Korean-Speaking World. https://blogs.transparent.com/korean/how-to-count-money-in-korean-post-1/

Future Learn. (n.d.). *A variety of Korean greeting expressions.* FutureLearn. https://www.futurelearn.com/info/courses/introduction-to-korean/0/steps/29390

Girlswanderlust. (2022, July 7). *How to prepare for a trip to South Korea -.* Girlswanderlust.com. https://girlswanderlust.com/how-to-prepare-for-a-trip-to-south-korea/

Go! go! Hanguk. (2021, November 3). *The main rules of etiquette in Korea.* Go! Go! Hanguk. https://gogohanguk.com/en/blog/rules-of-etiquette-in-korea/

GOV.UK. (n.d.). *Health - South Korea travel advice.* GOV.UK. https://www.gov.uk/foreign-travel-advice/south-korea/health

Health Tourism. (n.d.). *Medical Tourism to South Korea : Getting Medical Treatment in South Korea.* Www.health-Tourism.com. https://www.health-tourism.com/medical-tourism-south-korea/

International Citizens Insurance. (n.d.). *Safety Advice and Travel Insurance for South Korea.* International Citizens Insurance. Retrieved October 12, 2023, from https://www.internationalinsurance.com/travel-to/south-korea/

Jang, H. (2021, November 1). *Food culture and table manners in Korea - Koreanischkurs.* https://k-jang.com/en/food-culture-and-table-manners-in-korea/

Kaaloa, C. (2016). *42 Things to Know Before Traveling Korea - GRRRLTRAVELER.* https://grrrltraveler.com/things-to-know-before-traveling-korea/

Kazmi, S. (2022, December 11). *25+ Best Things To Know Before Going To Korea - Ling App.* https://ling-app.com/ko/things-to-know-before-going-to-korea/

Kimchi Mobile. (2023, February 26). *10 Tips for Navigating Public Transportation in Korea Like a Pro.* KIMCHI MOBILE. https://www.kimchimobile.com/10-tips-for-navigating-public-transportation-in-korea-like-a-pro/

KKday. (2019, September 11). *What You Should Know Before Visiting South Korea For The First Time.* KKday Blog. https://www.kkday.com/en/blog/24464/asia-what-you-should-know-before-visiting-south-korea-for-the-first-time

Klook Team. (2023). *The Only Seoul Subway Guide You'll Ever Need - Klook Travel Blog.* Www.klook.com. https://www.klook.com/blog/subway-guide-seoul/

KoreanClass101. (n.d.). *Hotels in Korea.* KoreanClass101. Retrieved October 12, 2023, from https://www.koreanclass101.com/lesson/survival-phrases-38-hotels?lp=37

kris. (2023a, January 9). *Planning a Trip to South Korea: a Step By Step Guide.* Wapiti Travel. https://www.wapititravel.com/blog/en/planning-a-trip-to-south-korea/

kris. (2023b, March 24). *Best South Korea Travel Tips For an Unforgettable Holiday.* Wapiti Travel. https://www.wapititravel.com/blog/en/south-korea-travel-tips/

Ladner, M. (2017, January 23). *Things to Know Before Traveling to South Korea.* Culture Trip. https://theculturetrip.com/asia/south-korea/articles/10-things-to-know-before-traveling-to-south-korea

Learn Korean. (2021, January 13). *Money In Korean - How To Count Korean Money - LearnKorean24.* https://learnkorean24.com/money-in-korean/

M, A. (2020, June 15). *Korean Greetings You Need to Know Before You Travel to South Korea.* KoreaTravelPost - South Korea's Leading Trip and Travel Media Publication. https://www.koreatravelpost.com/korean-greetings-you-need-to-know/

M, A. (2023, January 11). *Tips on Taking a Taxi in South Korea.* KoreaTravelPost - South Korea's Leading Travel Media Publication. https://www.koreatravelpost.com/taxi-south-korea/

Manselon, V. (n.d.). *Practical Guide : things to do and to avoid in South Korea -.* https://bonjour-coree.org/practical-guide-things-to-do-and-to-avoid-in-south-korea/

Marrinan, J. (2022, August 16). *Korean Etiquette, Culture And Manners: 35 Useful Insights.* In My Korea. https://inmykorea.com/korean-etiquette-culture-manners-insights/

Marrinan, J. (2023, February 19). *Complete South Korea Travel Guide 2023: Korean Travel Tips.* https://inmykorea.com/south-korea-travel-guide-korean-travel-tips/

Max. (2022, November 15). *19+ Things Not to Do in South Korea.* Seoul Korea Asia. https://seoulkoreaasia.com/things-not-to-do-in-south-korea/

MedicaltourismReviewCommunity. (2019, November 21). *Health Tourism in South Korea.* MedicalTourism.Review. https://medicaltourism.review/countries/south-korea

Mittal, B. (2021, November 16). *Take A Look At These Korea Travel Tips For A Smooth Vacation To The Korean Peninsula!* https://traveltriangle.com/blog/korea-travel-tips/

No, M. (2015). *The Dos and Don'ts of Eating Korean Barbecue.* Thrillist. https://www.thrillist.com/eat/nation/dos-and-donts-of-eating-in-a-korean-restaurant-korean-cuisine-etiquette

Ozonur, S. (2023, February 15). *10 Tips & Things To Know Before Traveling To Korea.* TheTravel. https://www.thetravel.com/things-to-know-before-traveling-to-korea/

Passport Symphony. (2020, March 22). *30 Important Things I Wish I Knew Before Visiting Korea.* Passportsymphony.com. https://passportsymphony.com/30-things-to-know-before-visiting-korea/

ProQuest. (2018). *7 Cultural Customs to Know Before Visiting South Korea.* About.proquest.com. https://about.proquest.com/en/blog/2018/7-cultural-customs-to-know-before-visiting-south-korea/

Ranjan, A. K. (2023). *The Most Spoken Words in the World: Insights and Cultural Differences.* Top Three US. https://www.topthreeus.com/2023/05/three-most-spoken-words-in-the-world.html

Rose. (2020, May 26). *30 South Korea Travel Tips To Know Before Going!* Where Goes Rose? https://www.wheregoesrose.com/south-korea-travel-tips/

Rough Rides. (n.d.). *Travel Tips South Korea for planning and on the go.* Rough Guides. https://www.roughguides.com/south-korea/travel-advice/

amantha. (2022, April 6). *50 South Korea Travel Tips*. There She Goes Again. https://thereshegoesagain.org/south-korea-travel-tips/

ieben, E. (2022, July 20). *Preparation South Korea | Practical information and travel tips*. Wereldreizigers.nl. https://www.wereldreizigers.nl/en/asia/South-Korea/preparation-best-travel-time-packing-list-information/

outhkorea. (2023, June 30). *How do you show respect in Korean? - Namhan South Korea*. https://www.namhansouthkorea.com/how-do-you-show-respect-in-korean/

sam, Y. (2019, November 18). *10 Things You Should Never Do in South Korea*. UBitto. https://ubitto.com/blog/10-things-you-should-never-do-in-south-korea/

ta. Maria, T., & Chang, C. (2023, March 23). *First Time in South Korea? Here Are 15 Travel Tips You Should Know Before Going!* TripZilla. https://www.tripzilla.com/south-korea-tips-first-time-travellers/133349

taff, H. (2023, July 11). *Important Tips When Traveling to Korea*. Haps Magazine. https://www.hapskorea.com/important-tips-when-traveling-to-korea/

usie. (2023, July 10). *South Korea Travel Tips – Things to Know Before Visiting Korea*. World Travel Toucan. https://worldtraveltoucan.com/south-korea-travel-tips/

ylvia. (2022, October 21). *Best Airbnb in Seoul: 15 amazing places to stay in 2023 (vacation homes, VRBOs, ..).* Wapiti Travel. https://www.wapititravel.com/blog/en/best-airbnb-seoul/

harp, C. (2016, December 9). *10 Korean customs to know before you visit Korea*. Matador Network; Matador Network. https://matadornetwork.com/abroad/10-korean-customs-to-know-before-you-visit-korea/

Traveling to South Korea for the first time: useful travel information. (n.d.). Zen Moments in Korea. Retrieved October 12, 2023, from https://zenmomentsinkorea.com/useful-information-south-korea-travel/

Tripadvisor. (2017). *Hotel or Airbnb? - South Korea Forum - Tripadvisor*. Www.tripadvisor.ca. https://www.tripadvisor.ca/ShowTopic-g294196-i8160-k10920217-Hotel_or_Airbnb-South_Korea.html

urla, F. (2020, April 20). *10 Things You Need to Know Before Visiting South Korea*. Two Monkeys Travel Group. https://twomonkeystravelgroup.com/dos-and-donts-before-visiting-south-korea/

J. S. Department of State. (2018). *South Korea International Travel Information*. State.gov. https://travel.state.gov/content/travel/en/international-travel/International-Travel-Country-Information-Pages/SouthKorea.html

Jsher, C. (2022a). *Tips for South Korea*. Lonely Planet. https://www.lonelyplanet.com/articles/things-to-know-before-traveling-to-south-korea

Jsher, C. (2022b, September 10). *Getting around in South Korea*. Lonely Planet. https://www.lonelyplanet.com/articles/getting-around-south-korea

Yeong. (2019). *Creatrip: 9 things to check for accommodation in South Korea!* Creatrip. https://www.creatrip.com/en/blog/5310/9-things-to-check-for-accommodation-in-South-Korea

Yeong. (2022). *Creatrip: Useful Tips on Taking a Taxi in Korea!* Creatrip. https://www.creatrip.com/en/blog/2487/Useful-Tips-on-Taking-a-Taxi-in-Korea

Yoon, H. (2022, July 3). *Getting around Seoul is easy for first-timers with these simple tips*. Lonely Planet. https://www.lonelyplanet.com/articles/getting-around-seoul

KOREAN SHORT STORIES FOR
Language Learners

Learn and Improve Your Korean Comprehension
and Vocabulary through 50 Short Stories Based
Off Korea's Long History

WorldWide Nomad

Introduction

The Korean language, with its delicate yet dynamic script and rhythmic cadences, is the heart of Korea's rich history and vibrant culture. To fully embrace it, you need not only understand its grammar and vocabulary but also immerse yourself in its stories—stories that have traversed through time, echoing the voices of ancestors and shaping the thoughts of its speakers.

This book offers you about 50 tales, each a small window into Korea's past. They start small, like the soft whisper of leaves, and gradually grow, like the robust winds of autumn, enabling you to grasp the complexity and beauty of the language step by step.

The tales within these pages aren't mere historical recounting; they are vibrant retellings of Korea's pivotal moments, brought to life in a folktale format. For instance, one story sheds light on King Sejong, believed to have crafted the Korean language during the Joseon Dynasty. It isn't a dry lecture on history; it's a vivid painting of the past, rich with colors and details, allowing the characters and events to dance before your eyes.

Now, you might wonder how to traverse this book to gain the most. It's simple. Engage with the stories. Let the words paint pictures in your mind. Let the emotions wrap around you like a warm blanket, and let the narratives guide you through the myriad lanes of Korea's past. Reflect on the stories, the characters, the conflicts, and resolutions. Ponder upon the morals and the values they portray.

The stories chosen reflect significant events and periods in Korea's timeline, offering you a taste of its cultural richness and historical depth. Each story, like a delicate piece of pottery, is molded with care, infused with elements from Korea's diverse timeline, and fired in the kiln of imagination, producing a piece of art ready to be admired and understood.

Your venture into these stories is not about memorizing facts; it's about living the moments. It's about seeing the world through the eyes of those who lived before us, feeling their joys and sorrows, and understanding their thoughts and dreams. It's about connecting with the culture, the people, and the land that is Korea.

Let's take, for example, the story of "A Father and His Two Daughters." It's not just a simple tale; it's a reflection of the dilemmas faced by individuals in Korean folklore, where conflicting interests often collide, portraying the intricacies of human desires and decisions. It reveals the essence of Korean folktales where conflicting elements often coexist, drawing a picture of Korean culture's nuances and depths.

This book is your gateway to understanding the Korean language and culture. Approach it with curiosity and an open mind. Absorb the words, the meanings, the emotions, and the essence of each story. See each tale as a stepping stone, leading you deeper into the vibrant world of Korean thought, philosophy, and art.

Remember, this is not a race; it's a journey of discovery. Take your time to explore, to understand, to reflect. Engage with the stories at your own pace, let them unfold their meanings to you, and slowly, you will see the beauty of the Korean language revealing itself, like the gentle blossoming of a flower.

As you walk through the enchanting forest of Korean stories, may you find joy in every leaf, learn from every twig, and discover the richness and the diversity of the ecosystem of Korean thought and expression. May every story be a gentle breeze, whispering the secrets of the past in your ears, and may you embrace the essence of Korea with every step.

Happy Reading!

Three Kingdoms Period
(1st - 7th Centuries CE)

삼국시대와 용의 선물
Samguk sidae wa Yong ui Seonmul

첫 번째 **왕국**, 고구려는 **북쪽**에 **위치**했습니다. **왕**은 **지혜로운 지도자**였으며, **국민**들은 그를 **존경**했습니다. 어느 날, 왕은 **꿈**을 꾸었습니다. 그 꿈에서 **용**이 **출현**했고, 용은 왕에게 **특별한** 선물을 주었습니다.

두 번째 왕국, 백제는 **남쪽**에 위치했습니다. 왕은 **공정**하고 **성실한** 지도자였으며, 국민들은 그를 사랑했습니다. 어느 날, 왕은 **같은** 꿈을 꾸었습니다. 그 꿈에서 용이 출현했고, 용은 왕에게 **동일한** 선물을 주었습니다.

세 번째 왕국, 신라는 **동쪽**에 위치했습니다. 왕은 **강력**하고 **용감한** 지도자였으며, 국민들은 그를 **두려워**했습니다. 어느 날, 왕은 같은 꿈을 꾸었습니다. 그 꿈에서 용이 출현했고, 용은 왕에게 동일한 선물을 주었습니다.

그 선물은 **각** 왕이 다른 왕국과 **통일**할 수 있도록 **도와주**는 **지도** 였습니다. **하지만** 세 왕국의 왕들은 서로 다른 **방식**으로 선물을 **사용**했습니다. 고구려의 왕은 선물을 **지혜롭게** 사용했고, 백제의 왕은 **공정하게** 사용했으며, 신라의 왕은 **강력하게** 사용했습니다.

결국, 세 왕국은 하나의 큰 나라, 삼국으로 **통합**되었습니다. 그리고 그 나라는 지금의 한국, 우리가 아는 그 나라가 되었습니다.

The Three Kingdoms Period and the Dragon's Gift

The first kingdom, Goguryeo, was located in the north. The king was a wise leader, and the people respected him. One day, the king had a dream. In that dream, a dragon appeared, and the dragon gave the king a special gift.

The second kingdom, Baekje, was located in the south. The king was a fair and diligent leader, and the people loved him. One day, the king had the same dream. In that dream, a dragon appeared, and the dragon gave the king the same gift.

The third kingdom, Silla, was located in the east. The king was a powerful and brave leader, and the people feared him. One day, the king had the same dream. In that dream, a dragon appeared, and the dragon gave the king the same gift.

The gift was a map that would help each king unify with the other kingdoms. However, the kings of the three kingdoms used the gift in different ways. The king of Goguryeo used the gift wisely, the king of Baekje used it fairly, and the king of Silla used it powerfully.

In the end, the three kingdoms became one large country, the Three Kingdoms. And that country became the Korea we know today.

Vocabulary

왕국 wang-guk - Kingdom

북쪽 buk jjok - North

위치 wi chi - Location

왕 Wang - King

지혜로운 ji hae ro woon - Wise

지도자 ji do ja - Leader

국민 gook min - Citizen

존경 jong kyung - Respect

꿈 - kkoom - Dream

용 yong - Dragon

출현 chool hyeon - Appear

특별한 teuk byeol han - Special

선물 seon mul - Gift

남쪽 nam jjok - South

성실한 seong sil han - Faithful

같은 gat eun - Same

동일한 dong il han - Same

동쪽 - dong jjok - East

강력하다 Ganglyeokhada - Powerful

용감하다 Yonggamhada - Brave

두려워하다 du ryeo wo ha da - To be scared

각 gak - Each

통일 tong il - Unify

도와 do wa - Help

지도 ji do - Map

하지만 ha ji man - However

방식 bang sik - Method

사용 sa yong - Use

공정하다 Gong jeong ha da - Fair

성실하다 Seong sil ha da – Diligent

Comprehension Questions

a.　　세 왕국의 왕들은 각각 어떤 꿈을 꾸었습니까? What dream did each of the kings of the three kingdoms have?

b.　　용이 선물한 것은 무엇이었습니까? What did the dragon gift?

c.　　세 왕국의 왕들은 어떻게 선물을 사용했습니까? How did the kings of the three kingdoms use the gift?

d.　　세 왕국은 어떻게 통합되었습니까? How did the three kingdoms unify?

Historical Notes

The Three Kingdoms Period marks the beginnings of Korea as we know it, as different tribes gathered together to form Kingdoms that dominated the land

고구려, 백제, 신라의 세 왕국
Goguryeo, Baekje, Silla-ui Se Wang-guk

고대 **시대**에 세 왕국이 있었습니다. 이왕국들은 고구려, 백제, 신라 왕국이었습니다. 이 세 왕국은 모두 강력하고 **강인**했지만, 각 왕국은 **독특한 성격**과 **문화**를 가지고 있었습니다. 고구려 왕국은 **군사적**으로 강력했으며, 백제 왕국은 **예술**과 문화에서 세계를 **선도**했고, 신라 왕국은 공정하고 **평화로운 사회**를 **추구**했습니다.

어느 날, 세 왕국의 왕들이 **모였습니다**. 그들은 자신들의 왕국이 얼마나 강력한지 서로 **과시하려고** 했습니다. 고구려의 왕은 자신의 **군대**의 힘을 **자랑**했고, 백제의 왕은 **화려한** 예술 작품을 **선보였고**, 신라의 왕은 평화롭고 공정한 사회를 자랑했습니다.

그러나 서로가 왕국의 힘을 **인정**하지 않았습니다. 그들은 **대회**를 열기로 **결정**했습니다. 각 왕국은 자신들의 힘과 능력을 **증명**하는 대회에서 **의미**있는 **공헌**을 했습니다. 고구려는 군대의 훈련과 **전술**을 보여주었고, 백제는 아름다운 예술 작품을 **전시**했고, 신라는 평화적인 **대화**와 **협상**을 위한 **회의**를 **개최**했습니다.

대회는 **몇일** 동안 계속되었고, 각 왕국은 자신의 **강점**을 보여주는 데 **최선**을 다했습니다. 그러나 결국, 그들은 자신들의 왕국이 가장 강력하다는 것을 증명할 수 없었습니다. 그들은 모두 자신의 왕국이 강력하고 독특하다는 것을 **깨달았습니다**.

이 **이야기**는 고구려, 백제, 신라의 세 왕국이 강력하고 독특하다는 것을 보여줍니다. 그들은 모두 강력하고 강인했지만, 그들 각각의 독특한 방식으로 특별했습니다. 이것은 우리가 자신의 힘과 능력을 인정하고 **서로**를 존중해야 함을 **상기**시켜줍니다.

The Three Kingdoms of Goguryeo, Baekje, and Silla

In the ancient times, there were three kingdoms. These were the kingdoms of Goguryeo, Baekje, and Silla. All three kingdoms were strong and resilient, but each kingdom had its unique character and culture. Goguryeo was militarily strong, Baekje led the world in arts and culture, and Silla pursued a fair and peaceful society.

One day, the kings of the three kingdoms gathered. They tried to show off how powerful their kingdoms were. The king of Goguryeo boasted of the strength of his army, the king of Baekje showed off splendid works of art, and the king of Silla bragged about a peaceful and just society.

However, they did not acknowledge each other's kingdom's power. They decided to hold a competition. Each kingdom made meaningful contributions in the competition to prove their strength and abilities. Goguryeo showed the training and tactics of its army, Baekje exhibited beautiful works of art, and Silla hosted a meeting for peaceful dialogue and negotiation.

The competition continued for several days, and each kingdom did their best to demonstrate their strengths. But in the end, they could not prove that their kingdom was the most powerful. They all realized that their kingdoms were powerful and unique.

This story shows that the three kingdoms of Goguryeo, Baekje, and Silla were strong and unique. They were all strong and resilient, but each was special in its unique way. This reminds us that we should acknowledge our strength and abilities and respect each other.

Vocabulary

시대 shi dae - Era

강인 - kang in - Strong

독특한 dok teuk han - Unique

성격 - seong gyeok - Personality

문화 mun hwa - Culture

군사적 gun sa juk - Military

예술 ye sool - Art

선도 seon do - Lead

평화 pyeong hwa - Peace

사회 sa hwae - Society

추구 choo goo - Pursue

모였습니다 mo yeot seub ni da - They gathered

과시하다 gwa shi ha da - To show off

군대 gun dae - Army

자랑 ja rang - Brag

화려한 hwa ryeo han - Fancy

선보이다 sun bo i da - To present

인정 in jeong - To acknowledge

대회 dae hwae - Competition

증명하다 jeung myeong ha da - To prove

의미 ui mi - Meaning

공헌 gong hun - Contribution

대화 dae hwa - Conversation

협상 hyeop sang - Compromise

회의 hwe yi - Meeting

개최 gae choi - Hold

며칠 myeot chil - Couple days

강점 kang jum - Strong point

최선 choi sun - Best effort

깨달았습니다 kkae dal aut seub ni da - Realized

이야기 yi ya gi - Story

서로 seo ro - Each other

상기 sang gi - Remind

공정하다 Gong jeong ha da: To be fair

Comprehension Questions:

a.   세 왕국의 왕들이 모인 이유는 무엇입니까? Why did the kings of the three kingdoms gather?

b.   왜 그들은 대회를 열었습니까? Why did they hold a competition?

c.   대회의 결과는 어떠했습니까? What was the result of the competition?

Historical Notes

The Three Kingdoms that held power over the country competed constantly in order to expand their own influence and domain

갈등과 연대, 그리고 문화 교류
Kaldeunggwa Yeondae Keurigo MunHwa Kyoryu

한 **전사**에게는 두 **아들**이 있었습니다. 모든 전사가 그렇듯이, 그는 그의 아들들에게 **건강**과 **힘**을 바랐습니다. 두 아들 모두 그의 **기대**를 **충족**시켰습니다. 첫째 아들은 **뛰어난** 전사가 되어, 그의 **부족**을 수많은 **전투**에서 **이끌**었습니다. 둘째 아들은 **탁월한 외교관**이 되어, 그의 부족을 다른 **지역**의 부족들과 **연결**시켜주었습니다.

어느 날, 전사는 첫째 아들에게 그의 꿈이 무엇인지 물었습니다. 첫째 아들은 그의 부족이 다른 부족들에게 두려움을 줄 수 있도록 힘을 원했습니다. 둘째 아들에게 **똑같은** 질문을 했습니다. 둘째 아들은 그의 부족이 다른 부족들과 평화롭게 **공존**할 수 있도록 **이해**를 원했습니다. 전사는 어느 아들의 꿈을 지지해야 할지 몰랐습니다.

그러다가 그는 아들 둘 중 누구의 꿈도 **선택**하지 않기로 **결정**했습니다. **대신**, 그는 두 아들에게 자신들의 꿈을 이루기 위해 서로 **협력**하도록 **교훈**을 줬습니다. 첫째 아들은 그의 힘을 사용해 부족을 **보호**하고, 둘째 아들은 그의 외교 능력을 사용해 부족의 **소통**을 **촉진**해야 했습니다.

그래서, 두 아들은 자신들의 능력을 **합치**고, 서로의 차이를 인정하면서 **공동**의 **목표**를 향해 나아갔습니다. 그들은 **갈등**과 **연대**, 그리고 **문화 교류**의 **중요성**을 알게 되었습니다. 그들의 이야기는 지금도 부족 사이에서 전해져 내려오며, 그들의 협력과 이해의 가치를 깨닫게 해줍니다.

Conflicts, Alliances, and Cultural Exchange

There was a warrior who had two sons. Like all warriors, he wished for his sons to be strong and healthy. Both sons exceeded his expectations. The first son became an outstanding warrior, leading his tribe in numerous battles. The second son became an excellent diplomat, connecting his tribe with other tribes in the region.

One day, the warrior asked the first son what his dream was. The first son wished for his tribe to instill fear in other tribes through its strength. He asked the same question to his second son. The second son wished for his tribe to coexist peacefully with other tribes through understanding. The warrior did not know which son's dream to support.

Then, he decided not to choose either son's dream. Instead, he taught his sons to cooperate with each other to achieve their dreams. The first son had to use his strength to protect the tribe, and the second son had to use his diplomatic skills to facilitate communication for the tribe.

Thus, the two sons combined their abilities and moved towards a common goal, acknowledging their differences. They learned about the importance of conflicts, alliances, and cultural exchange. Their story is still passed down among tribes, helping them realize the value of their cooperation and understanding.

Vocabulary

전사 jeonsa - Warrior

아들 adeul - Son

건강 gun kang - Health

힘 him - Strength

기대 ki dae - Expectation

충족 choong jok - Satisfy

뛰어난 twi eo nan - Exceptional

부족 bujok - Tribe

전투 jeon tu - Battle

이끌다 yi kkeul da - To lead

탁월한 tak wol han - Excellent

외교관 oegyogwan - Diplomat

지역 ji yeok - Region

연결 yeon gyeol - Connect

똑같은 ddok gat eun - Same

공존 gong jon - Coexistence

선택 seon taek - Choose

결정 gyeol jung - Decision

대신 dae shin - Instead

이해 ihae - Understanding

협력 hyeopryeok - Cooperation

교훈 kyo hoon - Lesson

보호 bo ho - Protect

소통 so tong - Communicate

촉진 chok jin - Promote

합쳐 hab chyeo - Combine

공동 gong dong - Mutual

목표 mok pyo - Goal

갈등 galdeung - conflict

연대 yeondae - Alliance

문화 교류 munhwa gyoryu - Cultural exchange

중요성 joong yo sung - Importance

Comprehension Questions

a.   전사는 왜 아들들에게 꿈을 물어봤습니까? Why did the warrior ask his sons about their dreams?

b.   첫째 아들의 꿈은 무엇이었습니까? What was the first son's dream?

c.   둘째 아들의 꿈은 무엇이었습니까? What was the second son's dream?

d.   왜 전사는 어느 아들의 꿈도 선택하지 않았습니까? Why did the warrior not choose either son's dream?

Historical Notes

Behind the scenes of the competition between the Three Kingdoms saw many different interactions that resulted in cultural exchange and separate alliances as well as conflicts. It is important to note that at this point, Korea is not unified under one "banner" and many differences between the kingdoms existed.

발해의 부상과 몰락
Balhaeui Busanggwa Mollak

한 때, **큰 땅**을 **지배**하던 발해 왕국이 있었습니다. 그들은 강력하고 **유능한** 지도자들의 지혜로 넓은 **영토**를 **장악**했습니다. 왕국은 **속성**과 문화의 **다양성**을 자랑했으며, 이는 그들의 뛰어난 외교 **능력**을 보여주었습니다. 그러나 왕국의 **성공**은 **영원히** 이어지지 않았습니다. 왕국의 힘은 시간이 지남에 따라 **약해졌**으며, 결국 왕국은 **몰락**했습니다. 발해 왕국의 몰락은 왕국의 지도자들이 자신들의 **권력**을 **유지**하는 데 어려움을 겪었음을 보여줍니다. 이는 왕국의 힘과 **영향력**이 얼마나 빠르게 사라질 수 있는지를 보여줍니다. 발해 왕국의 이야기는 그들이 어떻게 성공했는지, 그리고 그들이 어떻게 실패했는지를 보여줍니다. 이 이야기는 역사를 통해 우리가 배울 수 있는 중요한 교훈을 가지고 있습니다.

Rise and Fall of the Balhae Kingdom

There was once a kingdom of Balhae that ruled a vast land. They seized wide territories with the wisdom of their powerful and competent leaders. The kingdom boasted diversity in ethnicity and culture, showcasing their outstanding diplomatic skills. However, the success of the kingdom did not last forever. The strength of the kingdom weakened over time, and the kingdom eventually fell. The fall of the Balhae kingdom shows that the kingdom's leaders struggled to maintain their power. It shows how quickly the power and influence of a kingdom can disappear. The story of the Balhae kingdom shows how they succeeded and how they failed. This story holds important lessons we can learn through history.

Vocabulary

큰 keun - Large

땅 ddang - Land

지배 ji bae - Control

유능한 yu neung han - Capable

영토 yeong to - Territory

장악 jang ak - Hold

속성 sok sung - Property

다양성 da yang sung - Variety

능력 neung ryeok - Capability

성공 sung gong - Success

영원히 yeong won hi - Forever

약해져 yak hae jeo - To weaken

몰락 mol lak - Downfall

권력 kwol ryeok - Authority

유지 yu ji - Maintain

영향력 yeong hyang ryeok - Influence

Comprehension Questions

1. 발해 왕국은 어떻게 성공했습니까? How did the Balhae Kingdom succeed?

2. 왜 발해 왕국이 약해졌습니까? Why did the Balhae Kingdom weaken?

3. 발해 왕국의 몰락으로부터 어떤 교훈을 얻을 수 있습니까? What lessons can be learned from the fall of the Balhae Kingdom?

Historical Notes

The Balhae Kingdom is actually surrounded by controversy, as historians argue whether it belongs to Korean or Chinese history. As we are sticking to Korea, it is believed by some that Balhae is the successor state of the Goguryeo Kingdom. It lasted from the time period of 698-926.

통일 신라의 영웅

Tongil Silla-ui Yeongwoong

옛날 신라에는 국민들 사이에 **믿음**과 **희망**을 **불러**일으킨 한 **영웅**이 살았습니다. 이 영웅의 이름은 김유신이었으며, 그의 **지도력**과 **무예**로 신라는 세 왕국 중 하나가 되었습니다. 그는 통일 신라의 **창시자**이자 신라를 한 단계 업그레이드 시킨 **인물**로 **기억**됩니다.

김유신은 어릴 때부터 무예에 뛰어났으며, 그의 **용기**와 지혜로움으로 많은 전투에서 **승리**하였습니다. 그는 신라의 **장군**으로서 **국가**를 위해 몸 바쳤고, 그의 **전략**은 신라를 성공으로 이끌었습니다.

그는 신라의 대외 정책을 **책임**지며, 외국과의 **동맹**을 **구축**하였습니다. 이 동맹은 신라의 국력을 강화시키고, 신라가 다른 왕국들과 **대립**할 수 있게 하였습니다. 김유신의 **노력**으로 인해 신라는 힘을 얻었고, 그의 지도력 하에 **번영**하였습니다.

김유신은 또한, 국민들 사이에서도 존경과 사랑을 받았습니다. 그의 **의리**와 **충성**심은 국민들에게 **영감**을 주었으며, 그들이 그를 따르게 하였습니다. 김유신의 이러한 특성은 신라가 유일한 왕국이 될 수 있도록 도왔습니다.

김유신의 **기록**은 오늘날까지도 기억되고 있으며, 그의 **업적**은 한국 사람들에게 자랑스럽게 여겨집니다. 그는 통일 신라를 위한 **기반**을 마련한 영웅으로 기억됩니다.

The Hero of Unified Silla

In ancient Silla, lived a hero who kindled faith and hope among the people. This hero, named Kim Yu-sin, with his leadership and martial prowess, elevated Silla to be one of the Three Kingdoms. He is remembered as the founder of Unified Silla, the figure who upgraded Silla to a new level.

Kim Yu-sin excelled in martial arts from a young age and won many battles with his courage and wisdom. As a general of Silla, he dedicated himself to the state, and his strategies led Silla to success.

He was responsible for Silla's foreign policies and established alliances with foreign countries. These alliances strengthened Silla's national power and allowed it to compete with other kingdoms. Thanks to Kim Yu-sin's efforts, Silla gained strength and prospered under his leadership.

Kim Yu-sin also received respect and love among the citizens. His loyalty and sense of duty inspired the people, leading them to follow him. These characteristics of Kim Yu-sin helped Silla become the unique kingdom it was.

Kim Yu-sin's records are remembered to this day, and his achievements are a source of pride for Koreans. He is remembered as the hero who laid the foundation for Unified Silla.

Vocabulary

믿음 mi deum - Faith

희망 hee mang - Hope

불러 bool leo - Call

영웅 yeong woong - Hero

지도력 ji do ryeok - Leadership

무예 mu ye - Martial Arts

창시자 chang si ja - Founder

인물 in mul - Character

기억 ki eok - Memory

용기 yong gi - Courage

승리 seung ri - Victory

장군 jang goon - General

국가 guk ga - Nation

전략 jeon ryak - Strategy

책임 chaek im - Responsibility

동맹 dong maeng - Alliance

구축 gu chook - Build

대립 dae rip - Opposition

노력 no ryeok - Effort

번영 beon yeong - Prosperity

의리/충성심 - eu ri / choong sung shim - Loyalty

영감 yeong gam - Inspiration

기록 gi rok - Record

업적 eop juk - Achievements

기반 ki ban - Base

Comprehension Questions

a.   김유신은 어떤 영웅으로 기억되고 있습니까? How is Kim Yu-sin remembered as a hero?

b.   김유신은 신라에 어떤 영향을 미쳤습니까? What impact did Kim Yu-sin have on Silla?

c.   김유신의 전략은 어떻게 신라를 강화시켰습니까? How did Kim Yu-sin's strategies strengthen Silla?

Historical Notes

The unification of the three kingdoms finally occurred to begin the Unified Silla dynasty (668-935). It began with the fall of Baekje to Silla in 668 and lasted 267 years, falling to Goryeo in 935.

고려시대의 창립

Goryeo Shidae-ui Changlip

한때 **장엄한** 왕이 살았습니다. 그는 왕과 국민들 사이에 평화와 **조화**를 끌어올 수 있는 **방법**을 항상 **고민**하였습니다. 그 왕은 **왕좌**에 오르기 전에 용감한 전사였으며, 그의 이름은 왕건이었습니다. 그는 고려를 **창립**하였고, 그는 이렇게 하여 그의 국가가 한 편의 **아름다운 시**와 같이 번영하고 평화로워지기를 바랬습니다.

그러나 왕건의 나라는 아직 그의 꿈처럼 평화롭지 않았습니다. 그는 왕국을 두고 싸우는 다른 왕들과 계속 싸워야 했습니다. 왕건은 자신의 국가를 보호하고, 평화와 번영을 위해 싸울 **결심**을 하였습니다. 그래서 그는 자신의 전사들을 불러 모아, 그들에게 이렇게 말했습니다. "우리는 우리의 국가를 **지키기** 위해 싸울 것이다. 우리는 우리의 국가를 위해 싸울 것이다. 우리는 우리의 국민들을 위해 싸울 것이다."

그의 전사들은 왕건의 말에 **감동**하여, 그들은 왕건을 따라 싸우기로 결심했습니다. 그들은 왕건의 지도 하에 싸워, **결국** 그들은 왕국을 위한 평화와 조화를 이루어냈습니다. 그리하여, 고려는 한 편의 아름다운 시와 같이 번영하고 평화로워졌습니다. 왕건은 그의 국민들에게 사랑받는 왕이 되었고, 그의 왕국은 **오랫동안** 평화롭게 **지속**되었습니다.

Goryeo Dynasty (918-1392)

ounding of the Goryeo Dynasty

Once upon a time, there lived a magnificent king who constantly sought ways to bring peace and harmony between the king and the people. He was a brave warrior before he ascended the throne, and his name was Wang Geon. He founded Goryeo and wished for his country to flourish and be peaceful like a beautiful poem.

However, Wang Geon's country was not yet peaceful as he dreamed. He had to continue fighting with other kings fighting for the kingdom. Wang Geon decided to fight to protect his country and for peace and prosperity. So, he called his warriors and told them, "We will fight to protect our country. We will fight for our country. We will fight for our people."

Moved by Wang Geon's words, his warriors decided to fight with him. They fought under Wang Geon's leadership and eventually achieved peace and harmony for the kingdom. Thus, Goryeo flourished and became peaceful like a beautiful poem. Wang Geon became a king loved by his people, and his kingdom continued in peace for a long time.

Vocabulary

장엄한 jang um han - Sublime

조화 jo hwa - Harmony

방법 bang bup - Method

고민 go min - To think about/ worry

왕좌 wang jwa - Throne

창립 chang lip - Found (as in Founder)

아름다운 - a reum da woon - Beautiful

시 shi - Poem

결심 kyeol shim - Determine with conviction

지키기 ji ki gi - To protect

감동 gam dong - Moved

결국 kyeol guk - In the end

오랫동안 o raet dong an - For a long time

지속 ji sok – Continue

Comprehension Questions:

a.   왕건이 왕이 되기 전에는 어떤 사람이었나요? Who was Wang Geon before becoming a king?

b.   왕건이 자신의 국가를 위해 싸운 이유는 무엇인가요? Why did Wang Geon fight for his country?

c.   왕건의 왕국이 어떻게 변화하였나요? How did Wang Geon's kingdom change?

Historical Notes

Wang Geon actually became the King through a coup, in which Gungye was overthrown by four of his top generals. Wang Geon at the time had proven himself as a capable commander and was popular among the people He opposed the coup at first, but agreed later, taking the throne and renaming the kingdom to Goryeo and thus beginning the long dynasty.

왕 태조와 고려의 건설
Wang Taejo-wa Goryeo-ui Geonseol

고려를 세운 왕 태조는 왕으로서의 **자격**을 증명하기 위해 많은 **고난**을 겪었습니다. 그는 **장사꾼**의 아들로 태어나 **군인**이 되었고, 그 후에는 왕이 되었습니다. 그는 **공정함**과 **지혜**로움으로 **통치**하였고, 그의 지배는 평화로웠습니다. 그는 **세계**를 통합하고 국민들에게 **평등**과 평화를 **선사**하기 위해 노력하였습니다. 그는 국민들이 그를 사랑하며 존경하도록 만들었습니다. 그의 아들들은 그를 따르고, 그의 **가르침**을 따랐습니다. 그는 모든 것을 바치며, 그의 나라를 위해 최선을 다하였습니다. 그의 통치 기간 동안 그는 고려를 강력한 국가로 만들었습니다. 그는 왕으로서의 **책임**을 다하며, 그의 **민족** 으로서 존경받았습니다.

King Taejo, who established Goryeo, faced many hardships to prove his qualifications as a king. He was born a a merchant's son, became a soldier, and then became a king. He ruled with fairness and wisdom, and his reign was peaceful. He strived to unite the world and bring equality and peace to his people. He made his people love and respect him. His sons followed him, and they followed his teachings. He gave his all, and he did his best for his country. During his reign, he made Goryeo a powerful nation. He fulfilled his responsibilities as a king, and he was respected by his people.

Vocabulary

자격 ja gyeok - the right

고난 go nan - Hardship

장사꾼 jang sa kkun - Merchant

군인 gun-in - Soldier

공정함 gong jeong ham - Fairness

지혜 ji-hye Wisdom

통치 tong chi Rule

세계 se gye - World

평등 pyeong deung - Equality

선사 seon sa - Offering

가르침 ga reu chim - Teaching

책임 chaeg-im - Responsibility

민족 minjok – People

Comprehension Questions

1. 왕 태조는 어떤 배경으로 태어났습니까? What background was King Taejo born into?

2. 왕 태조는 어떻게 통치하였습니까? How did King Taejo rule?

3. 왕 태조의 주요 성취는 무엇이었습니까? What were the major accomplishments of King Taejo?

4. 왕 태조는 누구를 따랐습니까? Who did King Taejo follow?

Historical Notes

For those of you who have been following the historical notes, you are probably very confused right? How could there be two founders of Goryeo? In fact, there isn't. The full name of the founder is Taejo Wang Geon and the story above grants a bit of insight into his humble beginnings. Born into a merchant clan, King Taejo Wang Geon followed his father to serve under Gungye, becoming recognized and rising the ranks.

고려 왕자의 약속

Goryeo Wangjaeui Yaksok

고려 왕자는 아버지의 왕좌를 **계승**하려고 했습니다. 그러나 **형제**들은 그의 **계획**에 **반대**했습니다. 고려 왕자는 통치를 위해 지혜와 용기가 필요하다는 것을 알았습니다. 그는 문화적으로 번영하는 나라를 만들기 위해 **학문**을 촉진하고 예술을 **장려**하려고 노력했습니다. 그는 고려 시대의 **유명한 도예가**에게 아름다운 **청자**를 만들어 나라를 **장식**하라고 **요청**했습니다. 도예가는 왕자의 요청을 기꺼이 받아들였습니다. 그는 왕자의 **명령**을 따라 가장 아름다운 청자를 만들었습니다. 그 결과, 고려 청자는 전 세계에서 가장 아름다운 것으로 알려졌습니다. 왕자는 이를 통해 형제들에게 자신의 리더십을 **입증**했습니다. 그는 **나라**를 위해 가장 좋은 것을 원하는 사람이 **진정한** 왕이라는 것을 보여주었습니다.

The Promise of the Goryeo Prince

A prince of Goryeo was set to inherit his father's throne. However, his brothers opposed his plans. The Goryeo prince knew that wisdom and courage were needed to rule. He endeavored to promote scholarship and encourage the arts to create a culturally flourishing nation. He requested a famous potter from the Goryeo period to create beautiful celadon to decorate the country. The potter gladly accepted the prince's request. Following the prince's command, he created the most beautiful celadon. As a result, Goryeo celadon became known as the most beautiful in the world. The prince proved his leadership through this. He showed that the true king is the one who wants the best for the country.

Vocabulary

계승 gye seong - Succession

형제 hyeongje - Brothers

계획 gye hwaek - Plan

반대 ban dae - Oppose

학문 hak mun - Scholarship

장려 jang ryeo - Encourage

유명한 yu myeong han - Famous

도예가 do ye ga - Ppotter

청자 cheong ja - Celadon

장식 jang sik - Decoration

요청 yo cheong - Request

명령 myeong nyeong - Command

입증 ip jeung - Prove

나라 nara - Country

진정한 jin jeong han - True

Comprehension Questions

a.   왕자는 왕좌를 얻기 위해 어떤 노력을 했습니까? What efforts did the prince make to gain the throne?

b.   왕자는 왜 도예가에게 청자를 만들라고 요청했습니까? Why did the prince request the potter to make celadon?

c.   왕자의 리더십은 어떻게 입증되었습니까? How was the prince's leadership proven?

Historical Notes

During the Goryeo Dynasty, art and culture flourished, particularly celadon pottery. The celadon pottery from this era is highly regarded as among the finest pottery pieces produced anywhere and provides a look into the creative and dynamic aesthetics of the time.

예술가와 과학자의 이야기
Yesulgawa Gwahakja-ui Yiyagi

한때, **예술가**와 **과학자**가 있었습니다. 이들은 서로를 **경쟁자**로 생각하였으며, 자신이 더 중요하다고 주장하였습니다. 예술가는 자신의 **그림**이 사람들을 **위로**하고, **상상력**을 **자극**한다고 말하였습니다. **반면**, 과학자는 자신의 **발견**이 세상을 **이해**하고, **삶의 질**을 **향상**시킨다고 주장하였습니다. 이들의 **논쟁**은 왕에게 **도달**하였고, 왕은 이들에게 공평하게 **판단**하겠다고 약속하였습니다. 왕은 예술가에게 새로운 그림을 그리라고 요청하였고, 그는 아름다운 **풍경**을 그렸습니다. 그리고 왕은 과학자에게 새로운 발견을 하라고 요청하였고, 그는 어떻게 비가 **형성**되는지를 발견하였습니다. 왕은 이들의 **성과**를 보고, 두 분야가 모두 중요하다는 것을 깨달았습니다. 그는 예술가와 과학자에게 **역량**을 합쳐 더 큰 것을 만들어 내라고 **권유**하였습니다. 그 결과, 예술가는 과학자의 발견을 **바탕**으로 한 그림을 그려냈고, 과학자는 예술가의 그림에서 영감을 받아 새로운 **이론**을 제시하였습니다.

The Story of the Artist and the Scientist

Once upon a time, there was an artist and a scientist. They considered each other as competitors, each claiming they were more important. The artist argued that his paintings comfort people and stimulate their imagination. The scientist, on the other hand, insisted that his discoveries help understand the world and improve the quality of life. Their dispute reached the king, who promised to judge them fairly. The king asked the artist to paint new picture, and he painted a beautiful landscape. The king then asked the scientist to make a new discovery, and he found out how rain is formed. Seeing their achievements, the king realized the importance of both fields. He encouraged the artist and the scientist to combine their talents to create something greater. As a result, the artist painted a picture based on the scientist's discovery and the scientist proposed a new theory inspired by the artist painting.

Vocabulary

예술가 yesul ga - Artist

과학자 gwa hak ja - Scientist

경쟁자 gyeong jaeng ja - Competitor

그림 geu rim - Painting

위로 wi ro - Comfort

상상력 sang sang ryeok - Imagination

자극 ja geuk - Stimulate

반면 ban myeon - On the other hand

발견 balgyeon a discovery

삶의 질 salm ui jir - Quality of life

항상 hang sang - Always

논쟁 non jaeng - Argument

도달 do dal - Arrive

판단 pan dan - Judgement

풍경 poong kyung - View/Sight

형성 hyeong sung - Formation

성과 seong gwa - Result

역량 yeok ryang - Ability

권유 kwon yoo - Advice

바탕 ba tang - Background

이론 yi ron - Theory

Comprehension Questions

왕은 왜 예술가와 과학자에게 공평하게 판단하겠다고 약속하였습니까? Why did the king promise to judge the artist and the scientist fairly?

예술가와 과학자는 어떤 성과를 이루었습니까? What achievements did the artist and the scientist make?

왕의 제안은 무엇이었습니까? What was the king's suggestion?

Historical Notes

The Goryeo time period saw immense technological and artistic advancements. One such example is the invention of metal movable type printing in 1234, which greatly increased printing efficiency and led to a rise in literacy in general.

부처님의 가르침과 왕의 결정: 불교의 채택

Bucheonim-ui Gareuchim-gwa Wang-ui Gyeoljeong: Bulgyo-ui Chae-tak

한 때, 고구려의 왕 고가가 있었습니다. 그는 고구려의 사람들이 평화롭고 행복하게 살 수 있도록 원했습니다. 어느 날, 왕은 **부처님**의 가르침을 들었습니다. 그의 가르침은 평화, 사랑, 그리고 **자비에** 관한 것이었습니다. 왕은 이를 우리의 국가에 **적용**하고 싶었습니다.

그래서 왕은 명령을 내렸습니다. 그는 **불교**를 **공식적**으로 **국가 종교**로 **선포**하였습니다. 이는 그의 왕국에서는 전례 없는 사건이었습니다. 그러나 사람들은 왕의 결정을 존중하였습니다. 그들은 왕이 그들의 행복을 위해 결정을 내렸을 것이라 믿었습니다.

그래서 사람들은 불교를 배우기 시작했습니다. 그들은 부처님의 가르침을 따르기 시작했습니다. 사람들은 서로를 사랑하고 존중하며, 평화를 추구하기 시작했습니다. 그들은 이것이 그들의 삶을 **개선**하는 길임을 깨달았습니다.

그러나 불교를 받아들이지 않는 사람들도 있었습니다. 그들은 그들의 **전통적인 신앙**을 **보존**하고 싶었습니다. 그들은 왕에게 자신들의 신앙을 **준수**하게 해달라고 요청했습니다.

왕은 이를 이해했습니다. 그는 자신의 국민들이 자신들의 신앙을 **자유롭게** 표현하도록 **허용**했습니다. 그는 이를 통해 국민들이 행복하고 평화롭게 살 수 있도록 했습니다.

이와 같이, 불교는 고구려에서 국가 종교로 **설립**되었습니다. 그러나 그것은 사람들이 자신의 신앙을 자유롭게 선택하도록 허용하는 왕의 지혜로 인해 **가능**했습니다. 이 사건은 한국의 **역사**에서 중요한 순간으로 기억되었습니다.

The Teachings of Buddha and the King's Decision: Adoption of Buddhism

Once upon a time, there was a king of Goguryeo named King Goga. He wanted the people of Goguryeo to live in peace and happiness. One day, the king heard about the teachings of Buddha. His teachings were about peace, love, and mercy. The king wanted to apply this to our nation.

So the king issued a decree. He proclaimed Buddhism as the official state religion. This was an unprecedented event in his kingdom. But the people respected the king's decision. They believed that the king made the decision for their happiness.

So the people began to learn Buddhism. They began to follow the teachings of Buddha. People began to love and respect each other, and pursue peace. They realized that this was the way to improve their lives.

However, there were people who did not accept Buddhism. They wanted to preserve their traditional beliefs. They asked the king to allow them to adhere to their faith.

The king understood this. He allowed his people to freely express their faith. He made it possible for his people to live happily and peacefully.

In this way, Buddhism became established as the state religion in Goguryeo. But it was possible because of the king's wisdom, which allowed people to freely choose their faith. This event is remembered as an important moment in Korean history.

Vocabulary

부처님 bu cheo nim - Buddha

자비 ja bi - Mercy

관한 gwan han - Related to

적용 jeok yong - Utilize

불교 bul gyo - Buddhism

공식적 gong sik juk - Officially

국가 종교 guk ga jong gyo - State religion

선포 seon po - Proclaim

개선 gye sun - Improve

전통적인 jeon tong jeok in - Traditional

신앙 shin ang - Faith

보존 bo jon - Preserve

준수 jun su - Observe

허용 heo yong - Allow

설립 seol lip - Establish

가능 ga neung - Possible

역사 yeok sa - History

Comprehension Questions

a.   왕은 왜 부처님의 가르침을 우리의 국가에 적용하고 싶었나요? Why did the king want to apply the teachings of Buddha to our nation?

b.   사람들은 왜 왕의 결정을 존중했나요? Why did people respect the king's decision?

c.   왕은 왜 사람들이 자신들의 신앙을 자유롭게 표현하도록 허용했나요? Why did the king allow people to freely express their faith?

Historical Notes

The religious fervor during the Goryeo Dynasty was huge. There were many Buddhist temples and literature built and created during this period and many prominent families were encouraged to become monks. One of the most famous works created during this time is Korea's 32nd National Treasure, The Tripitaka Koreana, which is a collection of Buddhist scriptures carved onto over 80,000 wooden blocks.

몽골의 침략과 고려의 저항
Mongol-ui Chimrakgwa Goryeo-ui Jeohang

한 때, 고려라는 아름다운 나라가 있었습니다. 이 나라는 아름다운 **산과 강**, 그리고 **맑은 하늘**로 유명했습니다. 그러나 어느 날, 몽골이라는 강력한 **적**이 나타났습니다. 이들은 고려의 **풍요로운** 땅을 **탐내**어 **침략**하려 했습니다. 그러나 고려의 왕은 그의 나라를 보호하기 위해 용감하게 싸웠습니다. 왕은 전사들에게 용기를 북돋우며, 그들에게 나라를 지키는 것이 얼마나 중요한지를 **강조**했습니다. 전사들은 왕의 말을 듣고, 적을 **물리치기** 위해 싸웠습니다. 그들은 자신의 나라와 **가족을** 위해 목숨을 걸었습니다. 결국, 고려는 몽골의 침략을 **막아**냈고, 평화가 다시 찾아왔습니다.

Mongol invasions and Goryeo's resistance

Once upon a time, there was a beautiful country called Goryeo. This country was known for its beautiful mountains, rivers, and clear skies. However, one day, a powerful enemy called the Mongols appeared. They coveted the fertile lands of Goryeo and tried to invade. But the king of Goryeo fought bravely to protect his country. The king encouraged his warriors, emphasizing how important it was to protect their country. The warriors heard the king's words and fought to repel the enemy. They risked their lives for their country and their families. In the end, Goryeo fended off the Mongol invasion, and peace returned.

Vocabulary

산 san - Mountain

강 kang - River

맑은 malk eun - Clear

하늘 ha neul - Sky

적 jeok - Enemy

풍요로운 poong yo ro woon - Rich

탐내 tam nae - To covet

침략 chim ryak - To invade

강조 kang jo - Enforce

물리쳐 mul li chyeo - To defeat

가족 ga jok - Family

막아 mak a - To block

Comprehension Questions

a.　　몽골은 왜 고려를 침략하려 했습니까? Why did the Mongols try to invade Goryeo?

. 고려의 왕은 어떻게 그의 나라를 보호하려 했습니까? How did the king of Goryeo try to protect his country?

. 고려의 전사들은 왕의 말을 어떻게 받아들였습니까? How did the warriors of Goryeo react to the king's words?

Historical Notes

The Mongol invasion was a rough time for Goryeo that started because a Mongol envoy was killed after a trip to Goryeo in which tribute was demanded. It is surmised that while Goryeo refused to pay tribute, the envoy was actually killed by bandits on the way back. The envoy's death gave the Mongols an excuse to invade Goryeo on a large scale, as Goryeo had been fiercely resisting conquest attempts, determined to keep its independence no matter what.

고려 시대의 내부 분쟁과 그 끝

Goryeo Sidae-ui Naebu Bunjaenggwa Geu Kkeut

고려 시대에는 **임금**과 **고위 관리들** 사이에 권력 **다툼**이 있었습니다. 임금이 **본인**의 권력을 강화하려 했지만, 고위 관리들은 자신들의 **지위**를 지키기 위해 **저항**했습니다. 이러한 **내부 분쟁**은 국가를 약화시켰고, **외부**의 **위협**은 더욱 **심각**해졌습니다. 결국, 이러한 분쟁과 외부의 위협이 합쳐져 고려 시대의 마지막을 알렸습니다. **왕권**이 약화되고, 고위 관리들의 권력 다툼이 **격화**되자, 고려는 **붕괴 위기**에 처했습니다. 이는 결국 고려의 몰락을 가져왔으며, 새로운 조선 시대의 시작을 알렸습니다.

Internal Strife and the End of the Goryeo Dynasty

During the Goryeo Dynasty, there were power struggles between the king and high-ranking officials. The king tried to strengthen his power, but the high-ranking officials resisted to protect their position. This internal strife weakened the nation, and external threats became more serious. Eventually, these conflicts and external threats signaled the end of the Goryeo Dynasty. As the royal power weakened and the power struggle among high-ranking officials intensified, Goryeo was on the verge of collapse. This ultimately led to the fall of Goryeo and marked the beginning of a new Joseon era.

Vocabulary

임금 im geum - King

고위 관리들 go wi gwan li deul - High ranking officials

다툼 da toom - A struggle/fight

본인 bon in - Self

지위 ji wi - Status

저항 jeo hang - Resist

내부 nae bu - Internal

분쟁 boon jaeng - Dispute

외부 wae boo - Foreign

위협 wi hyeob - Threat

심각 sim gak - Serious

왕권 wang gwon - Royal Power

격화 gyeok hwa - exacerbate

붕괴 boong gwe - Collapse

위기 wi gi - Crisis

Comprehension Questions

a.   왜 임금과 고위 관리들 사이에 권력 다툼이 일어났습니까? Why was there a power struggle betwee the king and high-ranking officials?

b.   이 내부 분쟁이 고려에 어떤 영향을 미쳤습니까? What impact did this internal strife have o Goryeo?

c.   고려 시대의 끝을 알린 것은 무엇이었습니까? What signaled the end of the Goryeo Dynasty?

Historical Notes

Following the Mongol's invasion, Goryeo was under the influence of Mongol for a long time until the Mong Yuan began to collapse in the mid 14th century. Goryeo took this chance to fight to remove Mongolian influence and reform the government. The eventual downfall of Goryeo was mostly due to internal power struggles amids foreign threats.

고려의 마지막 왕과 황제의 눈물

Goryeo-ui Majimak Wanggwa Hwangjae-ui Noonmool

고려의 마지막 왕, 왕건,은 그의 왕국이 점점 약해지는 것을 보며 가슴이 아팠습니다. 그는 그의 왕국이 멍에에서 벗어나기를 원했습니다. 그러나 그의 왕국은 중국의 원나라에 의해 굴복하고 있었습니다. 왕건은 원나라의 황제에게 그의 왕국을 떠나게 해 달라고 기도했습니다. 그러나 황제는 그의 요청을 거부했습니다. 황제는 고려를 자신의 제국의 일부로 보았습니다. 왕건은 점점 절망감에 빠졌습니다. 그는 마침내 그의 왕국을 위해 전쟁을 시작하기로 결심했습니다. 어렵게 싸워서 조금씩 벗어나기 시작했습니다.

Goryeo's Last King and the Emperor's Tears

The last king of Goryeo, King Gongmin, was heartbroken to see his kingdom weakening. He wished for his kingdom to break free from Mongol Yuan. However, his kingdom was succumbing to the Mongol Empire of China. Gongmin prayed to the emperor of Yuan to let his kingdom go. However, the emperor refused his request. The emperor saw Goryeo as part of his empire. Gongmin fell into despair. He finally decided to start a war for his kingdom. He fought hard and began to escape little by little.

Vocabulary

Comprehension Questions

a.   왕건은 왜 황제에게 기도했습니까? Why did Gongmin pray to the emperor?

b.   황제는 왕건의 요청을 왜 거절했습니까? Why did the emperor refuse Gongmin's request?

c.   왕건이 전쟁을 시작하기로 결정한 이유는 무엇입니까? Why did Gongmin decide to start a war?

Historical Notes

King Gongmin was the last king of Goryeo, who had actually been forced into marriage to a Mongol princess. With the weakening of Mongol Yuan, Gongmin was able to remove pro-Mongol officials from their positions in the Goryeo court and worked towards reform. He fought to push back foreign influences and was successful. His biggest enemies were actually the deeply entrenched bureaucracy that did not want to escape from China and these issues would eventually lead to his demise and the end of Goryeo.

창립자와 그의 두 아들들
Changlipjawa geu-ui- du adeuldeul

한 **창립자**와 두 아들이 있었습니다. 그는 그의 아들들을 **매우** 사랑했습니다. 첫째 아들은 **대장장**이로, 둘째 아들은 농부였습니다. 어느 날, 창립자는 첫째 아들에게 무엇을 원하는지 물었습니다. 그는 **신**에게 그의 **소원**을 위해 기도하겠다고 말했습니다. 첫째 아들은 그의 대장간에서 불이 항상 타오르기를 원했습니다. 그는 둘째 아들에게 동일한 질문을 **던졌**습니다. 그는 그의 **농장**에서 **비**가 **자주** 내리기를 원했습니다. 창립자는 어느 소원을 위해 기도해야 할지 몰랐습니다.

Joseon Dynasty (1392-1910)

The Founder and His Two Sons

There was a founder who had two sons. He loved his sons very much. The first son was a blacksmith, and the second son was a farmer. One day, the founder asked the first son what he wanted. He said he would pray to God for his wish. The first son wished for the fire in his forge to always burn. He asked the same question to his second son. He wished for frequent rain on his farm. The founder did not know which wish to pray for.

Vocabulary

창립자 chang lip ja - Founder

매우 mae woo - Very much

대장장 - dae jang jang - Blacksmith

신 shin - God

소원 so won - Wish

던져 deon jyeo - To throw

농장 nong jang - Farm

비 bi - Rain

자주 ja ju - Often

Comprehension Questions

a.   창립자는 왜 아들들에게 소원을 물어봤습니까? Why did the founder ask his sons for their wishes?

b.   첫째 아들의 소원은 무엇이었습니까? What was the first son's wish?

c.   둘째 아들의 소원은 무엇이었습니까? What was the second son's wish?

d.   왜 창립자는 어떤 소원을 위해 기도해야 할지 몰랐습니까? Why didn't the founder know which wish to pray for?

Historical Notes

Yi Seong Gye was the name of one who overthrew the Goryeo Dynasty to found the Joseon Dynasty. He ascended to the throne in 1392 and abdicated the throne six years later due to conflicts between his sons.

태조 왕과 유교의 성립
Taejo Wanggwa Yugyo-ui Seongnip

태조 왕이 있었습니다. 그는 조선을 세우고 **유교**를 **국가 이념**으로 세웠습니다. 그의 첫 번째 **임무**는 왕국의 **기초**를 다지는 것이었습니다. 그는 **지식인**들을 모아 유교를 **기반**으로 한 새로운 **교육 체제**를 만들었습니다. 그 다음에, 그는 조선의 **법률 체계**를 개혁하고, 새로운 **사회 질서**를 세웠습니다. 그는 공정하고 공평한 사회를 만들기 위해 노력했습니다. 그의 통치는 평화로웠고, 국가는 번영했습니다 그러나, 그의 통치는 많은 **도전**과 **고비**를 겪었습니다. 유교는 그의 왕국에 큰 **영향**을 미쳤고, 그의 통치는 한반도에 깊은 영향을 끼쳤습니다.

King Taejo and the Establishment of Confucianism

There was a king named Taejo. He established Joseon and set up Confucianism as the national ideology. His first task was to lay the foundation of his kingdom. He gathered intellectuals and created a new educational system based on Confucianism. Next, he reformed the legal system of Joseon and established a new social order. He strived to build a fair and just society. His reign was peaceful, and the country prospered. However, his reign faced many challenges and crises. Confucianism greatly influenced his kingdom, and his reign had a profound impact on the Korean Peninsula.

Vocabulary

유교 yu gyo - Confucianism

국가 이념 gukga inyeom - National ideology

임무 im mu - Duty

기초 ki cho - Basics

지식인 Ji sik in - Intellectual

기반 ki ban - Base

교육 체제 kyo yoke che je - School system

법률 체계 Beop ryul che gye - Legal system

사회 질서 sa hwae jil seo - Social order

도전 do jeon - Challenge

고비 go bi - Crisis

영향 yeong hyang - Influence

Comprehension Questions

a. 왕이 왕국의 기초를 다지기 위해 어떤 것을 만들었습니까? What did the king create to lay the foundation of his kingdom?

b. 왕이 어떤 신사회 질서를 세웠습니까? What new social order did the king establish?

c. 유교는 왕국에 어떤 영향을 미쳤습니까? What influence did Confucianism have on the kingdom?

Historical Notes

For those who are confused, the name of "Taejo" is given to the first king of a new dynasty. That is why the founder, of Joseon, Yi Seong Gye, is also called King Taejo. King Taejo's reign was marked by the establishment of Confucianism as the state ideology. His commitment to this philosophy shaped the social, legal, and educational structures of Joseon.

조선왕조의 영광
Joseonwangjo-ui Yeong-gwang

조선시대의 한 왕이 있었습니다. 그의 이름은 세종대왕이었고, 그는 자신의 나라를 위해 아주 열심히 일했습니다. 그는 **학문**과 과학에 큰 **관심**을 가지고 있었고, 그의 시대에 많은 **발전**이 일어났습니다. 그러나 그의 가장 큰 업적 중 하나는 한글을 창제한 것이었습니다.

그는 국민들이 **읽고** 쓸 수 있는 **문자**를 만들고 싶었습니다. 그 때까지, **한자**가 주로 사용되었지만, 이것은 일반 국민들에게는 너무 어렵고 **복잡**했습니다. 세종대왕은 이 문제를 **해결**하기 위해 한글을 창제하였습니다.

한글은 **쉽게** 배울 수 있는 문자였습니다. 각 글자는 **입**의 모양과 같아서, 사람들은 빠르게 배우고 쓸 수 있었습니다. 세종대왕의 이런 노력 덕분에 많은 사람들이 읽고 쓸 수 있게 되었습니다.

그러나 세종대왕의 **행동**은 모든 사람들이 좋아한 것은 아니었습니다. 일부 **양반**들은 그의 행동이 그들의 지위를 위협하고 있다고 생각했습니다. 그래서 그들은 세종대왕에게 반대하였습니다.

세종대왕은 이러한 반대에도 불구하고 국민들을 위해 노력하였습니다. 그는 한글을 **보급**하려고 노력하였고, 결국 그의 노력은 성공하였습니다. 오늘날, 한글은 한국의 공식 언어이며, 전 세계의 많은 사람들이 한글을 배우고 있습니다.

세종대왕의 이야기는 그의 **헌신**과 가치를 보여줍니다. 그는 자신의 꿈을 이루기 위해 노력하였고, 그의 노력은 결국 성공하였습니다. 그는 조선시대의 **영광**을 보여주는 한 사람이었습니다.

세종대왕의 이야기는 우리에게 많은 것을 가르쳐줍니다. 우리는 그의 헌신과 노력을 보며, 우리 자신의 **목표**를 **성취**하기 위해 노력해야 함을 배울 수 있습니다. 그의 이야기는 조선시대의 중요한 부분이며, 그의 업적은 오늘날도 계속되고 있습니다.

세종대왕의 이야기는 조선왕조의 영광을 보여줍니다. 그는 그의 시대에 큰 **변화**를 가져왔고, 그의 업적은 오늘날도 계속되고 있습니다. 그의 이야기는 우리에게 그의 가치와 노력을 보여주며, 우리 모두에게 중요한 교훈을 가르쳐줍니다.

세종대왕은 그의 업적을 통해 우리 모두에게 가치와 헌신을 보여줍니다. 그의 이야기는 조선왕조의 영광을 보여주며, 그의 업적은 오늘날도 계속되고 있습니다. 그의 이야기를 통해, 우리는 그의 가치와 노력을 배울 수 있습니다.

The Glory of the Joseon Dynasty

There was a king in the Joseon Dynasty. His name was King Sejong, and he worked very hard for his country. He had a great interest in academia and science, and there was much progress in his time. However, one of his greatest achievements was the creation of Hangul.

He wanted to create a script that the people could read and write. Up until then, Chinese characters were mainly used, but they were too difficult and complicated for the common people. King Sejong created Hangul to solve this problem.

Hangul was an easy-to-learn script. Each character resembled the shape of the mouth, so people could quickly learn and write. Thanks to King Sejong's efforts, many people became literate.

However, not everyone liked King Sejong's actions. Some yangbans (aristocrats) thought his actions threatened their status. Therefore, they opposed King Sejong.

Despite this opposition, King Sejong worked for the people. He made efforts to spread Hangul, and eventually, his efforts were successful. Today, Hangul is the official language of Korea, and many people around the world are learning Hangul.

King Sejong's story shows his dedication and values. He worked to achieve his dream, and his efforts were ultimately successful. He was one person who represented the glory of the Joseon Dynasty.

King Sejong's story teaches us a lot. We can learn from his dedication and effort and strive to achieve our own goals. His story is an important part of the Joseon Dynasty, and his achievements continue today.

King Sejong's story demonstrates the glory of the Joseon Dynasty. He brought about great changes in his time, and his achievements continue today. His story shows us his values and efforts, providing important lessons for all of us.

King Sejong shows us values and dedication through his achievements. His story demonstrates the glory of the Joseon Dynasty, and his achievements continue today. Through his story, we can learn about his values and efforts.

Vocabulary

학문 hak mun - Scholarship

관심 kwan shim - Interest

발전 bal jeon - Development

읽고 ilk go - Read

문자 mun ja - Text

한자 han ja - Chinese Characters

복잡 bok jab - Complicated

해결 hae gyeol - Solve

쉽게 shwib gae - Easily

입 eep - Mouth

행동 haeng dong - Action

양반 yang ban - Aristocrat

헌신 hun shin - Dedication

영광 yeong gwang - Honor

목표 mok pyo - Goal

성취 sung chwi - Achievement

변화 byeon hwa - A change

Comprehension Questions

a.   왕이 한글을 창제한 이유는 무엇이었습니까? Why did the king create Hangul?

b.   왕의 행동에 대해 모든 사람들이 어떻게 반응했습니까? How did everyone react to the king's actions?

c.   왕의 이야기가 우리에게 무엇을 가르쳐주는가? What does the king's story teach us?

Historical Notes

King Sejong(1397-1450) is a hallmark figure that we cannot miss out on when discussing important Korean historical figures. Known as the father of Hangul, he created the Korean alphabet as we know and study it today.

"한글의 창조 Hangul-ui Changjo

조선 시대에 왕 세종이 있었습니다. 그는 자신의 나라 사람들이 **문해**를 **즐길** 수 있도록 하고 싶었습니다. 하지만, 그의 사람들은 한자를 배우는 것이 너무 어려웠습니다. 그래서 왕 세종은 새로운 **글자**를 만들기로 결정했습니다. 이것이 바로 한글이었습니다. 왕 세종은 가장 똑똑한 **학자**들을 모아 한글을 **개발**했습니다. 한글은 **소리**를 **표현**하는 것이었고, 모든 사람들이 쉽게 배울 수 있었습니다. 한글이 만들어진 후, 많은 사람들이 더 쉽게 읽고 쓸 수 있었습니다. 왕 세종의 한글은 그의 나라 사람들에게 문화와 교육의 문을 열어주었습니다. 그러나 한글은 조선 시대에는 **널리** 받아들여지지 않았습니다. 그러나 시간이 지나면서 한글은 한국 사람들에게 가장 중요한 글자가 되었습니다.

The Creation of Hangul

There was a king named Sejong during the Joseon Dynasty. He wanted his people to enjoy literacy. However, his people found it too difficult to learn Chinese characters. So, King Sejong decided to create a new script. This was Hangul. King Sejong gathered the brightest scholars to develop Hangul. Hangul was about representing sounds, and everyone could learn it easily. After Hangul was created, many people could read and write more easily. King Sejong's Hangul opened the doors of culture and education to his people. However, Hangul was not widely accepted during the Joseon Dynasty. But as time passed, Hangul became the most important script for the Korean people.

Vocabulary

문해 mun hae - Literacy

즐기다 jeul gi da - To enjoy

글자 geul ja - Letter

학자 hak ja - Scholar

개발 gae bal - Invent

소리 so ri - Sound

표현 pyo hyeon - Express

널리 nul li - Widely

Comprehension Questions

a. 왕 세종이 한글을 만들기 위해 누구를 모았습니까? Who did King Sejong gather to create Hangul?

b. 한글은 어떤 문제를 해결했습니까? What problem did Hangul solve?

c. 한글이 처음에는 어떻게 받아들여졌습니까? How was Hangul initially received?

Historical Notes

A bit of background into the creation of Hangul, which is arguably the most important historical moment for those reading this book. It was created in the mid fifteenth century as an attempt to increase literacy, but was not well received during its time. In fact, it wasn't even used by scholars or upper class Koreans until after 1945, over 400 years after its creation.

신자와 국가 건설의 신조학의 확산

Shinjawa Gukga Geonseol-ui Sinjohak-ui Hwaksan

한때, 신조학이라는 새로운 **철학**이 동양에 퍼져 나갔습니다. 그 철학은 **이성**과 **도덕**에 중점을 두었으며, 사람들이 자신의 생활을 개선하고 사회를 변화시키는 데 중요한 **역할**을 했습니다. 한 존경받는 학자가 이 철학을 **전파**하는 데 **앞장섰**습니다. 그는 **국가 건설**에 신조학의 **원칙**을 적용하려 노력했습니다. 그는 국가를 건설하면서 사람들에게 신조학의 가치를 가르쳤습니다. 그의 **훈련**은 사람들이 서로에 대해 이해하고 존중하는 사회를 만들었습니다. 그러나 그의 **접근**법은 모든 사람들이 받아들이지 못했습니다. 몇몇은 그의 철학을 이해하지 못하거나 받아들이지 않았습니다. 그러나 그는 **포기**하지 않고 계속 교육하고 가르쳤습니다. 그의 노력 덕분에 신조학은 점차 사람들 사이에 받아들여졌고, 그들의 생활에 **긍정적인** 변화를 가져왔습니다.

Spread of Neo-Confucianism and Statecraft

Once upon a time, a new philosophy, known as Neo-Confucianism, spread across the East. This philosophy emphasized on reason and morality, and it played a crucial role in improving people's lives and transforming societies. A respected scholar led the propagation of this philosophy. He strove to apply the principles of Neo-Confucianism to the construction of the nation. As he built the nation, he taught the values of Neo-Confucianism to the people. His teachings fostered a society where people understood and respected each other. However, his approach was not accepted by everyone. Some either did not understand or accept his philosophy. But he did not give up and continued to educate and teach. Due to his efforts, Neo-Confucianism was gradually accepted among the people, bringing positive changes to their lives.

Vocabulary

철학 chul hak - Philosophy

이성 yi sung - Reason

도덕 do deok - Morality

역할 yeok hal - Role

전파 jeon pa - Spread

앞장쓰다 ap jang sseu da - To take the lead

국가 건설 guk ga geon seol - National construction

원칙 won chik - Rule (noun)

훈련 hool ryeon - Training

접근 jeob geun - Approach

포기 po gi - To give up

긍정적인 geung jeong jeok in - Positively/ optimistically

Comprehension Questions

a.   이 학자는 어떤 철학을 전파하려고 노력했습니까? What philosophy did this scholar attempt to propagate?

신조학이 사람들의 생활에 어떤 영향을 미쳤습니까? What impact did Neo-Confucianism have on people's lives?

모든 사람들이 그의 철학을 받아들였습니까? Did everyone accept his philosophy?

Historical Notes

During the Joseon Dynasty, Neo-Confucianism was established as the state ideology and Buddhism was seen as a hindrance. Buddhism was restricted and occasional persecutions would occur as campaigns were launched to promote Neo-Confucianism

도전과 쇠퇴

Dojeongwa Swetwe

한 번은 **고요한** 마을에 두 형제가 살았습니다. 이들은 서로를 아주 사랑했지만, 그들의 생활 방식은 매우 다르게 나타났습니다. 첫째 형제는 **성실한** 농부였고, 땅을 기르는 것을 좋아했습니다. 둘째 형제는 **호기심** 많은 **여행자**였으며, 항상 새로운 지역을 **탐험**하는 것을 좋아했습니다.

어느 날, 마을이 **가뭄**에 시달리기 시작했습니다. 첫째 형제의 농장은 **수확**이 급격히 **감소**했고, 그는 고민에 빠졌습니다. 반면에 둘째 형제는 그의 여행을 계속하며, 물이 풍부한 새로운 땅을 찾아 나섰습니다.

첫째 형제는 자신의 농장을 다시 살리기 위해 기도했습니다. 그는 비가 오기를 원했습니다. 그러나 둘째 형제는 그의 여행을 계속하며, **타지**에서의 삶을 원했습니다. 그는 풍요로운 땅을 찾기를 원했습니다.

그런데 아이러니하게도, 첫째 형제의 농장에는 비가 내리지 않았습니다. 대신, 둘째 형제가 찾은 땅에는 비가 내렸습니다. 이런 상황에서 두 형제는 어떻게 해야 할지 몰랐습니다.

결국, 두 형제는 자신들의 선택을 받아들이고, 각자의 길을 따르기로 결정했습니다. 첫째 형제는 농장을 **포기**하고, 둘째 형제와 함께 새로운 땅으로 **이주**하였습니다. 둘째 형제는 그의 여행을 마치고 첫째 형제와 함께 땅을 **경작**하기 시작했습니다.

이 이야기는 도전과 **쇠퇴**, 그리고 변화에 대한 것입니다. 때로는 우리의 도전이 우리를 원하는 곳으로 이끌지 못하고, 우리의 삶이 예상치 못한 방향으로 흘러갈 수 있습니다. 그럼에도 불구하고, 우리는 우리의 상황을 받아들이고, 우리의 삶을 계속 나아가야 합니다.

Challenges and Decline

Once upon a time, there were two brothers living in a peaceful village. They loved each other very much, but their ways of life appeared very different. The older brother was a diligent farmer, who enjoyed nurturing the land. The younger brother was a curious traveler, who always liked to explore new areas.

One day, the village started to suffer from drought. The older brother's farm saw a drastic decrease in harvest and he fell into worry. Meanwhile, the younger brother continued his journey, setting out to find new lands abundant in water.

The older brother prayed to revive his farm. He wished for rain. However, the younger brother, continuing his journey, wished for a life in a foreign land. He wished to find a fertile land.

Ironically, rain did not fall on the older brother's farm. Instead, it rained on the land that the younger brother had found. In this situation, the two brothers did not know what to do.

In the end, the two brothers accepted their choices and decided to follow their own paths. The older brother gave up farming and migrated to the new land with the younger brother. The younger brother ended his journey, and began to cultivate the land with the older brother.

This story is about challenges and decline, and about change. Sometimes, our challenges do not lead us to where we want, and our lives can flow in unexpected directions. Nevertheless, we must accept our situation and continue our lives.

Vocabulary

고요한 ko yo han - Serene

성실한 sung shil han - Hardworking/faithful

호기심 ho gi shim - Curiosity

여행자 yeo haeng ja - Traveler

탐험 tam hum - Adventure

가뭄 ka mum - Drought

수확 soo hwak - Harvest

감소 kam so - Decreae

타지에 ta ji e - Out of town

포기 po gi - To give up

이주 lee joo - Migrate

경작 kyeong jak - Tillage

쇠퇴 swe twe - Decline

Comprehension Questions

a.   두 형제는 어떤 문제에 직면했습니까? What problems did the two brothers face?

b.   첫째 형제의 소원은 무엇이었습니까? What was the older brother's wish?

c.   둘째 형제의 소원은 무엇이었습니까? What was the younger brother's wish?

d.   두 형제는 결국 어떻게 해결했습니까? How did the two brothers solve the problem in the end?

Historical Notes

In the 16th century, Joseon was facing pressure from many different foreign sources. From Japan in the East, Manchuria in the North, and China in the West, Korea faced challenges all around and this was a tumultuous time

임진왜란과 두 형제

Imjin Waerangwa Du Hyeongje

한 나라에 두 형제가 있었습니다. 그들은 아버지와 함께 평화롭게 농사를 짓고 있었습니다. 그러나 그 해는 **임진왜란**이라는 무서운 **전쟁**이 **발발**했습니다. **일본군**은 그들의 마을을 공격하고, 그들의 평화를 깨뜨렸습니다. 두 형제는 일본군에 맞서 싸우기로 결심했습니다. 형은 **검**을 들고 직접 전장에 나갔습니다. 동생은 집에서 밥을 지키고, 형이 돌아올 때까지 기다렸습니다. 전쟁은 계속되었고, 형은 돌아오지 않았습니다. 결국, 동생은 형을 찾아 전장에 나갔습니다. 그러나 형을 찾을 수 없었습니다. 전쟁이 끝난 **후**, 동생은 형의 **희생**을 기억하며 평화를 **기원**했습니다."

The Imjin War and the Two Brothers

In a country, there were two brothers. They were farming peacefully with their father. However, that year, a terrible war called the Imjin War broke out. The Japanese army attacked their village and shattered their peace. The two brothers decided to fight against the Japanese army. The older brother took up a sword and went directly to the battlefield. The younger brother stayed at home, guarding the food and waiting for his brother to return. The war continued, and the older brother did not return. Eventually, the younger brother went to the battlefield to find his brother. But he could not find his brother. After the war ended, the younger brother wished for peace, remembering his brother's sacrifice."

Vocabulary:

임진왜란 Imjin Waeran - the Imjin War

전쟁 jeon jaeng - War

발발 bal bal - Outbreak

일본군 il bon gun - Japanese Soldier

검 gum - Sword

후 hoo - After

희생 hee saeng - Sacrifice

기원 ki won - Wish

Comprehension Questions:

a. 두 형제는 무엇을 하고 있었습니까? What were the two brothers doing?

b. 왜 형은 전장에 나갔습니까? Why did the older brother go to the battlefield?

c. 동생은 전쟁이 끝난 후 무엇을 기원했습니까? What did the younger brother wish for after the war ended?

Historical Notes

The Japanese invasions that occurred between 1592-1598 were known as the "Imjin Wars" and was actually started because of Japan's idea to invade China through Korea. Two major invasions were launched by Japanese leader Toyotomi Hideyoshi, but were successfully repelled by Joseon efforts

이순신의 전설적인 거북선
YiSunShin-ui Jeonseoljeokin Geobooksun

옛날에 한 고장에서 이순신이라는 **장군**이 살았습니다. 이순신 장군은 국가를 사랑하고, 그의 땅을 지키기 위해 인생을 바쳤습니다. 그의 전략과 용기로 인해, 그는 많은 전쟁에서 승리하였습니다. 그 중에서도 그의 **거북선**은 **전설적**으로 알려져 있습니다.

거북선은 **철**로 만들어져 적의 **화살**로부터 **병사**들을 보호할 수 있었습니다. 그 배의 모양은 **거북**을 닮아 있었고, 불을 내뿜어 적을 물리칠 수 있었습니다. 이순신 장군은 이 거북선으로 많은 **해전**에서 적을 무찔렀습니다.

그러나 그의 전투는 쉽지 않았습니다. 그는 수없이 많은 어려움과 고난을 겪었습니다. 그의 병사들은 **배고픔**과 **추위**, 그리고 적의 공격에 맞서 싸워야 했습니다. 그러나 이순신 장군의 **지도력**과 거북선의 힘으로, 그들은 승리하였습니다.

이순신 장군은 국민들에게 희망과 용기를 주었습니다. 그는 조선의 자랑이었고, 그의 이야기는 오늘날까지 전해지고 있습니다. 그의 **눈빛**은 굳센 의지를 담고 있었고, 그의 마음은 국가를 향한 깊은 사랑으로 가득 차 있었습니다.

이순신 장군의 전쟁에서의 승리는 그의 **통찰력**과 전략, 그리고 그의 거북선의 전설적인 힘에 의한 것이었습니다. 그는 적에게 두려움을 주었고, 그의 적들은 그의 이름을 듣기만 해도 떨었습니다. 그의 거북선은 **불패**의 전설로 남아, 조선의 영웅으로 기억됩니다.

The Legendary Turtle Ship of Yi Sun Shin

Once, in a distant land, lived a general named Yi Sun Shin. General Yi loved his country and dedicated his whole life to protecting his land. His strategies and courage led him to victory in many battles, among which his turtle ship became legendary.

The turtle ship was made of iron, shielding the soldiers from enemy arrows. The ship, resembling a turtle, could emit fire to defeat enemies. With this turtle ship, General Yi overcame enemies in numerous naval battles.

However, his battles were not easy. He faced countless difficulties and hardships. His soldiers had to fight against hunger, cold, and enemy attacks. Yet, under General Yi's leadership and the strength of the turtle ship, they achieved victory.

General Yi gave hope and courage to the people. He was the pride of Joseon, and his story is still told today. His eyes held steadfast will, and his heart was filled with deep love for his country.

The victories in General Yi's wars were due to his insight, strategy, and the legendary power of his turtle ship. He instilled fear in his enemies, who trembled at the mere mention of his name. His turtle ship remains an undefeated legend, remembered as a hero of Joseon.

Vocabulary

장군 jang gun - General

거북선 geo buk sun - Turtle ship

전설적 jeon seol juk - Legendary

철 chul - Steel

화살 hwa sal - Arrow

병사 byeong sa - Soldier

거북이 geo buk yi- Turtle

해전 hae jun - Sea fight

배고픔 bae go peum - Hunger

추위 choo wi - The cold

지도력 ji do ryuk - Leadership

눈빛 noon bit - The look in the eyes

통찰력 tong chal ryeok - Insight

불패 bul pae - Undefeated

Comprehension Questions

. 이순신은 왜 거북선을 만들었습니까? Why did Yi Sun Shin create the turtle ship?

. 거북선은 어떻게 적을 무찔렀습니까? How did the turtle ship defeat enemies?

. 이순신의 지도력은 어떠한 영향을 미쳤습니까? What impact did Yi Sun Shin's leadership have?

Historical Notes

The biggest obstacle to the Japanese threat in the East during the 16th century was the exceptional Korean navy, led by the legendary figure Yi Sun Shin. In Korea, his name is as known as King Sejong and everyone you meet will most likely know of this figure and his turtle ships

해와 달의 형제

Hae-wa Dal-ui Hyeongje

한때, **해**와 **달**이라는 두 형제가 있었습니다. 해 형제는 밝은 **빛**을 내며 사람들이 **일**할 수 있게 했습니다. 달 형제는 **은은한** 빛으로 밤에 길을 **밝혀**주었습니다. 그들은 **완벽한 균형**을 이루며 세상을 비춰주었습니다.

하지만 어느 날, 두 형제 사이에 갈등이 생겼습니다. 해는 자신의 밝은 빛이 더 중요하다며 달을 **무시**했습니다. 달은 해의 행동에 **기분**이 상하였습니다.

해는 자신의 빛이 더 크고 밝으니 더 중요하다고 **주장**했습니다. 그런데 달은 자신의 빛이 더 **부드럽고 편안**하니 더 중요하다고 **반박**했습니다.

인간들 사이에서도 이 문제에 대한 **의견**이 분분했습니다. **일부**는 해의 빛이 더 중요하다고 말했습니다. 다른 일부는 달의 빛이 더 중요하다고 주장했습니다.

결국, 두 형제는 하늘의 신에게 판단을 내려달라고 요청했습니다. 신은 두 형제를 보고 말했습니다. "당신들 둘 다 중요합니다. 해는 낮에 사람들이 일할 수 있게 해주고, 달은 밤에 길을 밝혀줍니다."

그래서 두 형제는 서로의 중요성을 인정하게 되었습니다. 그들은 이제 갈등을 끝내고 함께 하늘을 비추기로 결심했습니다.

Brothers of the Sun and Moon

Once upon a time, there were two brothers, the Sun and the Moon. The Sun brother shone brightly, enabling people to work. The Moon brother illuminated the path at night with a soft glow. They cast light on the world in perfect balance.

However, one day, a conflict arose between the two brothers. The Sun dismissed the Moon, asserting that his bright light was more important. The Moon was hurt by the Sun's behavior.

The Sun argued that his light was brighter and larger, thus more significant. However, the Moon countered that his light was softer and more comforting, thus more important.

Among humans, too, opinions were divided on this matter. Some said that the light of the Sun was more important. Others claimed that the light of the Moon was more important.

Eventually, the two brothers asked the god of the sky to make a decision. The god looked at the two brothers and said, "Both of you are important. The Sun allows people to work during the day, and the Moon lights the path at night."

So the two brothers came to acknowledge each other's importance. They decided to end their conflict and light the sky together.

Vocabulary

해 hae - Sun

달 dal - Moon

빛 bit - Light

일 il - Work

은은한 eun eun han - Subtle

밝혀 balk hyeo - Reveal

완벽한 wan byeok han - Perfect

균형 gyoon hyeong - Balance

무시 mu si - Ignore

기분 ki bun - Feeling

주장 ju jang - Insist

부드럽다 bu deu rup go - Soft

편안 pyeon an - Comfortable

반박 ban bak - Retort

의견 ui gyeon - Opinion

일부 il bu - Part/Some

Comprehension Questions

a. 해와 달은 왜 갈등이 생겼습니까? Why did a conflict arise between the Sun and the Moon?

b. 인간들의 의견은 어떠했습니까? What were the opinions of the humans?

c. 하늘의 신은 어떤 판단을 내렸습니까? What decision did the god of the sky make?

Historical Notes

During the time periods of 1640 -1840, Joseon saw a time of relative peace and prosperity, with man advancements in literature and art. Conuficianism inspired pieces of literature and art that adopted wester techniques to show "realism" were some of the achievements of this era.

서방의 병사와 서로의 욕망
Seobang-ui Byongsawa Seoro-ui Yokmang

서방의 **병사**가 한 마을로 **진입**했습니다. 그들은 강력하고 두려움을 불러일으켰습니다. 그러나 마을 사람들은 맞서 싸울 **준비**가 되어 있었습니다. 이들의 리더, 장군,은 마을 사람들에게 자신들의 **권리**를 지키도록 **교육**했습니다. 하루는 병사가 한 **여성**을 만났습니다. 그녀는 그의 눈에 눈이 떨어졌습니다. 그녀는 그와 **결혼**하길 바랐습니다. 그러나 그녀의 아버지는 그가 자신의 딸에게 해를 끼칠까봐 **경계**했습니다. 그는 딸에게 병사가 그녀에게만 관심이 있지 않을 수도 있다고 **경고**했습니다. 그는 딸이 **안전**하고 행복하길 원했습니다.

The Western Soldier and Their Desires

A western soldier entered a village. They were powerful and invoked fear. However, the villagers were prepared t
fight back. Their leader, a general, educated the villagers to protect their rights. One day, a soldier met a womar
He fell for her at first sight. She wished to marry him. However, her father was wary that he would harm hi
daughter. He warned his daughter that the soldier might not only be interested in her. He wished for his daughte
to be safe and happy.

Vocabulary

서방 seo bang - West

병사 byeong sa - Soldier

진입 jin ip - Enter

준비 jun bi - Prepare

권리 kwol lee - Rights

교육 kyo yook - Educate

여성 yeo seong - Woman

결혼 kyeol hon - Marry

경계 kyeong ge - To be wary

경고 kyeon go - Warn

안전 an jun - Safety

Comprehension Questions

a.　　왜 마을 사람들은 병사들을 두려워했습니까? Why were the villagers afraid of the soldiers?

b.　　여성이 병사와 결혼하길 원했습니까? Did the woman want to marry the soldier?

c.　　아버지는 왜 병사를 신뢰하지 않았습니까? Why didn't the father trust the soldier?

Historical Notes

The late 19th century saw the beginnings of Western powers making a move in Korea. The United States held an expedition that led to an armed conflict in 1871, in which the US won, but Korea refused to open the country to the US. The US forces did not continue and were unable to establish meaningful diplomatic relations.

조선의 마지막 왕과 그의 꿈

Joseon-ui Majimag Wang-gwa Geuui Kkum

조선의 **마지막** 왕 고종이었습니다. 그는 자신의 나라를 사랑하였고, 자유롭게 살 수 있는 조선을 꿈꾸었습니다. 그러나 그의 꿈은 일본의 **식민지 정책** 때문에 **무너져**버렸습니다. 왕은 국민들에게 이를 알리려고 노력했으나, 그의 **목소리**는 일본에 의해 짓눌려진 채였습니다. 그럼에도 불구하고 그는 **절망**하지 않았고, 조선의 **미래**를 위해 계속해서 싸웠습니다. 그는 일본의 식민지 정책을 끝내기 위해 모든 것을 희생하려고 결심했습니다. 하지만 그의 노력에도 불구하고, 그의 꿈은 이루어지지 않았습니다. 조선은 일본의 식민지로 빠져들었고, 왕은 **철썩 무너져** 내렸습니다. 그러나 그의 꿈은 아직도 많은 사람들에게 희망을 줍니다. 그의 꿈은 조선의 자유를 바라는 모든 사람들에게 영감을 줍니다.

The Last King of Joseon and His Dream

There was a king named Gojong, the last king of Joseon. He loved his country and dreamed of a free Joseon. However, his dream was shattered by Japan's colonial policies. The king tried to inform his people about this, but his voice was suppressed by Japan. Yet, he did not despair and continued to fight for the future of Joseon. He was determined to sacrifice everything to end Japan's colonial policies. Despite his efforts, his dream did not come true. Joseon fell into the hands of Japan as a colony, and the king was devastated. Yet, his dream still gives hope to many people. His dream inspires all those who wish for the freedom of Joseon.

Vocabulary

마지막 ma ji mak - Final

식민지 정책 sik min ji jeong chaek - Colonial policy

무너져 mu neo jyeo - fall

목소리 mok so ri - Voice

절망 jeol mang - Despair

미래 mi rae - Future

철썩 무너져 chul seok mu neo jyeo - completely fall apart

Comprehension Questions

1.   왕이 어떤 꿈을 가지고 있었습니까? What was the king's dream?

b.   왕의 꿈이 무엇 때문에 무너져 내렸습니까? Why did the king's dream fall apart?

c.   왕의 꿈이 현재에 어떤 영향을 미치고 있습니까? What impact does the king's dream have today?

Historical Notes

The fall of the Joseon Dynasty began in the late 19th century, as Korea struggled to maintain its independence from all of the foreign superpowers that were fighting for control around it. An example of this is the Sino-Japanese War that was fought between China and Japan, but much of it actually occurred on the Korean peninsula.

고종왕과 한국제국의 선포
Gojongwanggwa Hangukjeguk-ui Seonpo

어느 날, 고종왕은 **황제**의 자리에 오르게 되었습니다. 그는 자신의 나라를 보호하고자 자신의 나라를 한국제국으로 **선포**하였습니다. 그는 자신의 나라가 다른 나라에 의해 **침략**당하지 않도록 하려고 노력하였습니다. 그러나 그의 노력이 헛되지 않기 위해서는 그가 자신의 나라를 강하게 만들어야 했습니다. 그래서 그는 자신의 나라를 **발전**시키기 위해 많은 노력을 기울였습니다. 그는 국민들에게 교육을 받게 하고, **경제**를 **획기적**으로 **성장**시키고, **국방력**을 강화시켰습니다. 그의 노력 덕분에 한국은 다른 나라들에게 존경받는 나라가 되었습니다. 그러나 그는 항상 자신의 나라를 위해 더 많은 일을 하려고 노력했습니다. 그는 결국 자신의 나라를 위해 **전력**을 다하였습니다. 그의 선포는 한국의 역사를 바꾸는 중요한 순간이었습니다.

The Korean Empire
(1897-1910)

King Gojong and the Proclamation of the Korean Empire

One day, King Gojong ascended to the throne of the emperor. He declared his country as the Korean Empire t protect his nation. He strived to prevent his country from being invaded by other countries. However, to ensur his efforts were not in vain, he had to strengthen his country. So, he put a great deal of effort into developing h country. He allowed his citizens to receive education, dramatically grew the economy, and enhanced militar power. Thanks to his effort, Korea became a country respected by other nations. Yet, he always endeavored to d more for his country. He eventually exhausted all his power for his nation. His proclamation was a crucial momer that changed the history of Korea.

Vocabulary

황제 hwang je - Emperor

선포 seon po - Proclamation

침략 chim ryak - Invasion

발전 bal jun - Advancement/ Development

경제 kyeong jae - Economy

획기적 hwaek ki jeok - Groundbreaking

성장 sung jang - Growth

국방력 guk bang - ryeok Military power

전력 jeol ryeok - All one's power

Comprehension Questions

1.   고종왕은 왜 한국제국을 선포했습니까? Why did King Gojong proclaim the Korean Empire?

2.   고종왕이 자신의 나라를 어떻게 발전시키려고 노력했습니까? How did King Gojong strive t develop his country?

3.   고종왕의 선포는 한국 역사에 어떤 영향을 미쳤습니까? What impact did King Gojong' proclamation have on Korean history?

Historical Notes

King Gojong ended the Joseon Dynasty in 1897 by declaring the Korean Empire and himself as the emperor. This was actually done in an attempt to preserve Korean independence and promote national integrity. However, this did not last and Korea fell under Japan.

현대 국가로의 변형
Hyundae Gukgaro-ui Byeonhyeong

한 나라가 고려시대로부터 조선시대, 그리고 **최종적**으로는 **현대** 국가로 **변형**되었습니다. 이 변형은 매우 복잡하고 **신중한 과정**이었습니다. 이 과정에서, 그들은 **외래** 문화를 **수용**하고, 독특한 문화를 유지하며, 고유한 국가적 **정체성**을 찾아야 했습니다. 이 이야기는 그 과정을 통해 한 나라가 어떻게 현대 국가로 **변모**하게 되었는지를 보여줍니다.

그 나라의 왕은 국가를 현대화하고자 하는 **야망**에 찬 사람이었습니다. 그는 외부 세계와의 **접촉**을 통해 새로운 아이디어와 기술을 받아들이는 것이 중요하다는 것을 알았습니다. 그는 그의 나라가 세계에서 가장 발전된 나라 중 하나가 되기를 바랐습니다. 그러나 그는 그의 나라의 **고유한** 문화와 **전통**을 잃지 않도록 하기 위해 매우 노력했습니다.

왕은 왕국을 교육으로 **개혁**하기로 결정했습니다. 그는 새로운 학교를 설립하고, 모든 사람들이 읽고 쓸 수 있도록 국어를 개발했습니다. 그는 또한 국가를 관리하기 위한 복잡한 **체제**를 **설립**했습니다.

그러나 왕의 **혁신**은 모두가 기뻐하는 것은 아니었습니다. 몇몇 사람들은 변화를 두려워했고, 그들은 그의 계획에 대해 반대했습니다. 그들은 그의 혁신이 그들의 전통적인 생활 방식을 **파괴**할 것이라고 믿었습니다.

왕은 이 반대를 **극복**하기 위해 많은 노력을 기울였습니다. 그는 그의 계획이 국가를 강화하고 사람들의 삶을 **향상**시킬 것이라는 것을 사람들에게 **설명**했습니다. 그는 또한 그의 혁신이 그들의 문화를 파괴하지 않을 것이라고 **확신**시켰습니다.

시간이 지나면서, 사람들은 왕의 계획을 받아들이기 시작했습니다. 그들은 그의 혁신이 그들의 삶을 향상시키고 국가를 발전시키는 데 도움이 되는 것을 **목격**했습니다. 그들은 또한 그들의 문화와 전통이 그의 혁신에도 불구하고 **생존**하고 있음을 알게 되었습니다.

이 이야기는 한 나라가 어떻게 현대 국가로 변형되었는지를 보여줍니다. 그 과정은 매우 복잡하고 어려웠지만, 그들은 그 과정을 통해 그들의 정체성을 찾고 그들의 국가를 세계적 수준으로 발전시킬 수 있었습니다.

이 이야기를 통해, 우리는 변화와 **진보**의 중요성을 배울 수 있습니다. 그러나 우리는 또한 우리의 문화와 전통을 존중하고 보존하는 것이 얼마나 중요한지를 배울 수 있습니다.

Transformation into a Modern State

A country transformed from the Goryeo Dynasty to the Joseon Dynasty, and ultimately into a modern state. This transformation was a complex and careful process. In this process, they had to accept foreign cultures, maintain a unique culture, and find their own national identity. This story shows how a country has transformed into a modern state through this process.

The king of the country was a man filled with ambition to modernize the country. He knew the importance of accepting new ideas and technology through contact with the outside world. He wished his country to become one of the most developed countries in the world. However, he worked very hard to prevent his country from losing its unique culture and tradition.

The king decided to reform the kingdom through education. He established new schools and developed a national language so that everyone could read and write. He also established a complex system to manage the state.

However, not everyone was happy with the king's innovations. Some people feared change and opposed his plans. They believed his innovations would destroy their traditional way of life.

The king made a lot of effort to overcome this opposition. He explained to people that his plans would strengthen the state and improve people's lives. He also assured them that his innovations would not destroy their culture.

Over time, people began to accept the king's plans. They witnessed that his innovations were improving their lives and helping the country to develop. They also realized that their culture and traditions were surviving despite his innovations.

This story shows how a country has transformed into a modern state. The process was very complex and difficult, but they were able to find their identity and develop their country to a global level through this process.

Through this story, we can learn the importance of change and progress. However, we can also learn how important it is to respect and preserve our culture and traditions.

Comprehension Questions

1.   왕은 왜 국가를 현대화하고자 했습니까? Why did the king want to modernize the country?

2.   왕의 혁신에 대한 반대는 어떻게 극복되었습니까? How was the opposition to the king's innovation overcome?

3.   왕의 혁신이 국민들의 삶에 어떤 영향을 미쳤습니까? What impact did the king's innovation have on people's lives?

Vocabulary

최종적 chwae jong juk - Final

현대 hyun dae - Modern

변형 byeon hyeong - Transform

신중한 shin joong han - Careful

과정 kwa jeong - Process

외래 wae rae - Outside

수용 soo yong - Accept

정체성 jeong chae seong - Identity

변모 byeon mo - Transformation

야망 ya mang - Ambition

접촉 jeob chok - Contact

고유한 ko yoo han - Unique

전통 jeon tong - Traditional

개혁 kae hyuk - Reform

체제 che je - System

설립 seol lip - Establish

혁신 hyeok shin - Innovation

파괴 pa gwe - Destroy

극복 keuk bok - Overcome

향상 hyang sang - Elevate/improve

설명 seol myung - Explain

확신 hwak shin - Certainty

목격 mok kyuk - Witness

생존 saeng jon - Survive

진보 jin bo - Progress

Historical Notes

During the Korean Empire's time, King Gojong pushed for the Gwangmu Reform, which called for a partial modernization and westernization of various aspects of Korea. This reform was not well received by the people and resistances such as the Independence Club were formed to protest for civil rights.

현대화 노력과 외교 관계

Hyundaehwa Noryeokgwa Waegyo Gwanggye

한 나라가 있었습니다. 그 나라의 이름은 한국이었습니다. 한국은 시간이 지나며 변화하였습니다. 그들은 **현대화**를 추구하였습니다. 그러나 그들의 **이웃** 나라들은 그들을 이해하지 못하였습니다. 그래서 한국은 **외교관계**를 맺기 시작했습니다. 한국은 자신들의 문화와 **가치**를 설명하였습니다. 이웃 나라들은 그들을 이해하기 시작했습니다. 그리고 그들은 한국과 **친구**가 되었습니다. 이것이 현대화와 외교 관계의 이야기입니다.

Modernization Efforts and Diplomatic Relations

There was a country. The name of the country was Korea. As time passed, Korea changed. They pursue modernization. However, their neighboring countries did not understand them. So, Korea began to establis diplomatic relations. Korea explained their culture and values. The neighboring countries began to understan them. And they became friends with Korea. This is the story of modernization and diplomatic relations.

Vocabulary

현대화 hyun dae hwa - Modernization

이웃 lee oot - Neighbor

외교관계 wae gyo gwang gye - Diplomatic relations

가치 ga chi - Worth

친구 ching gu - Friend

Comprehension Questions

a.   한국은 왜 현대화를 추구했습니까? Why did Korea pursue modernization?

b.   한국은 왜 이웃 나라들과 외교관계를 맺었습니까? Why did Korea establish diplomatic relation with neighboring countries?

c.   이 이야기에서 배울 수 있는 교훈은 무엇입니까? What lesson can we learn from this story?

Historical Notes

In the beginning of the Korean Empire, the powerful nations in the world did not accept Korea's proclamation a an empire due to its claim for independence from foreign influences. As Korea had many influences in its politica and economic space prior to this, the proclamation was seen in a negative light. This image changed over time, a foreign powers began to acknowledge Gojong as emperor.

독립을 위한 저항

Donglib-eul Wihan Jeohang

ㅏ 때, 작은 마을에 한 **청년**이 살았습니다. 그의 이름은 민수였습니다. 민수는 마을 사람들에게 **ㅏ부심**을 느끼게 하는 **재주**있는 농부였습니다. 그러나 그의 마음은 언제나 마을 밖, **외부 세계**를 ㅑ했습니다. 어느 날, 마을에 외부에서 온 사람들이 도착했습니다. 그들은 **독립운동**가라고 자신을 ㅗ개했습니다. 민수는 그들의 이야기를 듣고 자신도 독립운동에 **참여**하고 싶다는 생각이 들었습니다. ㅗ는 마을 사람들을 **설득**해 독립운동에 참여하게 했습니다. 그들은 많은 어려움에 **직면**했지만, 항상 ㅗ망을 잃지 않았습니다. 그들의 노력 덕분에 마을은 성공적으로 독립을 **선언**할 수 있었습니다.

Japanese Colonial Rule (1910-1945)

esistance Efforts for Independence

nce upon a time, there was a young man living in a small village. His name was Minsu. Minsu was a skilled rmer who brought pride to his fellow villagers. However, his heart always yearned for the world beyond the llage. One day, a group of strangers arrived at the village. They introduced themselves as independence activists. earing their stories, Minsu felt a desire to join their independence movement. He persuaded his fellow villagers join the movement. They faced many challenges, but they never lost hope. Thanks to their efforts, the village as able to declare its independence successfully.

Vocabulary

청년 cheong nyeon - A young man

자부심 ja bu shim - Pride

재주 jae ju - Skill

외부 세계 we bu se gye - Outside world

독립운동 dok lip un dong - Independence movement

소개 so gye - Introduce

참여 cham yeo - Participate

설득 seol deuk - Convince

직면 jik myeon - Confrontation

선언 seon eon - Declare

Comprehension Questions

1. 민수는 왜 독립운동에 참여하고 싶어했습니까? Why did Minsu want to join the independence movement?

2. 민수는 어떻게 마을 사람들을 설득했습니까? How did Minsu persuade the villagers?

3. 마을이 독립을 선언하는 것은 어떤 의미였습니까? What did it mean for the village to declare independence?

Historical Notes

King Gojong was forced to abdicate the throne in 1907 and Korea was officially annexed by Japan in 1910 throug the Japan-Korea Treaty of 1910. During this colonial period, many Koreans volunteered to rise up in resistanc forming guerilla armies like the "righteous armies" to fight back against oppression.

해방의 소리

Haebang-ui Sori

1910 년부터 1945 년까지, 한 아이와 그의 **할머니**가 있었습니다. 그들은 일본의 **식민지 지배** 아래에서 살았습니다. 아이는 농사를 지으며 **가난한** 생활을 이어갔습니다. 하루가 멀다하고 일본군에게 **고역**을 당하고, 그들의 땅이 빼앗겼습니다. 그럼에도 불구하고 할머니는 **손자**에게 희망을 가지라고 가르쳤습니다.

어느 날, 아이는 할머니에게 자신이 원하는 것이 무엇인지 물었습니다. 할머니는 한국이 **자유**를 찾는 것을 바란다고 **대답**했습니다. 그녀는 식민지 지배에서 벗어나 한국이 **독립**을 이루는 날을 기다렸습니다. 아이는 할머니의 말에 **고개**를 끄덕였습니다. 그는 할머니의 꿈을 이해했습니다.

1945 년 8 월 15 일, **아침**에 일어난 아이는 할머니가 **눈물**을 흘리며 라디오를 듣고 있는 것을 보았습니다. 그 라디오에서는 한국의 독립을 선언하는 소리가 들렸습니다. 그날, 그들은 자유를 얻었습니다. 아이는 할머니의 꿈이 이루어진 것을 보았습니다. 그리고 그는 이 자유를 **소중히** 아껴야 한다는 것을 깨달았습니다.

The Sound of Liberation

From 1910 to 1945, there was a child and his grandmother. They lived under Japanese colonial rule. The child led a poor life, farming and suffering from forced labor by the Japanese. Their land was taken away, but the grandmother taught the child to hold on to hope.

One day, the child asked his grandmother what she wanted. The grandmother answered that she wished for Korea to find its freedom. She waited for the day Korea would break free from colonial rule and gain independence. The child nodded at his grandmother's words. He understood her dream.

On August 15, 1945, the child woke up to see his grandmother crying as she listened to the radio. The radio announced Korea's declaration of independence. That day, they gained their freedom. The child saw his grandmother's dream come true. And he realized that he must cherish this freedom.

Vocabulary

할머니 hal meo ni - Grandma

식민지 지배 sik min ji ji bae - Colonial rule

가난한 ga nan han - Humble/poor

고역 go yeok - Servitude

손자 son ja - Grandson

자유 ja yoo - Freedom

대답 dae dap - Response

독립 dok lip - Independence

고개 go gae - Head

아침 a chim - Morning

눈물 noon mul - Tears

소중히 so joong hee - Preciously

Comprehension Questions

a. 할머니와 아이는 어떤 상황에서 살았습니까? In what situation did the grandmother and child live?

b. 할머니의 소원은 무엇이었습니까? What was the grandmother's wish?

c. 1945년 8월 15일에 무엇이 발생했습니까? What happened on August 15, 1945?

d. 아이는 무엇을 깨달았습니까? What did the child realize?

Historical Notes

Korea was liberated from Japan's rule in 1945 due to an event that affected the whole world. This event was the surrender of Japan and the end of World War II. August 15 is the official day that Korea was liberated and is still celebrated as a holiday called "Gwangbokjeol", or Korea's Independence Day. The literal translation is restoration of light.

일본의 군주를 해방하다
Ilbon-ui Gunjooreur Haebanghada

한 시대가 끝나고 **새로운** 시대가 시작되었습니다. 한국은 일본의 군주에서 벗어나 자유를 찾았습니다. 그 해는 1945 년이었고, 모든 사람들은 **감격**에 찬 눈물을 흘렸습니다. 그들은 이제 자신의 나라를 스스로 통치할 수 있으며, 그들의 **언어**와 문화를 자유롭게 **연습**할 수 있었습니다. 그들은 더 이상 일본의 군주에 대한 **공포**에서 벗어나 자유를 누리게 되었습니다.

한 **소년**, 지환은 그의 아버지가 돌아오기를 기다렸습니다. 그의 아버지는 일본군에게 끌려가서 강제로 **노동**을 하게 된 이래로 몇 년 동안 가족을 보지 못했습니다. 지환의 아버지는 그의 가족에게 **편지**를 보냈지만, 그들은 그의 **상황**이 얼마나 나빴는지 알지 못했습니다. 지환은 그의 아버지가 돌아오면 다시 함께 **노래**하고 **춤**출 수 있을 것이라고 **상상**했습니다.

그러나 그의 아버지가 돌아올 때, 그는 다르게 보였습니다. 그의 눈은 희망과 기쁨이 아니라 **고통**과 **슬픔**으로 가득 차 있었습니다. 그는 노동에서 벗어나 자유를 찾았지만, 그의 마음은 여전히 **갇혀** 있었습니다. 그는 그의 가족을 보고 싶었지만, 그는 일본의 군주 아래에서 겪은 고통을 **잊을** 수 없었습니다.

지환은 그의 아버지가 다시 **웃을** 수 있을까요? 그의 아버지는 다시 자신의 나라에서 자유롭게 살아갈 수 있을까요? 이야기는 아직 끝나지 않았습니다. 한국은 자유를 찾았지만, 그들은 여전히 그들의 과거를 극복해야 했습니다. 그들은 그들의 **미래**를 위해 희망을 잃지 않고 계속해서 **투쟁**해야 했습니다.

iberation from Japanese Rule

n era ended and a new one began. Korea had found its freedom from Japanese rule. The year was 1945, and veryone shed tears of joy. They could now govern their own country, practice their language and culture freely. hey were no longer under the fear of Japanese rule, they were free.

 young boy, Ji-Hwan, waited for his father to return. His father had not seen his family for several years since he vas taken by the Japanese military and forced into labor. Ji-Hwan's father had sent letters to his family, but they lid not know how bad his situation was. Ji-Hwan imagined that they could sing and dance together again when is father returned.

lowever, when his father returned, he looked different. His eyes were filled with pain and sadness, not hope and oy. He had escaped from labor and found freedom, but his heart was still captive. He missed his family, but he ouldn't forget the pain he had experienced under Japanese rule.

could Ji-Hwan's father smile again? Could his father live freely in his country again? The story is not over yet. .orea had found freedom, but they still had to overcome their past. They had to continue to struggle without osing hope for their future.

Vocabulary

새로운 sae ro woon - New

감격 gam gyuk - Touched/ in effervescence

언어 eon eo - Language

연습 yeon seup - Practice

공포 gong po - Fear

소년 so nyeon - Boy

노동 no dong - Labor

편지 pyeon ji - Letter

상황 sang hwang - Situation

노래 no rae - Song

춤 choom - Dance

고통 go tong - Pain

슬픔 seul peum - Sadness

갇혀 gad chyeo - Trapped

잊다 eet da - To forget

웃다 woot da - To laugh

미래 mi rae - Future

투쟁 tu jaeng - Fight

Comprehension Questions

a. 지환은 왜 그의 아버지를 기다렸습니까? Why did Ji-Hwan wait for his father?

b. 지환의 아버지는 왜 다르게 보였습니까? Why did Ji-Hwan's father look different?

c. 이 이야기의 중요한 메시지는 무엇입니까? What is the important message of this story?

Historical Notes

The liberation of Korea is a celebrated moment that marks the end of 35 years of colonial rule. Under colonial rule, Korea suffered as many of their rights were taken away and they were forced to adopt aspects of Japanese culture. For example, Korean newspapers were heavily censored and many Koreans were forced to adopt Japanese names, abandoning the names of their ancestors.

태극의 이야기: 동과 서의 결합
Taegeuk-ui Leeyagi: Donggwa Seo-ui Kyeolhap

태극의 두 부분, 하나는 **빨간색**이고 다른 하나는 **파란색**입니다. 이 두 부분은 서로 다르지만 하나의 완전한 통일을 이룹니다. **하늘**에서 떨어진 **별**이 하나 있었습니다. 이 별은 이 세상에 풍요를 가져다 주었습니다. 별의 빛은 **동쪽**과 **서쪽**으로 나뉘어 졌습니다. 그러나 이 두 빛은 항상 서로를 **그리워**했습니다. 동쪽의 빛은 서쪽의 빛이 차고 **선명**하다고 생각했습니다. 반면에 서쪽의 빛은 동쪽의 빛이 따뜻하고 **밝다**고 생각했습니다. 어느 날 이 두 빛이 만났을 때, 그들은 서로에게 **환희**의 눈물을 흘렸습니다. 이들의 눈물은 태극이라는 새로운 **존재**를 **탄생**시켰습니다.

The Tale of Taegeuk: The Fusion of East and West

The Taeguk comprises two sections, one red and the other blue. Different, yet they form a complete unity. A sta had fallen from the sky, bringing abundance to this world. The light of the star split into the east and the wes However, the two lights always longed for each other. The light of the east believed that the light of the west w cool and clear. On the other hand, the light of the west thought the light of the east was warm and bright. Whe these lights met one day, they shed tears of joy upon each other. Their tears gave birth to a new entity known Taegeuk.

Vocabulary

태극 tae geuk - Korean flag symbol

빨간색 bbal gan saek - Red

파란색 pa ran saek - Blue

하늘 ha neul - Sky

별 byeol - Star

동쪽 dong jjok - Eastside

서쪽 seo jjok - Westside

그리워 geu ri wo - To miss

선명 seon myung - Clear

밝다 bark da - Bright

환희 hwan hee - Joy

존재 jon jae - Existence

탄생 tan saeng - Birth

Comprehension Questions

a.   왜 두 빛은 서로를 그리워했습니까? Why did the two lights long for each other?

b.   태극은 어떻게 탄생했습니까? How was the Taegeuk born?

c.   동쪽의 빛과 서쪽의 빛이 어떻게 다르게 생각되었습니까? How were the light of the east and the light of the west perceived differently?

Historical Notes

There are a lot of beliefs surrounding the meaning of the Taegeuk symbol, but the name itself translates to "Supreme Ultimate". The meaning behind the symbol mostly correlates to a balance of two opposing forces in harmony, much like yin and yang. Many different sources state different interpretations, one example being blue for heaven and red for earth, but most agree that the idea behind the symbol is unification and harmony. The taegeukgi, or Korean flag as we know it today, was officially adopted when Korea gained independence from Japan in August 1945.

제이차 세계 대전 이후의 분열
Jeleecha Segye Daejeon Ihu-ui Bunyeol

세계 대전이 끝난 후, 한반도는 **미국**과 **소련**의 이데올로기적 대립에 휘말렸습니다. 전쟁에서 승리한 두 나라는 한반도를 **임시**로 **분할**하고, 서로 다른 이데올로기를 **확립**하려 했습니다. 미국은 자유롭고 **민주적인** 사회를 위해 남한에 힘을 실었고, 소련은 **공산주의**를 북한에 **도입**했습니다. 이 나라들은 각자의 방식으로 한반도를 통치했으며, 그 과정에서 많은 갈등과 분쟁이 발생했습니다.

하루 아침에 나라가 두 개로 나뉘어진 것은 한반도의 사람들에게 큰 **충격**이었습니다. 가족들은 **분리**되고, 친구들은 서로 다른 이데올로기에 흩어졌습니다. 이 사이에서 한 소년이 있었습니다. 그의 이름은 민준이었습니다. 민준은 북한에 살던 소년이었지만, 그의 아버지는 남한에 살고 있었습니다. 민준은 아버지에게서 **오랜만에** 편지를 받았습니다. 편지에는 그의 아버지가 그를 사랑하고 **그리워**한다는 말이 적혀있었습니다.

민준은 남한에 있는 아버지를 **만나**고 싶었습니다. 그는 힘든 **여정**을 떠나기로 결심했습니다. 그러나 그의 여정은 위험하고 어려웠습니다. 그는 **국경**을 넘어가려 했지만, 군인들이 그를 막았습니다. 민준은 절망했지만, 그는 포기하지 않았습니다. 그는 계속해서 아버지를 만나기 위한 방법을 찾았습니다.

일년 후, 민준은 결국 남한에 **도착**했습니다. 그는 아버지를 만나게 되어 기뻤습니다. 그들은 서로를 꼭 안았고, 많은 이야기를 나누었습니다. 그러나 민준은 북한에 있는 어머니와 여동생을 그리워했습니다. 그는 가족이 다시 **한자리에** 모이는 날을 기다리기로 결심했습니다.

그 이후로 **수십** 년이 지났지만, 한반도는 여전히 분열된 **상태**입니다. 민준처럼 많은 사람들이 가족과 친구들을 만나기 위해 힘든 여정을 떠났습니다. 그들의 이야기는 세계에게 한반도의 분열에 대한 깊은 이해를 **제공**하고, 통일을 향한 희망을 키우는데 **도움**을 주었습니다."

Korean War (1950-1953)

Post-World War II Division

After World War II, the Korean Peninsula was caught in the ideological confrontation between the United States and the Soviet Union. The two victorious countries temporarily divided the peninsula and attempted to establish their own ideologies. The United States bolstered the South for a free and democratic society, while the Soviet Union introduced communism in the North. These countries ruled the peninsula in their own ways, causing many conflicts and disputes in the process.

The overnight division into two countries was a great shock for the people of the peninsula. Families were separated, and friends dispersed under different ideologies. Amidst this, there was a boy named Minjun. Minjun lived in North Korea, but his father lived in South Korea. Minjun received a letter from his father after a long time. The letter read that his father loved and missed him.

Minjun wanted to meet his father in South Korea. He decided to embark on a difficult journey. However, his journey was dangerous and challenging. He tried to cross the border, but the soldiers stopped him. Minjun was desperate, yet he didn't give up. He continued to search for a way to meet his father.

A year later, Minjun finally arrived in South Korea. He was delighted to meet his father. They hugged each other tightly and shared many stories. But Minjun missed his mother and younger sister in North Korea. He decided to await the day his family could be together again.

Decades have passed since then, but the peninsula is still divided. Like Minjun, many people embarked on difficult journeys to meet their families and friends. Their stories provided the world with a deep understanding of the division of the peninsula and helped foster hope for reunification.

Vocabulary

세계 대전 se gye dae jeon - World War

미국 mi guk - United States

소련 so ryeon - Soviet Union

임시 im shi - Temporary

분할 bun hal - Division

확립 hwak rip - Establish

민주적인 min ju jeok in - Democratic

공산주의 gong san joo ee - Communism

도입 do ip - Introduction

충격 choong gyeok - Shock

분리 bun li - Separate

오랜만에 o raen man ae - In a long time

그리워 geu ri wo - To miss

만나 man na - To meet

여정 yeo jeong - Journey

국경 guk kyeong - Border

도착 do chak - Arrive

한자리에 han ja ri ae - In one spot

수십 su sib - Many

상태 sang tae - Condition

제공 jae gong - Distribute/Offer

도움 do oom - Help

Comprehension Questions

a. 민준이 왜 남한에 가기로 결심했습니까? Why did Minjun decide to go to South Korea?

b. 민준의 여정은 어떠했습니까? What was Minjun's journey like?

c. 민준이 아버지를 만난 후에는 어떤 생각을 했습니까? What did Minjun think after meeting his father?

Historical Notes

Right after gaining independence, Korea was split along the 38th parallel. This was done in agreement between the US and the Soviet Union, with the US occupying South Korea and the Soviet Union in the north. This division of Korea into occupation zones was originally meant to be temporary until an international trusteeship could be implemented.

동맹국의 점령과 한국의 분단

Dongmaengguk-ui Jeomryeonggwa Hangguk-ui Bundan

동맹국이 한국을 **점령**하고 **분단**되었을 때, 한 마을에는 분단의 고통을 겪는 두 형제가 있었습니다. 첫째 형제는 북한에 있었고, 둘째 형제는 남한에 있었습니다. 첫째 형제는 북한에서 살기 위해 **강**을 건너야 했습니다. 그는 강을 건너기 위해 매일 **밤** 노력했습니다. 그러나 강은 너무 크고 강했으므로 그는 매번 **실패**했습니다. 그런 다음 그는 남한에 있는 둘째 형제에게 편지를 보냈습니다. 그는 둘째 형제에게 도움을 **청**하고, 그의 **상황**을 설명했습니다. 둘째 형제는 편지를 받고 매우 슬펐습니다. 그는 첫째 형제를 도와주기 위해 많은 방법을 생각했습니다. 하지만 그는 두 형제가 다시 만날 수 있는 방법을 찾지 못했습니다.

Allied Occupation and the Division of Korea

During the time when Korea was occupied by the Allied powers and divided, there were two brothers in a village who were experiencing the pain of division. The eldest brother was in North Korea, and the second brother was in South Korea. The eldest brother had to cross the river to survive in North Korea. He tried to cross the river every night. But the river was too large and strong, so he failed every time. Then he sent a letter to his second brother in South Korea. He asked his second brother for help and explained his situation. The second brother was very sad when he received the letter. He thought of many ways to help his first brother. But he couldn't find a way for the two brothers to meet again.

Vocabulary

동맹국 dong maeng guk - Ally country

점령 jeom ryeong - Occupy

분단 bun dan - Division

강 kang - River

밤 bam - Night

실패 shil pae - To fail

청하다 chung ha da - To request

상황 sang hwang – Situation

Comprehension Questions

a.   첫째 형제는 왜 강을 건너려고 했습니까? Why did the first brother try to cross the river?

b.   둘째 형제는 첫째 형제에게 어떻게 도움을 주려고 했습니까? How did the second brother try to help the first brother?

c.   이 이야기의 결말은 어떻게 됩니까? What happens at the end of this story?

Historical Notes

As mentioned before, the original plan for Korea was for it to be placed under an international trusteeship until Korea was deemed to have the ability to govern itself. In December 1945, a four power, five year trusteeship was drafted. However, it was unable to be implemented due to a variety of factors, including Korean opposition and the onset of the Cold War.

전쟁의 발발과 국제 개입
Junjaeng-ui Balbalgwa Gukjae Gaeib

한때 한 나라에서 평화롭게 살던 **동네** 사람들이 있었습니다. 그러나 어느 날, 전쟁이 **도래**했고 그들의 생활은 **불안정**해졌습니다. 나라는 분열되었고, 사람들은 두려워했습니다. 그들은 삶을 잃을까 봐 두려웠습니다. 그런데 그들에게는 희망이 있었습니다. 바로 **국제 사회**의 **개입**이었습니다.

국제 사회는 그들의 고통을 보았습니다. 그들은 이 나라의 사람들을 돕기 위해 모였습니다. 그들은 먼저 평화를 위한 **협상**을 시작했습니다. 그러나 이것은 쉽지 않았습니다. 각 나라는 자신의 **이익**을 위해 싸웠습니다. 그럼에도 불구하고, 그들은 계속해서 평화를 위해 노력했습니다.

결국 그들은 평화 **협정**에 **서명**하기로 결정했습니다. 그들은 이것이 전쟁을 끝내고, 사람들이 다시 평화롭게 살 수 있게 할 것이라 믿었습니다. 그러나 이것은 **시간**이 걸렸습니다. 그들은 많은 날들을 함께 보냈고, 많은 **어려움**을 겪었습니다.

그럼에도 불구하고, 그들은 포기하지 않았습니다. 그들은 이 나라의 사람들에게 평화를 가져다 주기 위해 **끊임없이** 노력했습니다. 그들은 그들의 노력이 결국은 성공할 것이라고 믿었습니다.

그리하여 그들은 마침내 평화 협정에 서명했습니다. 그들은 이것이 이 나라에 평화를 가져다 줄 것이라고 믿었습니다. 그들은 이것이 사람들의 삶을 바꿀 것이라고 믿었습니다. 그들은 이것이 이 나라의 미래를 바꿀 것이라고 믿었습니다.

Outbreak of the War and International Involvement

Once upon a time, there were ordinary people living peacefully in a country. However, one day, war broke ou and their lives became unstable. The country was divided, and the people were scared. They were afraid of losin their lives. But they had a hope. It was the intervention of the international community.

The international community saw their suffering. They gathered to help the people of this country. They fir started negotiations for peace. But it was not easy. Each country fought for its own interests. Nevertheless, the continued to strive for peace.

Eventually, they decided to sign a peace agreement. They believed that this would end the war and allow peopl to live peacefully again. But it took time. They spent many days together and faced many difficulties.

Yet, they did not give up. They tirelessly worked to bring peace to the people of this country. They believed tha their efforts would eventually succeed.

And so, they finally signed the peace agreement. They believed that this would bring peace to this country. The believed that this would change the lives of the people. They believed that this would change the future of thi country.

Vocabulary

동네 dong nae - Neighborhood

도래 do rae - Advent

불안정 bul an jung - Anxious/Instability

국제 사회 guk jae sa hwe - International Community

개입 gae ip - Intervention

협상 hyeop sang - Negotiation

이익 i ik - Profit/Gain

협정 hyeop jeong - Agreement

서명 seo myung - Signature

시간 shi gan - Time

려움 eo ryeo oom - Hardship

임없이 kkeun im up shi - Endlessly

Comprehension Questions

왜 사람들은 전쟁을 두려워했습니까? Why were the people afraid of the war?

국제 사회는 어떻게 도와주려고 했습니까? How did the international community try to help?

평화 협정을 서명하는 것은 어떤 의미가 있었습니까? What was the significance of signing the peace agreement?

Historical Notes

The Korean War (1950-1953) began as the division of Korea in 1945 led to two different governments forming. The Republic of Korea, backed by the US, was formed in the south, while The Democratic People's Republic of Korea, backed by the Soviet Union, was formed in the North.

용사의 결정

Yongsa-ui Kyeoljeong

한 마을에 용감한 청년이 있었습니다. 그는 나라를 사랑하는 마음이 **깊었**으며, 전쟁의 위협이 **닥쳐**을 때 그는 두려워하지 않았습니다. 그는 나라를 위해 싸울 결정을 내렸습니다. 그는 부모님에게 이 **소식**을 전했고, 그들은 슬픔에 빠졌지만 그의 결정을 존중했습니다. 청년은 **전선**으로 떠났고, 그의 **용기**는 **동료들**에게 큰 힘이 되었습니다. 전쟁은 힘들었지만 그는 포기하지 않았습니다. 그는 친구들을 지키기 위해 자신의 생명을 **위험**에 빠뜨렸습니다. 그의 용기와 희생**정신**은 전쟁이 끝날 때까지 계속되었습니다. 그의 이야기는 여전히 우리의 **마음속**에 살아있습니다. 그는 우리 모두에게 용기와 희생의 가치를 가르쳤습니다.

The Hero's Decision

There once was a brave young man in a village. He had a deep love for his country, and when the threat of war loomed, he did not fear. He decided to fight for his country. He shared this news with his parents, and though they were saddened, they respected his decision. The young man left for the front lines, and his courage was a great strength to his comrades. The war was tough, but he did not give up. He risked his life to protect his friends. His bravery and spirit of sacrifice continued until the end of the war. His story still lives in our hearts. He taught us all the value of courage and sacrifice.

Vocabulary

깊다 gip da - Is deep

닥쳐와 dak chyeo wa - It is coming

소식 so sik - News

전선 jeon seon - Front lines

용기 yong gi - Bravery

동료들 dong ryo deul - Comrades

위험 wi heom - Danger

정신 jeong shin - Mindset

마음속 ma eum sok - In (our) heart

Comprehension Questions

a.   청년은 왜 전쟁에 참여하기로 결정했습니까? Why did the young man decide to participate in the war?

b.   청년의 부모는 어떻게 반응했습니까? How did the young man's parents react?

c.   청년의 용기는 어떻게 표현되었습니까? How was the young man's bravery expressed?

Historical Notes

The Korean War was a brutal time that began with North Korea's invasion in an attempt to reunify the peninsula. Beginning on June 25, 1950, the war saw back and forth fighting along the peninsula as both forces fought to gain sovereignty. The war saw many Korean refugees and many split families, with foreign forces utilizing their resources to fight on the peninsula.

북남분단 이후의 휴전과 계속되는 분열

Buknambundan Yihoo-ui Hyoojeongwa Gyesokdwaeneun Bunyeol

두 나라의 분단은 가난한 어머니와 그녀의 두 아들로 **대표**될 수 있습니다. 어머니는 아들들을 **매우** 사랑했지만, 아들들은 서로 **원수**처럼 살았습니다. 어떤 날, 어머니가 하나님에게 기도했습니다. 첫째 아들은 농부였고, 풍요로운 땅을 원했습니다. 둘째 아들은 **어부**였고, **깨끗한** 바다를 원했습니다. 어머니는 하느님에게 두 아들의 소원을 들어주기를 기도했습니다. 그러나 두 아들의 소원은 서로 **충돌**했습니다. 첫째 아들이 원하는 풍부한 땅은 둘째 아들의 바다를 **말라**버렸습니다. 둘째 아들이 원하는 깨끗한 바다는 첫째 아들의 땅을 물에 잠기게 했습니다. 어머니는 이 충돌을 어떻게 **해결**해야 할지 알지 못했습니다.

Divided Korea (1953-Present)

Armistice and the Ongoing Division of North and South Korea

The division of two countries can be represented by a poor mother and her two sons. The mother loved her sons very much, but the sons lived like enemies. One day, the mother prayed to God. The first son was a farmer and wanted fertile land. The second son was a fisherman and wanted a clean sea. The mother prayed to God to grant both sons' wishes. But the wishes of the two sons conflicted. The fertile land that the first son wanted dried up the second son's sea. The clean sea that the second son wanted flooded the first son's land. The mother did not know how to resolve this conflict.

Vocabulary

대표 dae pyo - Represent

매우 mae woo - Very

원수 won soo - Enemy (mortal enemy)

어부 eo boo - Fisherman

깨끗한 Kkae kkeut han - Clean

충돌 choong dol - Conflicting/Crash

말라 mal la - Dry

해결 hae gyeol - Solve

Comprehension Questions

a. 어머니는 왜 아들들의 소원을 위해 기도했습니까? Why did the mother pray for her sons' wishes?

b. 첫째 아들의 소원은 무엇이었습니까? What was the first son's wish?

c. 둘째 아들의 소원은 무엇이었습니까? What was the second son's wish?

d. 왜 어머니는 충돌을 해결하지 못했습니까? Why couldn't the mother resolve the conflict?

Historical Notes

The Korean War ended in 1953 in a stalemate, with the Korean Armistice Agreement. This agreement established the DMZ (demilitarized zone) line as we know it today and Korea has stayed separated ever since. One thing to note is that this agreement was not a peace treaty, but simply an agreement to stop the fighting.

두 개의 코리아: 발전의 길
Du Gae-ui Korea: Baljeon-ui Gil

한때 북한과 남한이라는 두 나라가 있었습니다. 이 두 나라는 같은 땅에서 나왔지만, 서로 다른 **길**을 선택했습니다. 북한은 강력한 **주체사상**을 추구하며, 자신들만의 길을 가기로 결정했습니다. 반면에 남한은 자유롭고 **개방**된 사회를 추구하며, 세계와 **협력**하려는 길을 선택했습니다. 북한은 **굳건하게** 자기 길을 걸었지만, 그 길은 **고립**과 **굶주림**으로 이어졌습니다. 반면 남한은 협력과 교류를 통해 성장하였으며, 그 결과 오늘날 세계 강대국 중 하나가 되었습니다. 두 나라는 서로 다른 길을 걷고 있지만, 같은 땅에서 온 한민족이라는 점에서는 **변함**이 없습니다. 그들의 길이 다를지라도, 그들은 여전히 같은 **뿌리**를 가지고 있습니다. 이 이야기는 우리에게 선택의 중요성을 **교훈**으로 남기지만, 그보다 더 중요한 것은 우리가 어떠한 선택을 하더라도, 우리는 여전히 한 사람이라는 **사실**을 잊지 않아야 한다는 것입니다.

Two Koreas: Paths of Development

Once upon a time, there were two countries named North and South Korea. These two countries emerged from the same land, but each chose a different path. North Korea pursued a strong Juche ideology and decided to g their own way. On the other hand, South Korea pursued a free and open society, choosing the path of cooperatio with the world. North Korea walked its path firmly, but that path led to isolation and starvation. On the contrar South Korea grew through cooperation and exchange, which resulted in becoming one of the world's stron nations today. Although the two countries are walking different paths, they remain unchanged as one Korea people from the same land. Even though their paths differ, they still have the same roots. This story leaves us wit the lesson of the importance of choice, but what's more important is that no matter what choices we make, w should never forget that we are still one people.

Vocabulary

길 gil - Path/road

주체사상 joo chae sa sang - Juche ideology

개방 gae bang - Open/opening

협력 hyeob ryeok - Cooperation

굳건하게 goot gun ha gae - Firmly

고립 go rib - Isolation

굶주림 goorm joo rim - Starvation

변함 byeon ham - Change

뿌리 bbu ri - Root

교훈 kyo hoon - Lesson

사실 sa shil - Truth

Comprehension Questions

a.　　북한과 남한은 어떤 길을 선택했습니까? What paths did North and South Korea choose?

b.　　북한의 길은 어떤 결과를 가져왔습니까? What were the results of North Korea's path?

남한의 길은 어떤 결과를 가져왔습니까? What were the results of South Korea's path?

이 이야기에서 어떤 교훈을 얻었습니까? What lesson did you learn from this story?

Historical Notes

The stances and ideologies that the separated Koreas would pursue root back to 1948. With the establishment of the governing system set in both countries, the path that each country would take was clear. The North set up a system with a leader who had consolidated power, while the South set up a system of electing presidents.

북한: 주체 이데올로기와 고립
Bukhan: Juche Ideollogiwa Goriip

북한에는 한 명의 **천재**적인 과학자가 있었습니다. 그의 이름은 민준이었고, 그는 **주체 이데올로기**를 따르는 국가에서 살았습니다. 민준은 자신의 나라를 **더욱** 강력하게 만들 수 있는 **무기**를 **개발**하고 있었습니다. 그러나 그는 또한 그의 나라가 세계에서 **고립**되어 있다는 것을 알고 있었습니다. 그는 이 **현실**을 변경하고 싶었지만, 그의 나라의 **규칙**과 이데올로기 때문에 그는 어려움에 직면했습니다. 그러나 그는 **회복력의 정신**으로, 그의 고민을 극복하려고 노력했습니다. 그는 그의 나라가 세계와의 **외교 관계**를 갖게 되면, 그의 나라가 더욱 발전하고, 그의 나라의 사람들이 더욱 행복해질 수 있을 것이라고 믿었습니다. 그는 그의 꿈을 **실현**하기 위해 끝없는 노력을 기울였습니다. 그의 노력에도 불구하고, 그는 그의 국가의 이데올로기와 그의 꿈 사이에서 충돌을 겪었습니다. 그는 결국 그의 꿈을 포기하고, 그의 나라의 이데올로기를 따르기로 결정했습니다.

North Korea

North Korea: Juche Ideology and Isolation

In North Korea, there was a genius scientist named Minjun. He lived in a country that followed the Juche ideology. Minjun was developing weapons that could make his country even stronger. However, he also knew that his country was isolated from the world. He wanted to change this reality, but he faced difficulties due to his country's rules and ideology. Nevertheless, with a spirit of resilience, he tried to overcome his concerns. He believed that if his country were to have diplomatic relations with the world, his country would develop further and the people of his country would be happier. He made tireless efforts to realize his dream. Despite his efforts, however, he experienced conflicts between his country's ideology and his dream. In the end, he decided to give up his dream and follow his country's ideology.

Vocabulary

천재 cheon jae - Genius

주체 이데올로기 -Juche Ideology

더욱 deo wook - More

무기 mu gi - Weapon

개발 gae bal - Invent/develop

고립 go rip - Isolation

현실 hyeon shil - Reality

규칙 kyu chik - Rules

회복력의 정신 hwe bok ryeok ui jeong shin - Spirit of resilience

외교 관계 we gyo gwan gae - Diplomatic relations

실현 shil hyeon - Realize

Comprehension Questions

. 민준은 어떤 일을 하고 있었습니까? What was Minjun doing?

. 민준의 꿈은 무엇이었습니까? What was Minjun's dream?

. 민준은 왜 그의 꿈을 포기했습니까? Why did Minjun give up his dream?

Historical Notes

uche ideology became the official state ideology of North Korea in 1972. It embodies the spirit of self reliance nd aims for complete independence, rejecting any sort of dependence on others. This does not mean that North Korea did not want any interaction in the world, as it attempted to promote cooperation between other socialist ountries, such as the USSR and China. This cooperation would stress limited dependence and each country would remain politically independent. However, attempting to be free from any influences has led North Korea o be more isolated than not.

핵의 꿈과 국제 긴장감
Haek-ui Kkumgwa Gukje Ginjang-gam

한 나라의 왕자가 있었습니다. 그의 이름은 동진이었습니다. 동진은 어릴 때부터 **핵**에 대한 **열망**을 가지고 있었으며, 그의 나라를 세계에서 가장 강력한 국가로 만들고자 했습니다. 그는 그의 나라를 위해 핵을 개발하려는 **계획**을 세웠습니다. 그러나 이것은 그의 나라와 세계의 다른 나라들 사이의 **긴장감**을 **높였**습니다.

세계의 다른 나라들은 동진의 계획에 **불안감**을 느꼈습니다. 그들은 그의 나라가 **국제 안전**을 위협할 수 있다고 느꼈습니다. 그러나 동진은 그의 나라의 권력을 위해 계속해서 핵 개발을 **추진**했습니다.

한편, 동진의 나라의 사람들은 그의 계획에 대해 **갈등감**을 느꼈습니다. 그들 중 일부는 그의 꿈을 이해하고 지지했지만, 다른 일부는 그의 계획이 그들의 안전을 위협할 수 있다고 느꼈습니다.

동진은 자신의 계획에 대해 세계에 **공개적**으로 말했습니다. 그는 핵을 무기로 사용하는 것이 아니라 평화를 위해 사용하겠다고 말했습니다. 그러나 세계의 다른 나라들은 그의 말을 믿지 못했습니다.

결국, 세계의 다른 나라들은 동진의 나라에 대해 **제재**를 가하기로 결정했습니다. 그들은 그의 나라에게 **경제 제재**를 가하고, 그의 나라를 국제 사회에서 **배제**하기로 결정했습니다. 그러나 동진은 그의 계획을 포기하지 않았습니다.

Nuclear Dreams and International Tensions

There was a prince of a country. His name was Dong-jin. Since he was young, Dong-jin had a passion for nuclear power and wanted to make his country the most powerful in the world. He made plans to develop nuclear power for his country. However, this heightened tensions between his country and other countries in the world.

Other countries in the world felt uneasy about Dong-jin's plans. They felt that his country could threaten international safety. However, Dong-jin continued to push for nuclear development for the power of his country.

Meanwhile, the people of Dong-jin's country felt conflicted about his plans. Some of them understood and supported his dream, but others felt that his plans could threaten their safety.

Dong-jin spoke publicly to the world about his plans. He said he would use nuclear power for peace, not as a weapon. However, other countries in the world could not believe his words.

In the end, other countries in the world decided to impose sanctions on Dong-jin's country. They decided to impose economic sanctions on his country and exclude his country from the international community. However, Dong-jin did not give up his plans.

Vocabulary

핵 haek - Nuclear

열망 yeol mang - Yearning

계획 gye hwaek - Plan

긴장감 gin jang gam - Nervousness/tension

높여 no pyeo - To raise

불안감 bul an gam - Anxiety

국제안전 guk jae an jeon - International safety

추진 chu jin - Propel/pursue

갈등감 gal deung gam - Feeling of conflict

공개적 gong gae jeok - Public

제재 je je - Sanctions

경제 제재 kyeong je je je - Economic sanctions

배제 be je - Exclude

Comprehension Questions

a.   왕자 동진의 꿈은 무엇이었습니까? What was Prince Dong-jin's dream?

b.   왕자 동진의 계획에 대한 세계의 반응은 무엇이었습니까? What was the world's reaction to Princ Dong-jin's plan?

c.   왕자 동진의 나라의 사람들은 그의 계획에 대해 어떻게 생각했습니까? What did the people o Prince Dong-jin's country think about his plans?

d.   세계의 다른 나라들이 왕자 동진의 나라에 대해 어떤 조치를 취했습니까? What action did othe countries in the world take against Prince Dong-jin's country?

Historical Notes

North Korea's interest in nuclear powered weapons dates back to the 1980s, where they first began running programs and tests. This is when their conflicts with other countries began, as North Korea refused inspections and left multiple international societies. Other countries responded by attempting to persuade North Korea to give up nuclear weapon development through various means, but North Korea kept going and this has led to many sanctions being laid against it by countries around the world.

한국: 경제적 기적과 민주화
Hangguk: Gyeongjaejeok Gijeokgwa Minjuhwa

한 때 한 나라가 있었습니다. 그 나라의 이름은 한국이었습니다. 한국은 오랫동안 **가난**과 **압제**에 시달렸습니다. 그러나, 한국 사람들은 항상 희망을 잃지 않았습니다. 그들은 자신의 나라를 더 나은 곳으로 만들기 위해 끊임없이 노력했습니다. 그 노력의 결과로, 한국은 **놀라운** 변화를 이루었습니다. 한국은 가난한 나라에서 경제적 **기적**을 이룬 나라로 변했습니다. 또한, 그들은 **민주화**를 통해 자유와 **정의**를 찾았습니다. 그들은 자신의 권리를 위해 싸웠고, 그 싸움을 이겼습니다. 한국의 이야기는 용기와 **결의**의 이야기입니다.

South Korea

South Korea: Economic Miracle and Democratization

There was once a country. The name of that country was South Korea. South Korea had long suffered from poverty and oppression. However, the people of South Korea never lost hope. They worked tirelessly to make their country a better place. As a result of their efforts, South Korea underwent an astonishing transformation. South Korea changed from a poor country to a country that achieved an economic miracle. Also, they found freedom and justice through democratization. They fought for their rights and won their fight. The story of South Korea is a story of courage and determination.

Vocabulary

가난 ga nan - Poverty

압제 ap je - Oppression

놀라운 nol la woon - Surprising/astonishing

기적 gi jeok - Miracle

민주화 min ju hwa - Democratization

정의 jeong ui - Justice

결의 kyeol ui - Resolution

Comprehension Questions

한국 사람들은 어떤 노력을 통해 그들의 나라를 더 나은 곳으로 만들었습니까? Through what efforts did the people of South Korea make their country a better place?

한국이 경제적 기적을 이루게 된 원인은 무엇이었습니까? What caused South Korea to achieve an economic miracle?

한국 사람들은 자신의 권리를 어떻게 획득했습니까? How did the people of South Korea gain their rights?

Historical Notes

South Korea's rapid rise from an underdeveloped, war torn country to one of the most developed, thriving countries is known as the "Miracle of the Han River". Due to a hard working labor force and external assistance, South Korea's economy was able to boom and large conglomerates began to emerge. During this time, the child mortality rate greatly dropped while life expectancy greatly rose.

박청희와 산업화의 꿈
Park Chung-heewa Saneobhwa-ui Kkum

박정희 **대통령**은 국가를 **산업화**하려는 강력한 의지를 가지고 있었습니다. 그는 나라의 미래를 확실히 믿았고, 그 미래는 산업화를 통해 이루어질 것이라고 확신했습니다. 그는 이 목표를 **달성**하기 위해 나라 **전체**를 통합하고, 국가 계획을 통해 모든 **자원**을 이용했습니다. 그의 **정책**은 많은 도전과 어려움에 직면했지만, 그는 **결코** 흔들리지 않았습니다. 그는 농민들에게 **농업 기계화**를 **권장**하고, **도시**에서는 **공장**을 지어 산업화를 추진했습니다. 결과적으로, 그의 정책은 한국의 경제 성장을 촉진하고 국민들의 삶의 질을 향상시켰습니다.

Park Chung-hee and the Dream
of Industrialization

President Park Chung-hee possessed a powerful will to industrialize the nation. He had a clear vision of th country's future, and he was certain that this future would be achieved through industrialization. To accomplis this goal, he unified the entire nation and utilized all resources through a national plan. His policies faced man challenges and difficulties, but he never wavered. He encouraged farmers to mechanize agriculture, and in citie he built factories to promote industrialization. As a result, his policies promoted South Korea's economic growt and improved the quality of life for its people.

Vocabulary

대통령 de tong ryung - President

산업화 san eop hwa - Industrialization

달성 dal seong - Attain/accomplish

전체 jeon chae - Entire

자원 ja won - Resource

정책 jeong chaek - Policy

결코 gyeol ko - In the end

농업 기계화 nong eop gi gae hwa - Agricultural mechanization

권장 kwon jang - Encourage

도시 do shi - City

공장 gong jang – Factory

Comprehension Questions

박정희 대통령이 산업화를 추진하려고 했던 이유는 무엇이었습니까? What was the reason why President Park Chung-hee wanted to promote industrialization?

그의 산업화 정책에는 어떤 도전과 어려움이 있었습니까? What were the challenges and difficulties in his industrialization policy?

그의 정책이 한국에 어떤 영향을 미쳤습니까? What impact did his policies have on Korea?

Historical Notes

Park Chung-hee is a controversial figure in South Korean history, but there is no denying that he had the biggest impact in South Korean politics during the twentieth century. He led the country from 1961 to 1979, implementing many policies through authoritarian rule. These policies enabled South Korea to escape from poverty following the Korean War, but his authoritarian methods of ruling were criticized for holding back the development of democratization.

21 세기의 화해와 도전
21 Segi-ui Hwahaewa Dojeon

한 나라의 왕이 있었습니다. 왕은 자신의 나라가 분열되어 있음을 슬퍼했습니다. 북쪽은 **성장**하고 있다고 믿었지만, 불안정한 정치 상황으로 **인해** 고립되어 있었습니다. 반면에, 남쪽은 경제적으로 번영했지만, 분열로 인해 사람들은 불안해했습니다. 왕이 북쪽의 **대표**에게 물었습니다. "우리는 어떻게 **화해**할 수 있을까요?" 북쪽의 대표는 "우리는 우리의 **독립성**을 **보장**받아야 합니다,"라고 말했습니다. 왕이 남쪽의 대표에게 같은 질문을 했습니다. 남쪽의 대표는 "우리는 안전을 보장받아야 합니다,"라고 대답했습니다. 왕은 이 두 **요구 사항**이 서로 충돌함을 깨달았습니다. 그는 어떻게 이 두 가지 요구 사항을 **동시에** 만족시킬 수 있을까 고민했습니다.

21st Century

Reconciliation and Challenges in the 21st Century

There was a king of a country. The king was saddened by the division within his country. The North believed was progressing, but it was isolated due to a volatile political climate. Meanwhile, the South prospere economically, but the division made people feel uneasy. The king asked the representative of the North, "Ho can we reconcile?" The representative of the North said, "We need to be assured of our independence." The kin asked the same question to the representative of the South. The representative of the South replied, "We need t be assured of our safety." The king realized that these two demands were in conflict with each other. He pondere on how he could satisfy these two demands at the same time.

Vocabulary

성장 seong jang - Progress/growth

인해 in hae - Through

대표 de pyo - Representative

화해 hwa hae - Reconcile

독립성 dok lip seong - Independence

보장 bo jang - Guarantee

요구 사항 yo goo sa hang - Demands/requirements

동시에 dong si ae - At the same time

Comprehension Questions

a.   왕이 왜 북쪽과 남쪽 대표에게 질문을 했습니까? Why did the king ask questions to the representatives of the North and South?

b.   북쪽 대표의 요구 사항은 무엇이었습니까? What was the demand of the representative of the North?

c.   남쪽 대표의 요구 사항은 무엇이었습니까? What was the demand of the representative of the South?

d.   왜 왕은 이 두 요구 사항이 충돌한다고 생각했습니까? Why did the king think that these two demands were in conflict?

Historical Notes

The reunification of Korea back into one peninsula has been a goal ever since the end of the Korean War in 1953. However, the meaning of reunification and the idea behind it has greatly changed over time. Back in the 1950s, reunification was seen as needing military force, as both governments could not give up their individual ideologies. As this separation deepended, opinions on reunification have shifted up and down through the years.

한반도의 두 형제
Hanbando-ui Du Hyeongje

한반도에는 두 형제가 살았습니다. 그들은 아주 **친했**지만, 여러 가지 **이유**로 서로 다른 길을 가기 시작했습니다. 어느 날, 두 형제는 각자의 **방향**으로 가기로 결정했습니다. 하나는 북쪽으로, 다른 하나는 남쪽으로 가기로 했습니다. 그들은 각각의 세계에서 살아갔지만, 그들은 여전히 서로의 형제였습니다. 그들은 서로를 그리워했지만, 그들의 길은 서로 **다르게 퍼지고** 있었습니다. 그러나 그들은 알고 있었습니다. **언젠가는** 그들이 다시 만날 수 있을 것이라는 것을. 그들은 그 날을 기다렸습니다. 그 날이 오면, 그들은 다시 형제로서, 한반도의 두 형제로서 서로를 받아들일 수 있을 것입니다.

he Two Brothers of the Peninsula

his story is about two brothers who lived on the Korean peninsula. They were very close, but they started to go
eir separate ways for various reasons. One day, the two brothers decided to go in their directions. One decided
go north, and the other decided to go south. They each lived in their worlds, but they were still brothers. They
issed each other, but their paths were spreading differently. But they knew. That they would meet again
meday. They waited for that day. When that day comes, they could accept each other again as brothers, as two
rothers of the peninsula.

Vocabulary

친해 chin hae - Close (relationship wise)

이유 lee yoo - Reason

방향 bang hyang - Direction

다르게 퍼져 da reu gae peo jyeo - Spread differently

언젠가는 eon jaen ga neun - One day

Comprehension Questions

. 두 형제가 왜 서로 다른 길을 가게 됐습니까? Why did the two brothers go their separate ways?

. 형제들이 어떤 방향으로 갔습니까? In which directions did the brothers go?

. 형제들이 다시 만날 수 있을까요? Can the brothers meet again?

Historical Notes

Although many families were split apart and many saw reunification as necessary and very possible, opinions on
reunification swayed. In the 1980s, with the advent of hostile events like terrorist attacks from North Korea, many
South Koreans deemed unification as impossible and many began to stray from the goal of reunification.

통일을 원하는 대중의 여론과 소망

Tongileul Wonhaneun Daejoong-ui Yeorongwa Somang

한반도에서는 북과 남이 **통일**을 꿈꾸는 사람들의 이야기가 있었습니다. 철수는 북쪽에서 살았고 영희는 남쪽에서 살았습니다. 그들은 **어린시절부터** 서로의 **존재**를 알지 못했습니다. 그러나 어느 날 철수는 남쪽에서 온 편지를 발견했습니다. 편지에는 '통일을 원하는 사람이 있다면 답장을 주세요.'라고 **적혀** 있었습니다. 철수는 편지에 답장을 써서 남쪽으로 보냈습니다. 영희는 철수의 답장을 받고 **기뻐**했습니다.

그들은 편지를 **주고받으며** 서로를 알게 되었습니다. 철수는 북쪽의 삶을, 영희는 남쪽의 삶을 설명했습니다. 그들은 서로의 삶이 얼마나 다른지를 깨달았습니다. 그러나 그들은 한 가지 **공통점**을 발견했습니다. 그것은 바로 통일을 원하는 마음이었습니다. 그들은 통일을 통해 서로의 삶이 얼마나 변화할지 상상했습니다.

그들은 편지를 통해 각자의 지역에서 통일을 원하는 사람들을 모으기로 했습니다. 철수와 영희는 각자의 지역에서 통일을 원하는 사람들을 **찾아**냈습니다. 그들은 모두 통일을 원하는 마음을 가지고 있었습니다. 그들은 편지를 통해 서로의 마음을 **나누었**습니다.

그들은 통일을 위한 **모임**을 만들기로 결정했습니다. 철수와 영희는 서로의 지역에서 통일을 원하는 사람들을 **초대**했습니다. 그들은 모두 한 자리에 모여 통일을 위한 노력을 나누었습니다. 그들은 각자의 생각과 아이디어를 **공유**하며 통일의 길을 찾았습니다.

그들의 노력은 서서히 퍼져 나갔습니다. 철수와 영희의 이야기는 많은 사람들에게 전해졌습니다. 그들은 통일을 원하는 많은 사람들이 있다는 것을 알게 되었습니다. 그들의 이야기는 **대중**의 마음에 통일의 **소망**을 일으켰습니다.

The Public Opinion and Desire for Reunification

There was a story of people in the Korean peninsula who dreamt of reunification. Chulsoo lived in the North, and Younghee lived in the South. They did not know of each other's existence since they were young. However, one day, Chulsoo found a letter from the South. The letter read, 'If there is someone who wants reunification, please reply.' Chulsoo wrote a reply and sent it to the South. Younghee was delighted when she received Chulsoo's reply.

They got to know each other through exchanging letters. Chulsoo described life in the North, and Younghee described life in the South. They realized how different their lives were. However, they found one thing in common. It was the desire for reunification. They imagined how much their lives would change through reunification.

They decided to gather people who wanted reunification in their respective regions through letters. Chulsoo and Younghee found people in their respective regions who wanted reunification. They all had a desire for reunification. They shared their feelings with each other through letters.

They decided to create a meeting for reunification. Chulsoo and Younghee invited people from their respective regions who wanted reunification. They all gathered in one place and shared efforts for reunification. They found the way to reunification by sharing their thoughts and ideas.

Their efforts slowly spread. The story of Chulsoo and Younghee was passed on to many people. They realized that there are many people who want reunification. Their story sparked a hope for reunification in the hearts of the public.

Vocabulary

통일 tong il - Reunification

어린시절부터 - eo rin shi jeol bu teo - Since childhood

존재 jon jae - Existence

적혀 jeok hyeo - Written

기뻐 gi bbeo - Happy

주고받으며 joo go ba deu myeo - Exchanging

공통점 gong tong jeom - Common ground

찾아 cha ja - Find

나누어 na noo eo - To share

모임 mo im - Meeting

초대 cho dae - Invite

공유 gong yoo - Share

대중 de joong - Public

소망 so mang - Hope

Comprehension Questions

a.   철수와 영희는 왜 통일을 원하였는가? Why did Chulsoo and Younghee want reunification?

b.   철수와 영희가 만든 모임의 목적은 무엇인가? What was the purpose of the meeting that Chulsoo and Younghee created?

c.   이 이야기를 통해 배운 교훈은 무엇인가? What is the lesson learned from this story?

Historical Notes

Public opinion began to shift again in a hopeful manner in the 1990s, especially with the election of a president from the liberal faction in 1998. This was the first time a president from the liberal side had been elected, and this sparked expectations to improving relations with North Korea.

화해와 협력의 시도
Hwahaewa Hyeobryeok-ui Shido

한 나라에 전쟁으로 인해 분열된 두 마을이 있었습니다. 한 마을은 '북촌'이라 불릴 정도로 북쪽에 **위치해** 있었고, 다른 마을은 '남촌'이라 불릴 정도로 남쪽에 위치해 있었습니다. 이 두 마을 사이에는 깊고 **넓은** 강이 흐르고 있었습니다. 전쟁 이후, 북촌과 남촌은 서로를 적으로 **여기**며, 강을 넘어가지 않았습니다. 그러나 어느 날, 강가에서 두 마을의 어린이들이 **우연히** 만나게 되었습니다. 그들은 강가에서 놀면서 친구가 되었고, 서로의 마을에 대해 이야기하며 서로를 이해하려고 노력했습니다. 이 어린이들의 만남은 두 마을 사이에 화해의 **기회**를 **제공**했습니다. 어린이들은 각자의 마을에서 이야기를 나누며, 서로를 **적대**시하는 것이 아니라 이해하고 협력해야 한다는 사실을 깨달았습니다. 이 후, 두 마을은 서로를 이해하고 협력하는 길을 찾아나갔습니다.

Attempts at Reconciliation and Cooperation

There were two villages in a country that were divided due to war. One village was located in the north, enough to be called 'North Village,' and the other village was in the south, enough to be called 'South Village.' A deep and wide river flowed between the two villages. After the war, the North Village and the South Village regarded each other as enemies, and did not cross the river. However, one day, children from both villages coincidentally met by the river. They became friends while playing by the river and tried to understand each other by talking about their villages. Their encounter provided an opportunity for reconciliation between the two villages. The children shared their stories in their respective villages, realizing that they should not be hostile, but understand and cooperate with each other. Afterward, the two villages sought ways to understand and cooperate with each other.

Vocabulary

위치해 wi chi hae - Located

넓은 neol beun - Wide/large

여겨 yeo gyeo - Consider

우연히 woo yeon hee - Coincidentally/ by chance

기회 ki hwae - Opportunity

제공 je gong - Provide

적대 jeok de - Hostility

Comprehension Questions

a.   북촌과 남촌은 왜 서로를 적으로 여겼나요? Why did the North Village and the South Village regard each other as enemies?

b.   어린이들의 만남이 어떻게 화해의 기회를 제공했나요? How did the meeting of the children provide an opportunity for reconciliation?

c.   두 마을은 어떻게 서로를 이해하고 협력하게 되었나요? How did the two villages come to understand and cooperate with each other?

Historical Notes

The reunification of Korea is still an ongoing effort today, with there even being a government ministry in South Korea fully dedicated to it. However, many people have grown accustomed to the communist neighbor in the North and the younger generation has been leaning more towards a peaceful coexistence between the two countries.

기술 발전과 경제력
Gisool Baljeongwa Gyeongjeryeok

한 나라에 **장인**과 그의 아들이 살았습니다. 장인은 **손재주**가 뛰어나 **여러 가지 기술**을 가르쳤고 아들은 그의 **부친**처럼 기술을 **배워**나갔습니다. 하지만 아들은 더 나아가 그의 나라를 세계적인 **경제력**을 가진 나라로 만들고자 했습니다.

장인은 아들에게 기술의 중요성을 알려주었습니다. 그는 아들에게 **도구**와 **재료**를 다루는 법, 또한 기술과 과학의 **원리**를 가르쳤습니다. 아들은 이러한 지식을 가지고 새로운 **발명**을 **창출**했습니다.

아들은 그의 나라를 위해 새로운 기술을 개발했습니다. 그는 기계와 **전자 장비**를 만들어 농업과 산업을 혁신하였습니다. 이러한 변화는 그의 나라의 경제에 큰 영향을 미쳤습니다.

아들의 발명이 세계로 퍼져나가기 시작했습니다. 다른 나라들은 그의 기술을 **구매**하고, 그의 나라는 경제적인 부를 얻게 되었습니다. 이러한 성과는 아들을 **훌륭한 발명가**로 만들었고, 그의 나라를 세계의 중심으로 만들었습니다.

하지만 아들은 계속해서 학문을 공부하고 새로운 아이디어를 찾아내었습니다. 그는 기술의 발전이 그의 나라의 경제 발전에 **필수적**이라는 것을 알고 있었습니다. 그는 그의 나라가 세계에서 가장 강력한 경제력을 갖도록 노력했습니다.

그의 노력은 결국 성공하였습니다. 그의 나라는 세계에서 가장 강력한 경제력을 가진 나라가 되었습니다. 그의 나라는 기술 발전과 경제 발전 덕분에 세계의 **주목**을 받게 되었습니다.

그의 나라는 오늘날에도 세계에서 가장 강력한 경제력을 가지고 있습니다. 그의 나라는 기술의 **선두주자**가 되었고, 세계의 다른 나라들은 그의 나라를 본받으려고 노력하게 되었습니다.

이것은 장인과 그의 아들의 이야기입니다. 이 이야기는 기술과 경제의 중요성을 보여줍니다. 기술과 경제는 나라의 발전에 필수적인 **요소**입니다.

이 이야기는 우리에게 기술 발전이 경제력을 높이는 방법을 보여줍니다. 이 이야기는 우리에게 우리 자신의 능력과 지식을 최대한 **활용**해야 한다는 것을 가르쳐줍니다.

이야기는 또한 우리에게 **연구**와 학문의 중요성을 보여줍니다. 우리는 항상 새로운 것을 배우고, 우리의 지식을 **확장**해야 합니다. 이것은 우리의 나라와 세계에 대한 우리의 이해를 향상시키고, 우리의 나라를 더 강력하게 만들 수 있습니다.

South Korea's Global Influence

echnological Advancements and
conomic Prowess

1 a country, there lived a craftsman and his son. The craftsman was skilled and taught various skills, and the son earned his father's skills. However, the son aimed to make his country a globally powerful economy.

he craftsman taught the importance of technology to his son. He taught his son how to handle tools and materials nd the principles of technology and science. With this knowledge, the son created new inventions.

he son developed new technologies for his country. He made machines and electronic equipment to innovate griculture and industry. These changes had a significant impact on his country's economy.

he son's inventions began to spread worldwide. Other countries purchased his technology, and his country ained economic wealth. These achievements made the son a great inventor and made his country the center of he world.

However, the son continued to study and find new ideas. He knew that the advancement of technology was essential for the economic development of his country. He strived to make his country the most powerful economy n the world.

His efforts eventually succeeded. His country became the most powerful economy in the world. His country eceived global attention thanks to the advancement of technology and economic development.

His country still has the most powerful economy in the world today. His country has become a leader in technology, and other countries in the world strive to emulate his country.

This is the story of the craftsman and his son. This story shows the importance of technology and economics. Technology and economics are essential elements for the development of a country.

This story shows us how technological advancements can boost economic power. This story teaches us to maximize our abilities and knowledge.

This story also shows us the importance of research and scholarship. We must always learn new things and expand our knowledge. This can improve our understanding of our country and the world and make our country stronger.

Vocabulary

장인 jang in - Skilled expert

손재주 son je ju - skilled at craft

여러 가지 yeo reo ga ji - Several

기술 gi sul - Skills

부친 bu chin - Father

배워 be woa - To learn

경제력 gyeong je ryeok - Economic power

도구 do gu - Tool

재료 je ryo - Materials

원리 won ri - Principle

발명 bal myeong - Invent

창출 chang chul - Create

전자 장비 - jeon ja jang bi - Electric equipment

구매 gu me - Buy

훌륭한 hul ryong han - Great

발명가 bal myeong ga - Inventor

필수적 pil su jeok - Essential

주목 ju mok - Attention

선두주자 seon du ju ja - Leader

요소 yo so - Element

활용 hwal yong - Utilize

연구 yeon goo - Research

확장 hwak jang - Expand

Comprehension Questions

아들은 왜 새로운 기술을 개발하였습니까? Why did the son develop new technologies?

아들의 발명은 그의 나라에 어떤 영향을 미쳤습니까? What impact did the son's inventions have on his country?

아들은 왜 계속해서 학문을 공부하였습니까? Why did the son continue to study?

Historical Notes

South Korea has experienced one of the largest economic growths in a short time period. This was possible mainly because of technological innovations. With the US donating immense amounts of money after the Korean war, along with tax concessions to companies with potential, many jobs were created and South Korea's rigid education system helped to push innovation. These companies would take the lead in pushing South Korea's economic growth, eventually becoming companies that are known around the world.

한국의 아이돌 그룹과 그들의 성공 이야기
Hankuk-ui Aidol Geuroopgwa Geudeul-ui Seong-gong Iyagi

어느 날 한국의 **아이돌 그룹**이 있었습니다. 그들은 **음악**과 춤으로 사람들의 마음을 **사로잡았**습니다. 그들의 **인기**는 한국을 넘어 세계적으로 퍼져나갔습니다. 그들의 음악은 감동적이었고, 춤은 **화려하고 열정적**이었습니다. 소년들은 꿈을 이루기 위해 많은 **시련**을 겪었습니다. 그들은 힘든 연습과 오랜 기다림 끝에 성공을 이루었습니다. 세계의 사람들은 그들의 음악을 사랑하고, 그들의 문화를 이해하기 시작했습니다. 이로 인해 한국의 문화는 세계에 알려지게 되었고, **한류**가 시작되었습니다. 한류는 한국의 음악, **영화**, 드라마 등을 세계에 전파하였습니다.

orean Idol Group Success Story

ne day, there was an idol group in Korea. They captivated people's hearts with music and dance. Their popularity pread globally beyond Korea. Their music was touching, and their dance was vibrant and passionate. The boys ent through many trials to fulfill their dreams. They achieved success after hard practice and long waiting. People round the world loved their music and began to understand their culture. As a result, Korean culture was known o the world, and Hallyu began. Hallyu spread Korean music, movies, dramas, etc., to the world.

Vocabulary

아이돌 그룹 a i dol geu rup - Idol group

음악 eum ak - Music

사로잡아 sa ro jab ah - Captivate

인기 in gi - Popularity

화려 hwa ryeo - Fancy/vibrant

열정적 yeol jeong jeok - Passionate

시련 shi ryeon - Hardship/test

한류 hall yu - term to describe Korean wave

영화 yeong hwa - Movie

Comprehension Questions

a.   이 아이돌 그룹이 어떤 성공을 거두었습니까? What success did this idol group achieve?

b.   세계의 사람들이 그들의 음악에 어떻게 반응했습니까? How did people around the world react to their music?

c.   한류가 무엇을 세계에 전파했습니까? What did Hallyu spread to the world?

Historical Notes

The Hallyu wave is a phenomenon that put South Korea's name on the map. Beginning in the mid-2000s, Korean music and culture began to spread in popularity around the world, garnering global interest towards this small country. Its influence has only grown larger over time, and the amount of people who want to understand Korean culture and language has increased in proportion.

한국 음식의 인기
Hanguk-ui Eumshik-ui Iyagi

옛날 옛적에, 한국 **음식**은 세계적으로 알려지지 않았습니다. 그러나 어느 날, 세계 각지의 사람들이 한국 음식의 **맛**과 **다양성**에 빠져들었습니다. 이 맛있는 음식들은 한국의 역사와 문화를 담고 있었으며, 세계인들의 마음을 사로잡았습니다.

비빔밥, **김치**, **불고기**와 같은 한국 음식들은 전 세계적으로 사랑받게 되었고, 많은 사람들이 이러한 음식들을 찾아 여러 나라로 **여행**하기 시작했습니다. 이러한 음식들은 한국 문화의 아름다움과 다양성을 세계에 알렸습니다.

한국 음식의 인기는 **한류 열풍**과 함께 더욱 커졌습니다. 케이팝 스타들과 드라마는 전 세계의 **젊은이들**에게 한국 문화를 **소개**했고, 이러한 문화현상은 한국 음식에 대한 **관심**을 높였습니다.

이 인기로 인해 한국 음식점이 세계 곳곳에 생겨났습니다. 이러한 음식점들은 한국의 맛과 전통을 세계에 전하며, 많은 사람들이 한국 음식의 팬이 되었습니다. 이러한 **음식점**들은 한국의 전통을 계승하며, 세계 사람들에게 한국의 맛을 알렸습니다.

이러한 한국 음식의 인기는 한국 문화와 언어에 대한 관심도 **증가**시켰습니다. 많은 사람들이 한국어를 배우고, 한국의 역사와 전통에 대해 알아가고자 했습니다. 이러한 관심은 한국 문화의 **국제적인 인지도**를 높였습니다.

The Popularity of Korean Food

Once upon a time, Korean cuisine was not known worldwide. However, one day, people from around the world fell in love with the taste and diversity of Korean food. These delicious dishes, encapsulating Korean history and culture, captivated the hearts of people worldwide.

Korean foods such as Bibimbap, Kimchi, and Bulgogi began to be loved around the world, and many people started traveling to various countries to seek these foods. These foods spread the beauty and diversity of Korean culture to the world.

The popularity of Korean food increased even more with the Hallyu wave. K-pop stars and dramas introduced Korean culture to the youth worldwide, and this cultural phenomenon heightened interest in Korean cuisine.

Due to this popularity, Korean restaurants sprouted in various parts of the world. These restaurants conveyed the taste and traditions of Korea, turning many into fans of Korean cuisine. They carried on Korean traditions and introduced the flavors of Korea to people worldwide.

This popularity of Korean food also increased interest in Korean culture and language. Many people started learning Korean and sought to understand Korea's history and traditions. This interest elevated the international recognition of Korean culture.

Vocabulary

음식 eum shik - Food

맛 mat - Taste

다양성 da yang sung - Variety

비빔밥 bi bim bap - Famous Korean dish with rice and variety of side dishes mixed

김치 kim chi - Korean spicy cabbage

불고기 bul go gi - Korean style marinated beef

여행 yeo haeng - Travel/Vacation

한류열풍 hall yu yeol poong - Korean wave

젊은이들 jeol meu ni deul - Young people

소개 so ge - Introduce

관심 kwan shim - Interest

음식점 eum shik jeom - Restaurant

증가 jeung ga - Increase

국제적인 guk je jeok in - International

인지도 in ji do - Recognition

Comprehension Questions

a.   한국 음식이 세계적으로 인기를 얻게 된 이유는 무엇인가요? Why has Korean food gained popularity worldwide?

b.   한류 열풍이 한국 음식의 인기에 어떤 영향을 미쳤나요? How has the Hallyu wave impacted the popularity of Korean food?

c.   한국 음식의 인기는 어떻게 한국 문화와 언어에 대한 관심을 증가시켰나요? How has the popularity of Korean food increased interest in Korean culture and language?

Historical Notes

Another factor that has led to the increase in South Korea's influence is the popularity of Korean cuisine. As people began to take an interest in Korean culture, Korean cuisine was naturally explored and this has led to the spread of Korean cuisine around the world. Today, Korean cuisine style restaurants can be found all over the world, and variations and combinations continue to emerge.

꿈의 나무와 두 친구들

Kkum-ui Namuwa Du Chingudeul

한 마을에는 친구인 두 소년이 살았습니다. 그들은 어린 시절부터 함께 자라며, 서로의 꿈을 공유하였습니다. 첫 번째 소년은 과학자가 되어 세상을 바꾸는 발명을 하고 싶었습니다. 두 번째 소년은 작가가 되어 이야기로 사람들의 마음을 움직이고 싶었습니다. 어느 날, 그들은 나무 아래서 꿈에 대해 이야기하다가 나무가 그들의 꿈을 듣고 있다는 사실을 깨달았습니다. 그래서 그들은 나무에게 자신들의 꿈을 말해주었습니다. 첫 번째 소년은 나무에게 세상을 바꾸는 발명품을 만들 것이라고 말했습니다. 두 번째 소년은 나무에게 감동적인 이야기를 쓸 것이라고 말했습니다. 그러나 나무는 그들에게 미래는 예측할 수 없다고 말했습니다. 미래는 그들이 꿈꾸는 것보다 더 많은 것을 가지고 있을 수 있다고 말했습니다.

Future Prospects

The Tree of Dreams and Two Friends

In a village, there lived two boys who were friends. They grew up together from their childhood, sharing each other's dreams. The first boy wanted to become a scientist and invent something that could change the world. The second boy wanted to become a writer and move people's hearts with his stories. One day, as they were talking about their dreams under a tree, they realized that the tree was listening to their dreams. So, they told the tree about their dreams. The first boy told the tree that he would invent something that could change the world. The second boy told the tree that he would write touching stories. However, the tree told them that the future was unpredictable. The future could hold more than what they were dreaming of.

Comprehension Questions

a.   두 소년의 꿈은 무엇이었습니까? What were the two boys' dreams?

b.   어떤 나무가 그들의 꿈을 듣고 있었습니까? Which tree was listening to their dreams?

c.   나무는 그들에게 무엇을 말했습니까? What did the tree tell them?

Closing Notes

We have taken a tiny glimpse into the long history of Korea. The future of Korea remains unknown, with reunification still in the air and declining birth rates. However, the global influence of Korea continues to grow, and more and more people strive to learn about the Korean language and culture everyday! We hope that this book was a helpful resource in expanding your knowledge of Korean language comprehension and vocabulary, as well as in learning a bit about the background of the country and its origins.

Conclusion

We hope that you've enjoyed this little glimpse into the captivating history of Korea. We believe language learning is a process that must include understanding the culture, and learning a bit about the history behind the culture never hurts.

Hopefully, this book has been a fun, informative way to expand your Korean comprehension and vocabulary, as language learning is often seen as a tedious, boring task.

Thank you for choosing our book along your path to Korean mastery and we hope that you obtained a lot of useful information! If you have any questions, comments, or even suggestions we would love to hear from you by email at Contact@worldwidenomadbooks.com. We greatly appreciate the feedback and this allows us to improve our books and provide the best language learning experience we can.

Thank you,

Worldwide Nomad Team

Made in the USA
Coppell, TX
01 February 2024

28453235R00240